D1532432

Marvel Digests

MARVEL UNIVERSE AVENGERS: UNITED. Contains material originally published in magazine form as SUPER HEROES #17 and #19, and MARVEL ADVENTURES THE AVENGERS #1-2. First printing 2012. ISBN# 978-0-7851-5585-0. Published by MARVEL WORLDWIDE, INC., a subsidiary of MARVEL ENTERTAINMENT, LLC. OFFICE OF PUBLICATION: 135 West 50th Street, New York, NY 10020. Copyright © 2006, 2011 and 2012 Marvel Characters, Inc. All rights reserved. $9.99 per copy in the U.S. and $10.99 in Canada (GST #R127032852); Canadian Agreement #40668537. All characters featured in this issue and the distinctive names and likenesses thereof, and all related indicia are trademarks of Marvel Characters, Inc. No similarity between any of the names, characters, persons, and/or institutions in this magazine with those of any living or dead person or institution is intended, and any such similarity which may exist is purely coincidental. **Printed in the U.S.A.** ALAN FINE, EVP - Office of the President, Marvel Worldwide, Inc. and EVP & CMO Marvel Characters B.V.; DAN BUCKLEY, Publisher & President - Print, Animation & Digital Divisions; JOE QUESADA, Chief Creative Officer; DAVID BOGART, SVP of Business Affairs & Talent Management; TOM BREVOORT, SVP of Publishing; C.B. CEBULSKI, SVP of Creator & Content Development; DAVID GABRIEL, SVP of Publishing Sales & Circulation; MICHAEL PASCIULLO, SVP of Brand Planning & Communications; JIM O'KEEFE, VP of Operations & Logistics; DAN CARR, Executive Director of Publishing Technology; SUSAN CRESPI, Editorial Operations Manager; ALEX MORALES, Publishing Operations Manager; STAN LEE, Chairman Emeritus. For information regarding advertising in Marvel Comics or on Marvel.com, please contact John Dokes, SVP Integrated Sales and Marketing, at jdokes@marvel.com. For Marvel subscription inquiries, please call 800-217-9158. **Manufactured between 1/30/2012 and 2/20/2012 by SHERIDAN BOOKS, INC., CHELSEA, MI, USA.**

10 9 8 7 6 5 4 3 2 1

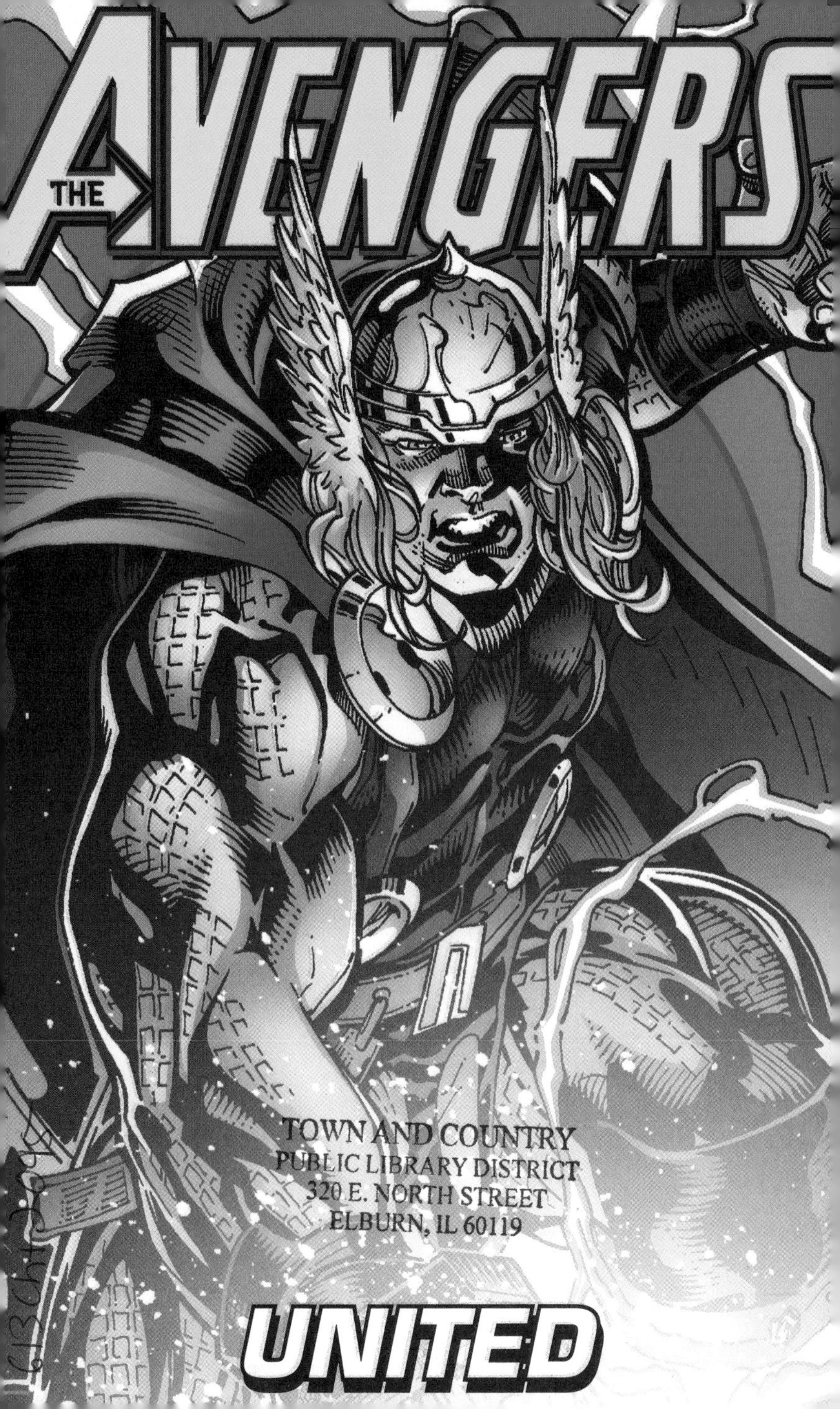
THE AVENGERS
UNITED

THE AVENGERS

UNITED

Writers: Paul Tobin, Joe Caramagna,
Eugene Son & Jeff Parker
Pencilers: Ronan Cliquet, Marcio Takara,
Amilcar Pinna, Kevin Sharpe, Wes Craig
& Manuel Garcia
Inkers: Amilton Santos, Marcio Takara,
Amilcar Pinna, Terry Pallot, Wes Craig
& Scott Koblish
Colorists: Chris Sotomayor & Val Staples
Letterer: Dave Sharpe
Cover Artists: Barry Kitson & Val Staples;
Stephen Segovia; and Aaron Lopresti & Guru-eFX
Assistant Editors: Ellie Pyle & Nathan Cosby
Editors: Rachel Pinnelas & Mark Paniccia
Contributing Editor: Tom Brennan
Consulting Editor: Mackenzie Cadenhead
Senior Editor: Stephen Wacker

Collection Editor: Cory Levine
Assistant Editors: Alex Starbuck & Nelson Ribeiro
Editors, Special Projects: Jennifer Grünwald & Mark D. Beazley
Senior Editor, Special Projects: Jeff Youngquist
Senior Vice President of Sales: David Gabriel
SVP of Brand Planning & Communications: Michael Pasciullo

Editor in Chief: Axel Alonso
Chief Creative Officer: Joe Quesada
Publisher: Dan Buckley
Executive Producer: Alan Fine

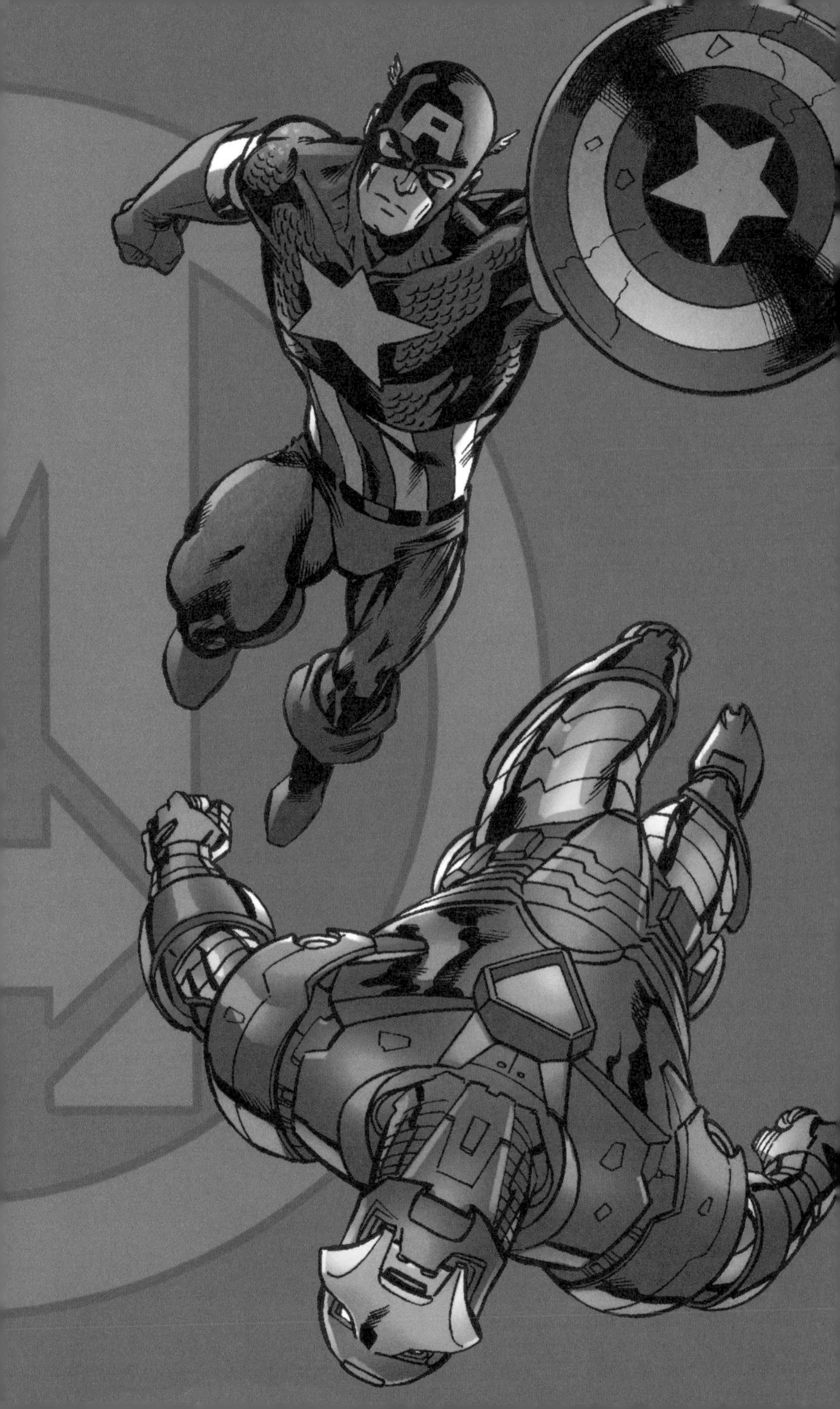

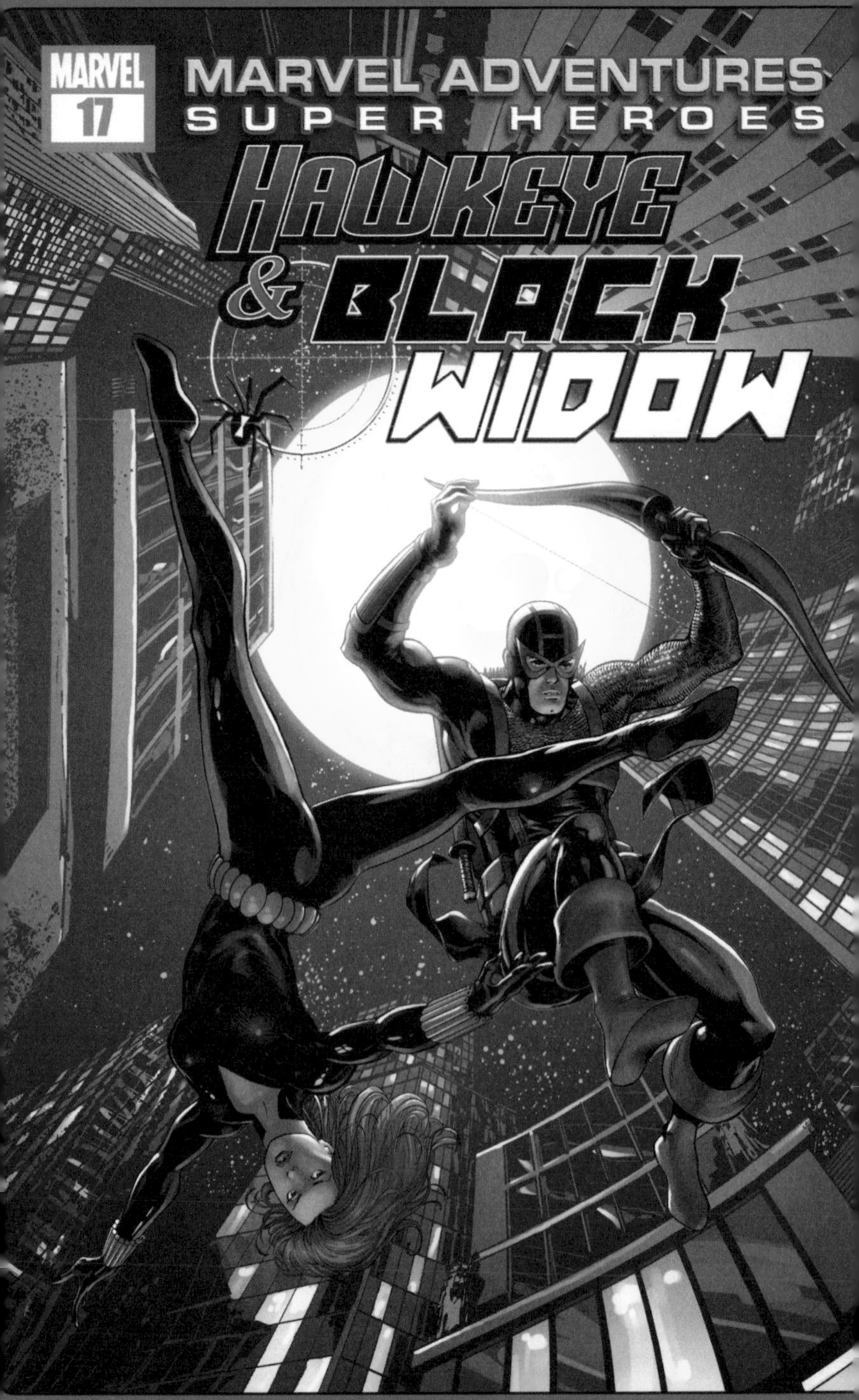

MARVEL
17
MARVEL ADVENTURES
SUPER HEROES
HAWKEYE
& BLACK
WIDOW

HAWKEYE & BLACK WIDOW

THE BLACK WIDOW
ATASHA ROMANOVA, SUPER-SPY, COVERT SPECIALIST

IRON MAN
TONY STARK, BILLIONAIRE INVENTOR, ONE-MAN ARMORED TANK

HAWKEYE
CLINT BARTON, THE ARCHING AVENGER

THERE ARE DANGERS THAT MANKIND CANNOT CONQUER. A MIGHTY FEW WOULD RISK THEIR LIVES TO DEFEND US ALL. THEY ARE

SUPER HEROES

HAWKEYE & IRON MAN IN **"RABID DOG"** AND THE BLACK WIDOW IN **"TELL NO SECRETS"**

PAUL TOBIN
WRITER

RONAN CLIQUET, MARCIO TAKARA & AMILCAR PINNA
PENCILERS

AMILTON SANTOS, MARCIO TAKARA & AMILCAR PINNA
INKERS

SOTOCOLOR
COLORIST

DAVE SHARPE
LETTERER

MANNY MEDEROS
PRODUCTION

BARRY KITSON & VAL STAPLES
COVER

RACHEL PINNELAS
EDITOR

STEPHEN WACKER
SENIOR EDITOR

AXEL ALONSO
DITOR IN CHIEF

JOE QUESADA
CHIEF CREATIVE OFFICER

DAN BUCKLEY
PUBLISHER

ALAN FINE
EXECUTIVE PRODUCEI

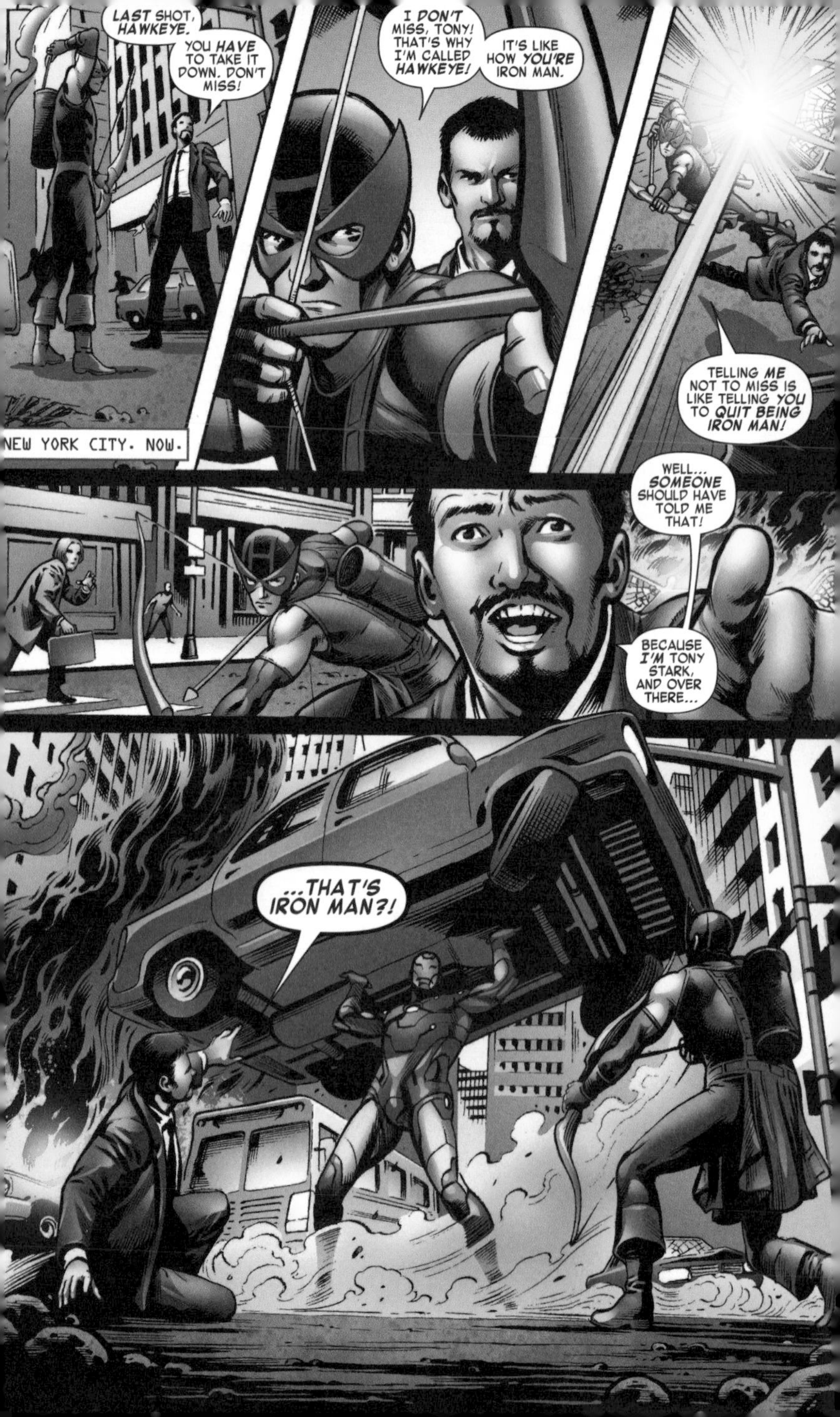
LAST SHOT, HAWKEYE.
YOU HAVE TO TAKE IT DOWN. DON'T MISS!
NEW YORK CITY. NOW.
I DON'T MISS, TONY! THAT'S WHY I'M CALLED HAWKEYE!
IT'S LIKE HOW YOU'RE IRON MAN.
TELLING ME NOT TO MISS IS LIKE TELLING YOU TO QUIT BEING IRON MAN!
WELL... SOMEONE SHOULD HAVE TOLD ME THAT!
BECAUSE I'M TONY STARK, AND OVER THERE...
...THAT'S IRON MAN?!

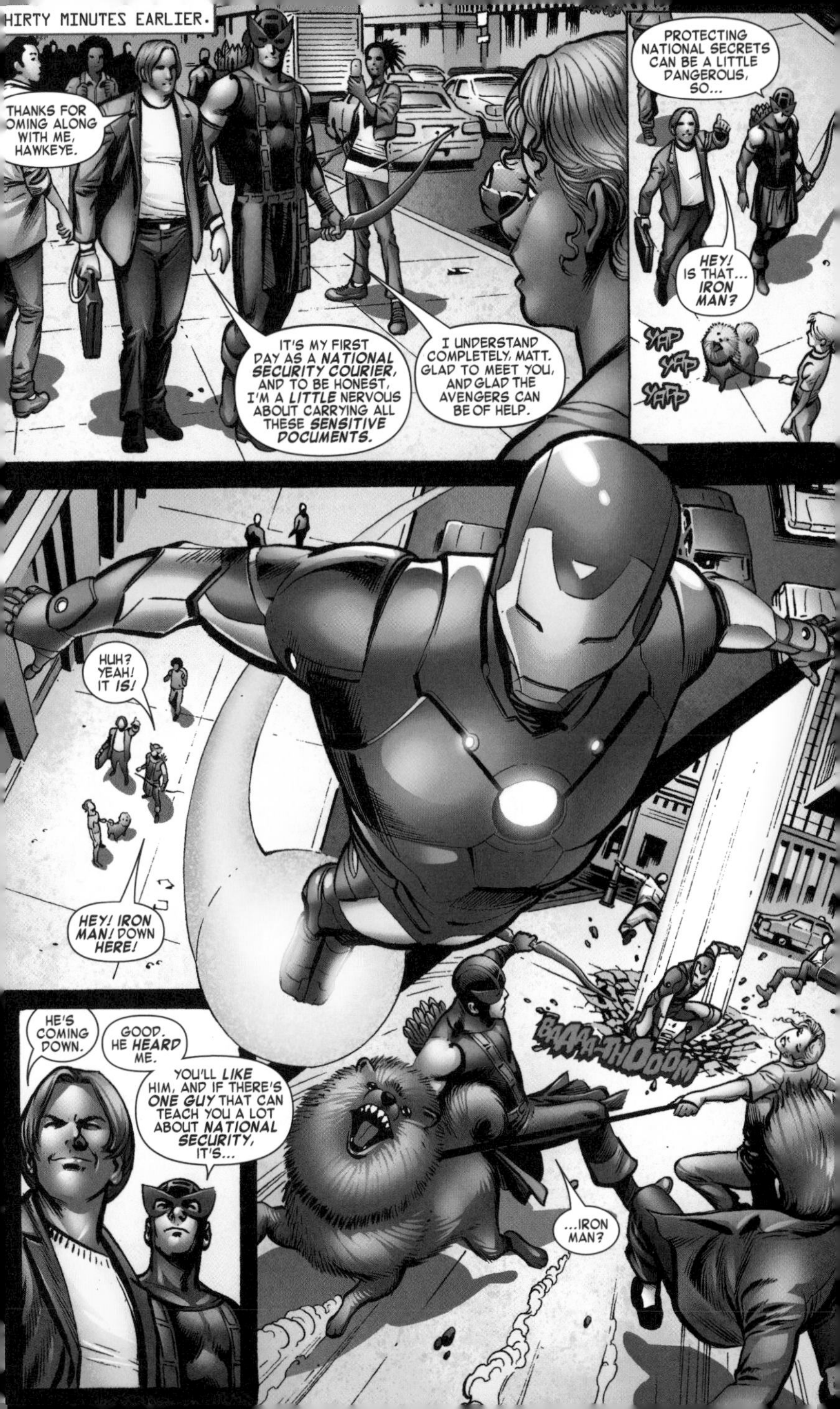
HIRTY MINUTES EARLIER.
THANKS FOR OMING ALONG WITH ME, HAWKEYE.
IT'S MY FIRST DAY AS A NATIONAL SECURITY COURIER, AND TO BE HONEST, I'M A LITTLE NERVOUS ABOUT CARRYING ALL THESE SENSITIVE DOCUMENTS.
I UNDERSTAND COMPLETELY, MATT. GLAD TO MEET YOU, AND GLAD THE AVENGERS CAN BE OF HELP.
PROTECTING NATIONAL SECRETS CAN BE A LITTLE DANGEROUS, SO...
HEY! IS THAT... IRON MAN?
YAP
YAP
YAP
HUH? YEAH! IT IS!
HEY! IRON MAN! DOWN HERE!
HE'S COMING DOWN.
GOOD. HE HEARD ME.
YOU'LL LIKE HIM, AND IF THERE'S ONE GUY THAT CAN TEACH YOU A LOT ABOUT NATIONAL SECURITY, IT'S...
BAAAA-THOOOM
...IRON MAN?

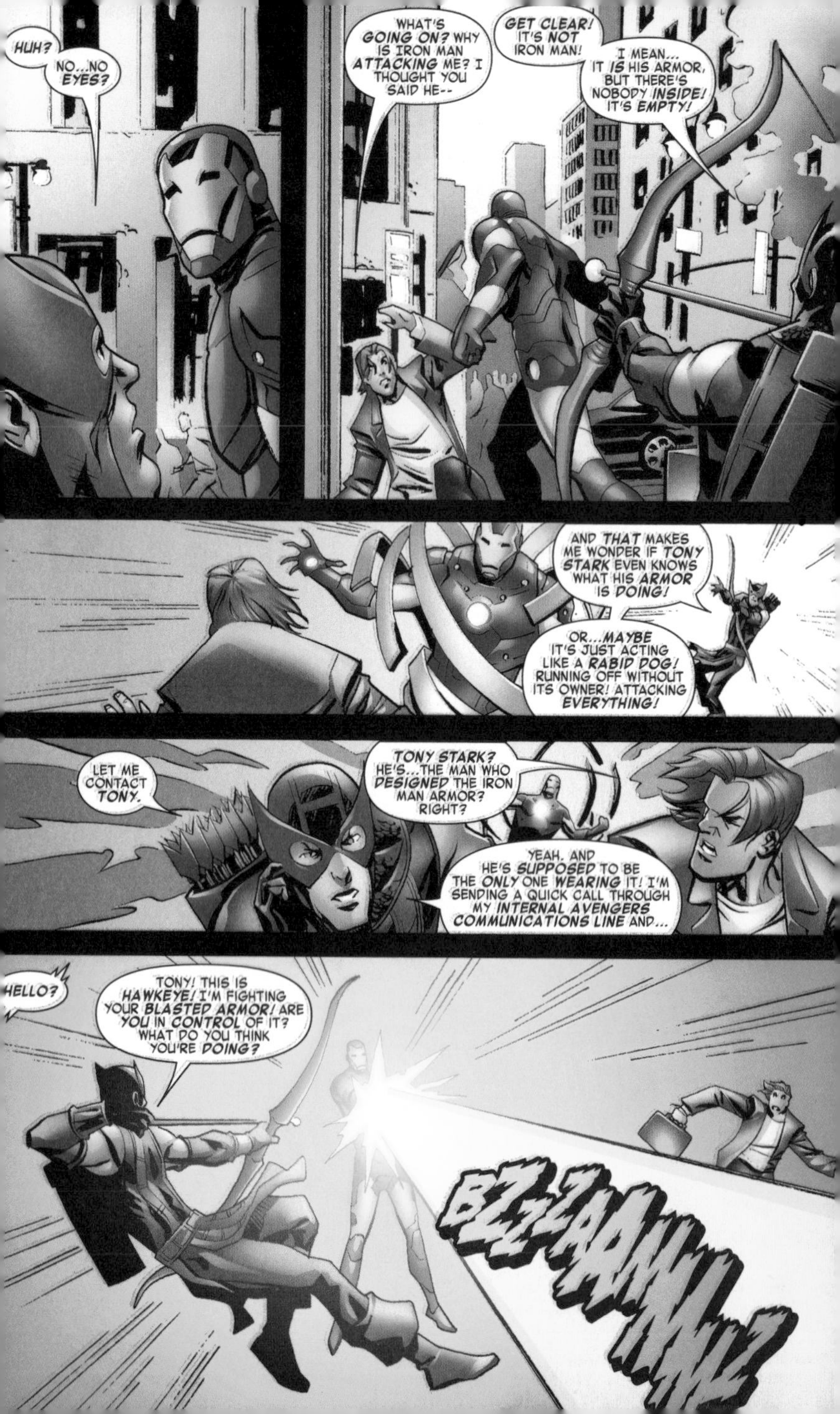
HUH?
NO...NO EYES?
WHAT'S GOING ON? WHY IS IRON MAN ATTACKING ME? I THOUGHT YOU SAID HE--
GET CLEAR! IT'S NOT IRON MAN!
I MEAN... IT IS HIS ARMOR, BUT THERE'S NOBODY INSIDE! IT'S EMPTY!
AND THAT MAKES ME WONDER IF TONY STARK EVEN KNOWS WHAT HIS ARMOR IS DOING!
OR...MAYBE IT'S JUST ACTING LIKE A RABID DOG! RUNNING OFF WITHOUT ITS OWNER! ATTACKING EVERYTHING!
LET ME CONTACT TONY.
TONY STARK? HE'S...THE MAN WHO DESIGNED THE IRON MAN ARMOR? RIGHT?
YEAH. AND HE'S SUPPOSED TO BE THE ONLY ONE WEARING IT! I'M SENDING A QUICK CALL THROUGH MY INTERNAL AVENGERS COMMUNICATIONS LINE AND...
HELLO?
TONY! THIS IS HAWKEYE! I'M FIGHTING YOUR BLASTED ARMOR! ARE YOU IN CONTROL OF IT? WHAT DO YOU THINK YOU'RE DOING?
BZZZARAKK!

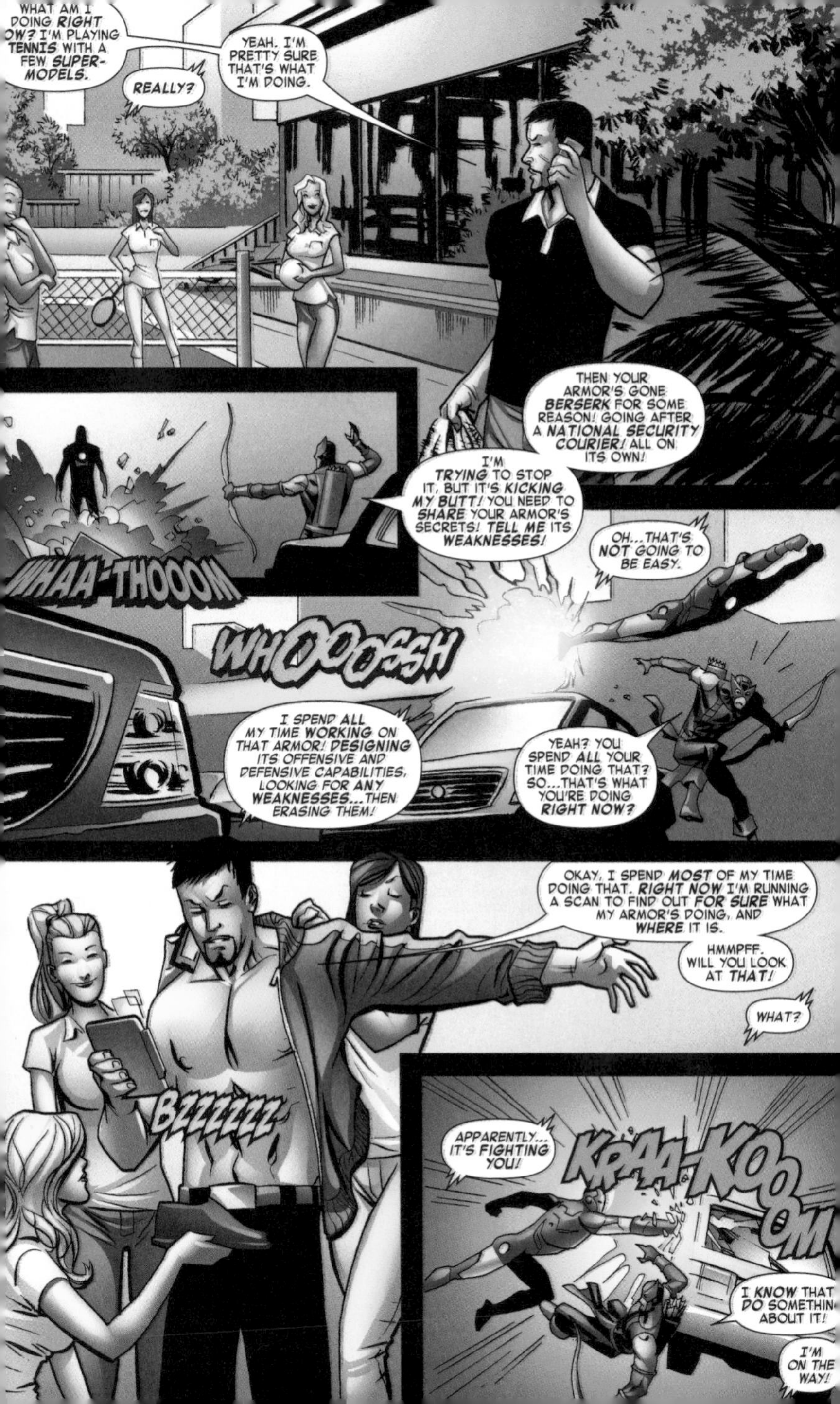

WHAT AM I DOING RIGHT OW? I'M PLAYING TENNIS WITH A FEW SUPER-MODELS.
REALLY?
YEAH. I'M PRETTY SURE THAT'S WHAT I'M DOING.
THEN YOUR ARMOR'S GONE BERSERK FOR SOME REASON! GOING AFTER A NATIONAL SECURITY COURIER! ALL ON ITS OWN!
I'M TRYING TO STOP IT, BUT IT'S KICKING MY BUTT! YOU NEED TO SHARE YOUR ARMOR'S SECRETS! TELL ME ITS WEAKNESSES!
WHAA-THOOOM
OH...THAT'S NOT GOING TO BE EASY.
WHOOOSSH
I SPEND ALL MY TIME WORKING ON THAT ARMOR! DESIGNING ITS OFFENSIVE AND DEFENSIVE CAPABILITIES, LOOKING FOR ANY WEAKNESSES...THEN ERASING THEM!
YEAH? YOU SPEND ALL YOUR TIME DOING THAT? SO...THAT'S WHAT YOU'RE DOING RIGHT NOW?
OKAY, I SPEND MOST OF MY TIME DOING THAT. RIGHT NOW I'M RUNNING A SCAN TO FIND OUT FOR SURE WHAT MY ARMOR'S DOING, AND WHERE IT IS.
HMMPFF. WILL YOU LOOK AT THAT!
WHAT?
BZZZZZZ
APPARENTLY... IT'S FIGHTING YOU!
KRAA-KOOOOM
I KNOW THAT DO SOMETHIN ABOUT IT!
I'M ON THE WAY!

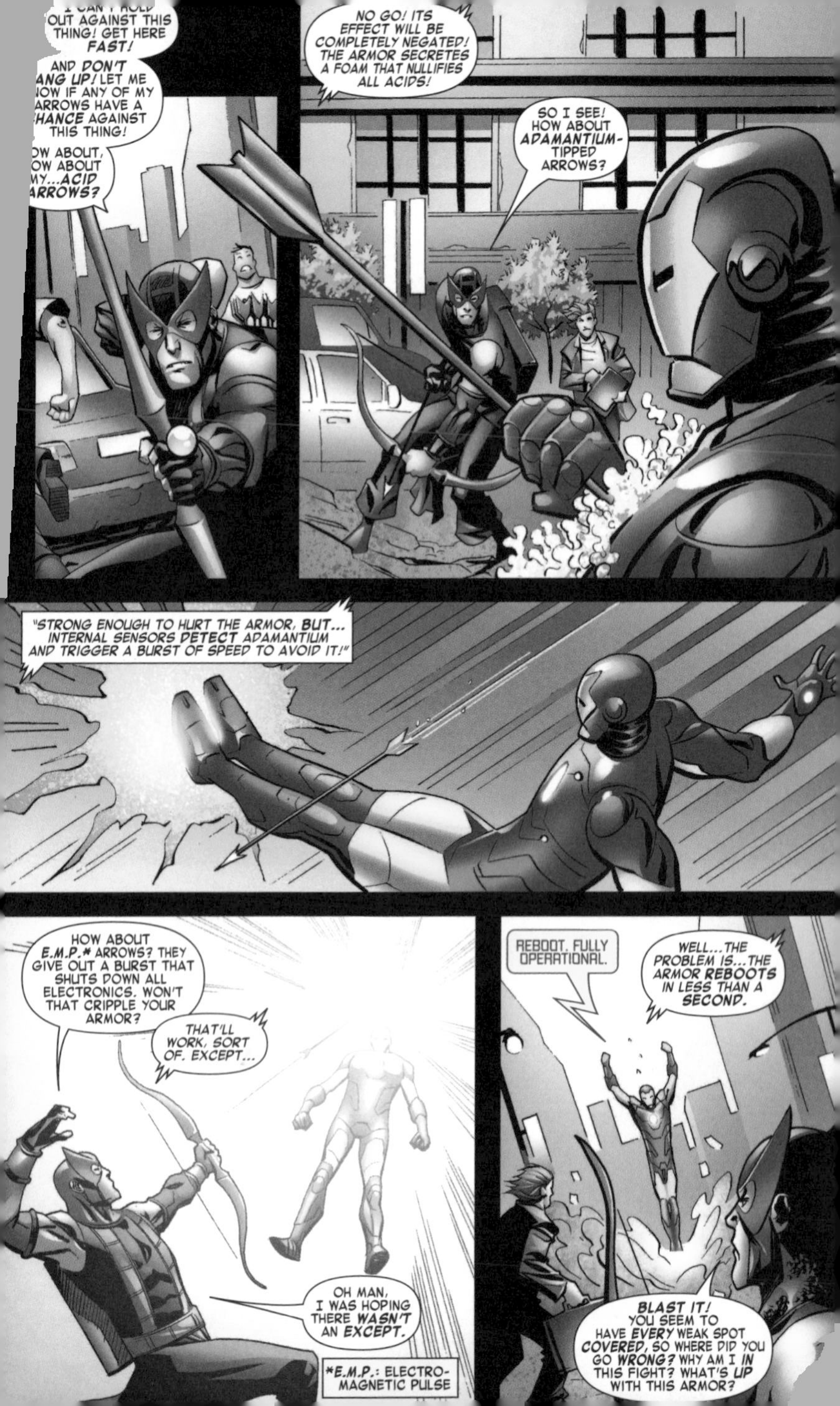

OUT AGAINST THIS THING! GET HERE FAST!
AND DON'T ANG UP! LET ME OW IF ANY OF MY ARROWS HAVE A HANCE AGAINST THIS THING!
OW ABOUT, OW ABOUT MY...ACID ARROWS?
NO GO! ITS EFFECT WILL BE COMPLETELY NEGATED! THE ARMOR SECRETES A FOAM THAT NULLIFIES ALL ACIDS!
SO I SEE! HOW ABOUT ADAMANTIUM-TIPPED ARROWS?
"STRONG ENOUGH TO HURT THE ARMOR, BUT... INTERNAL SENSORS DETECT ADAMANTIUM AND TRIGGER A BURST OF SPEED TO AVOID IT!"
HOW ABOUT E.M.P.* ARROWS? THEY GIVE OUT A BURST THAT SHUTS DOWN ALL ELECTRONICS. WON'T THAT CRIPPLE YOUR ARMOR?
THAT'LL WORK, SORT OF. EXCEPT...
OH MAN, I WAS HOPING THERE WASN'T AN EXCEPT.
*E.M.P.: ELECTRO-MAGNETIC PULSE
REBOOT. FULLY OPERATIONAL.
WELL... THE PROBLEM IS... THE ARMOR REBOOTS IN LESS THAN A SECOND.
BLAST IT! YOU SEEM TO HAVE EVERY WEAK SPOT COVERED, SO WHERE DID YOU GO WRONG? WHY AM I IN THIS FIGHT? WHAT'S UP WITH THIS ARMOR?

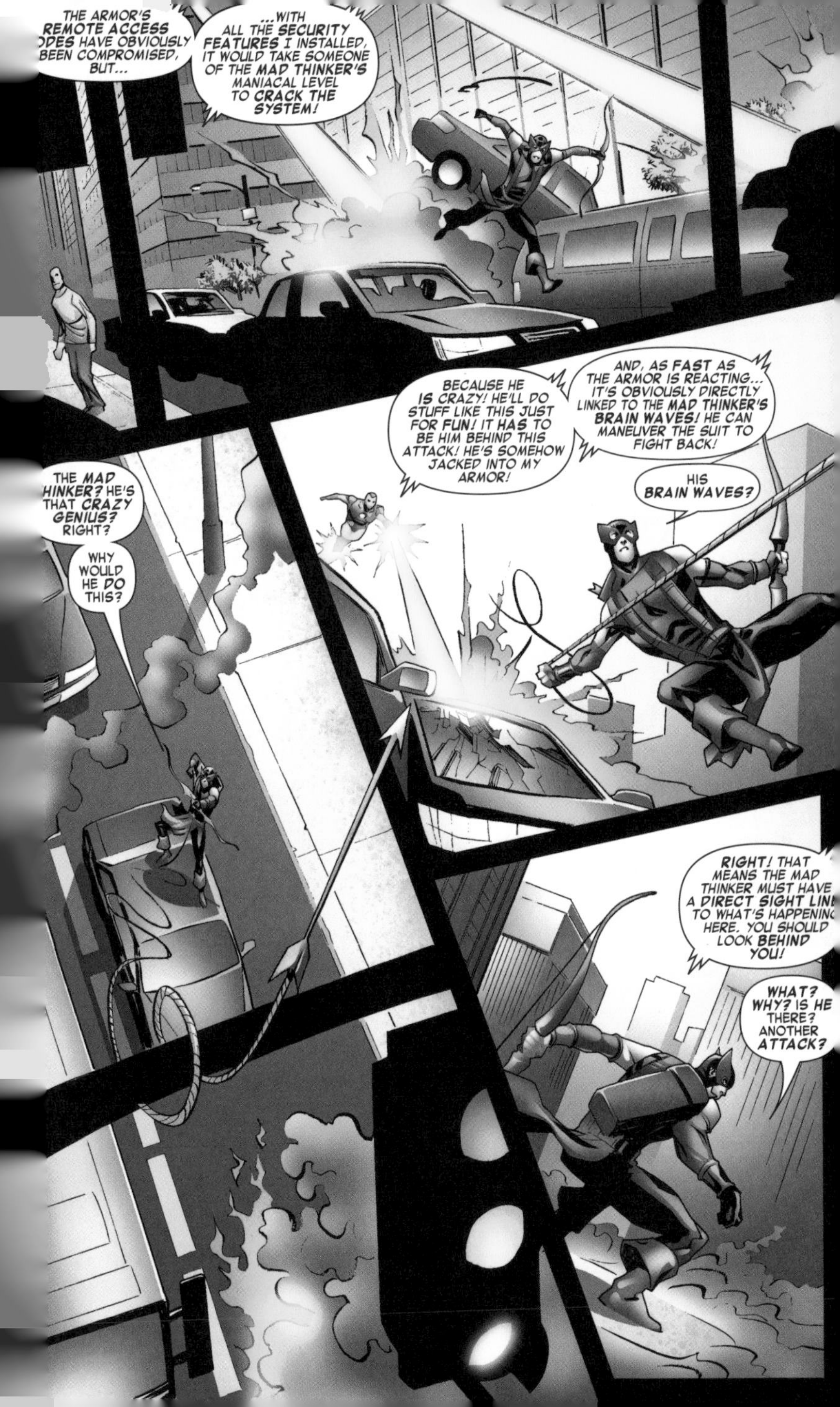
THE ARMOR'S REMOTE ACCESS ODES HAVE OBVIOUSLY BEEN COMPROMISED, BUT...
...WITH ALL THE SECURITY FEATURES I INSTALLED, IT WOULD TAKE SOMEONE OF THE MAD THINKER'S MANIACAL LEVEL TO CRACK THE SYSTEM!
THE MAD HINKER? HE'S THAT CRAZY GENIUS? RIGHT?
WHY WOULD HE DO THIS?
BECAUSE HE IS CRAZY! HE'LL DO STUFF LIKE THIS JUST FOR FUN! IT HAS TO BE HIM BEHIND THIS ATTACK! HE'S SOMEHOW JACKED INTO MY ARMOR!
AND, AS FAST AS THE ARMOR IS REACTING... IT'S OBVIOUSLY DIRECTLY LINKED TO THE MAD THINKER'S BRAIN WAVES! HE CAN MANEUVER THE SUIT TO FIGHT BACK!
HIS BRAIN WAVES?
RIGHT! THAT MEANS THE MAD THINKER MUST HAVE A DIRECT SIGHT LIN TO WHAT'S HAPPENIN HERE. YOU SHOULD LOOK BEHIND YOU!
WHAT? WHY? IS HE THERE? ANOTHER ATTACK?

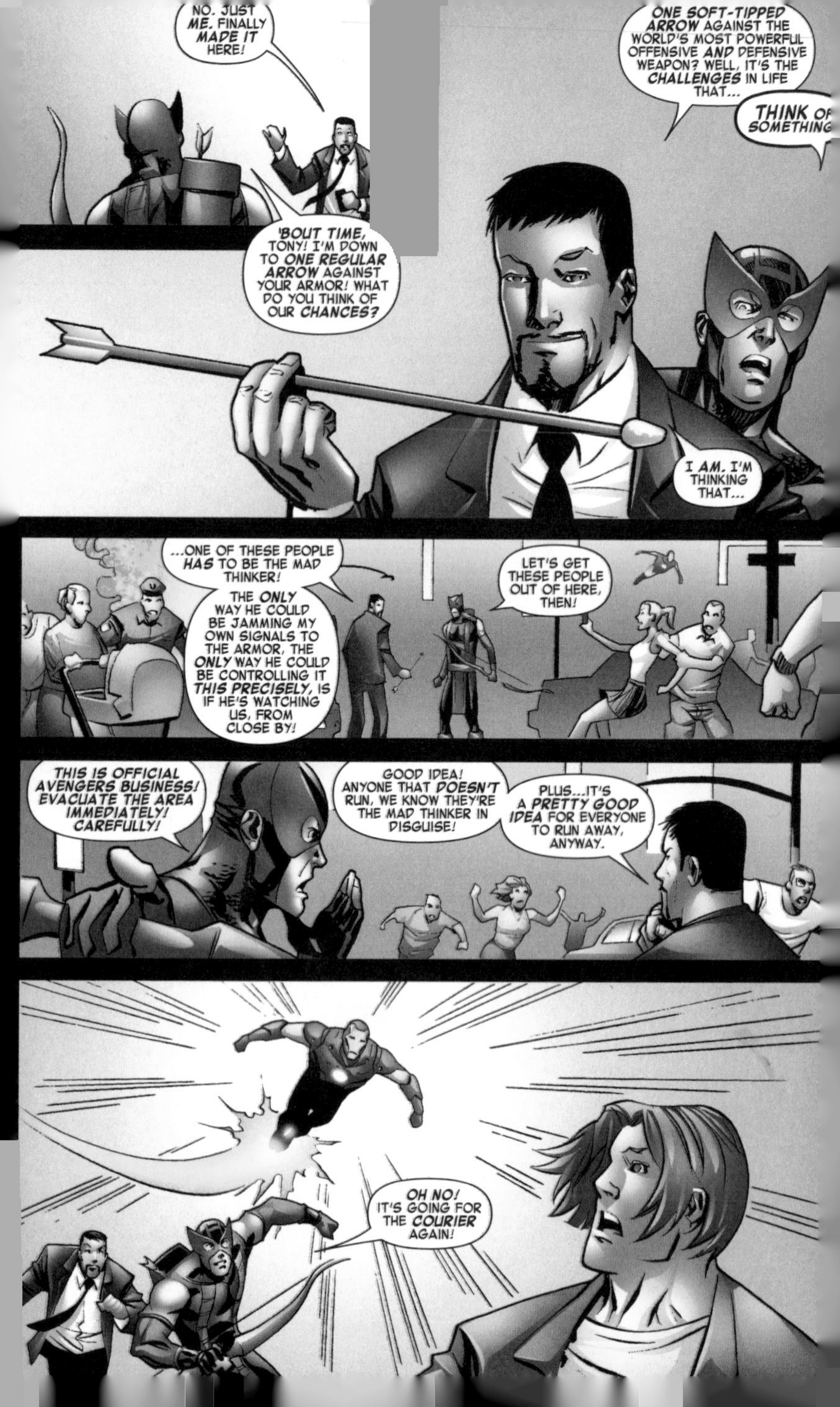
NO. JUST ME. FINALLY MADE IT HERE!
ONE SOFT-TIPPED ARROW AGAINST THE WORLD'S MOST POWERFUL OFFENSIVE AND DEFENSIVE WEAPON? WELL, IT'S THE CHALLENGES IN LIFE THAT...
THINK OF SOMETHING
'BOUT TIME, TONY! I'M DOWN TO ONE REGULAR ARROW AGAINST YOUR ARMOR! WHAT DO YOU THINK OF OUR CHANCES?
I AM. I'M THINKING THAT...
...ONE OF THESE PEOPLE HAS TO BE THE MAD THINKER!
THE ONLY WAY HE COULD BE JAMMING MY OWN SIGNALS TO THE ARMOR, THE ONLY WAY HE COULD BE CONTROLLING IT THIS PRECISELY, IS IF HE'S WATCHING US, FROM CLOSE BY!
LET'S GET THESE PEOPLE OUT OF HERE, THEN!
THIS IS OFFICIAL AVENGERS BUSINESS! EVACUATE THE AREA IMMEDIATELY! CAREFULLY!
GOOD IDEA! ANYONE THAT DOESN'T RUN, WE KNOW THEY'RE THE MAD THINKER IN DISGUISE!
PLUS...IT'S A PRETTY GOOD IDEA FOR EVERYONE TO RUN AWAY, ANYWAY.
OH NO! IT'S GOING FOR THE COURIER AGAIN!

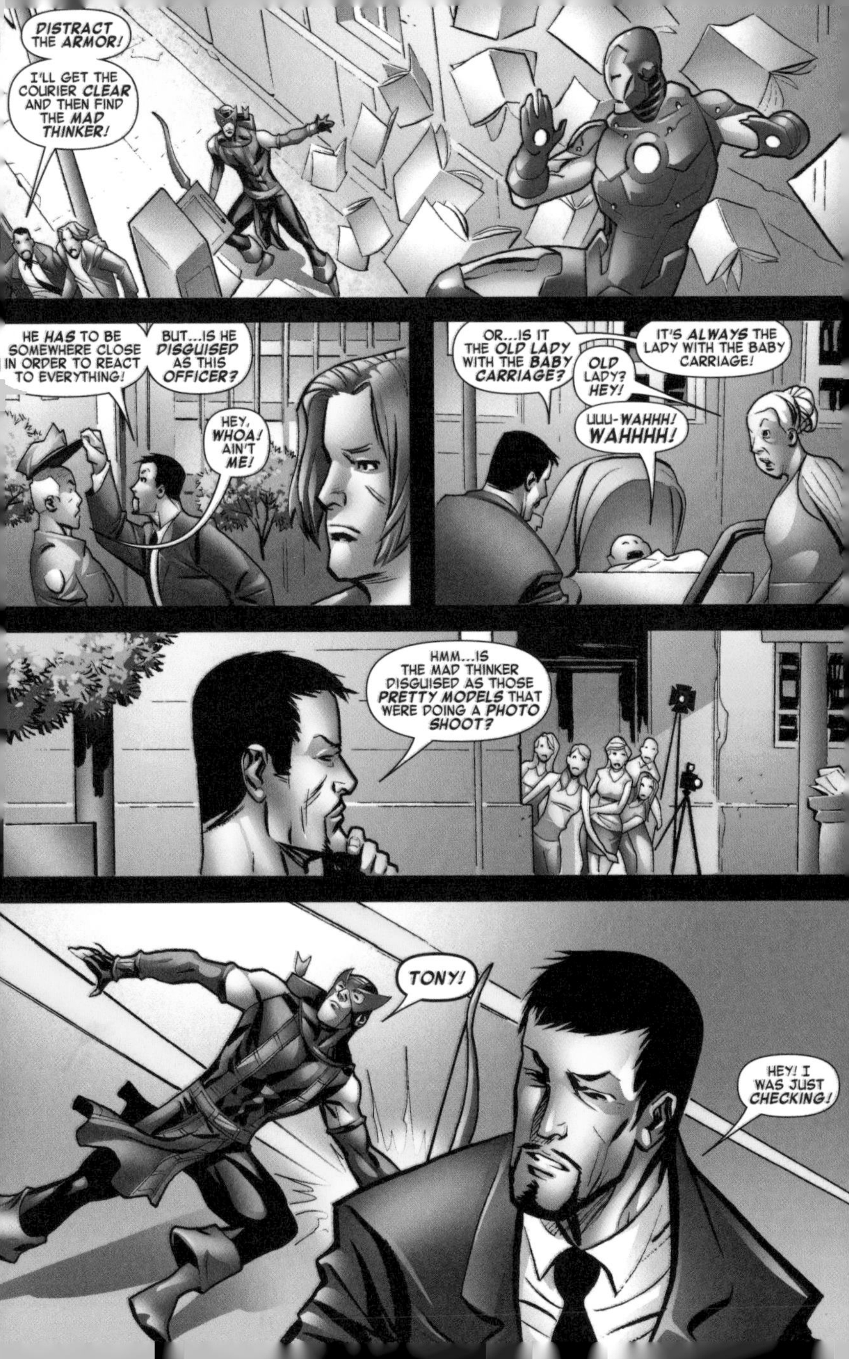
DISTRACT THE ARMOR!
I'LL GET THE COURIER CLEAR AND THEN FIND THE MAD THINKER!
HE HAS TO BE SOMEWHERE CLOSE IN ORDER TO REACT TO EVERYTHING!
BUT...IS HE DISGUISED AS THIS OFFICER?
HEY, WHOA! AIN'T ME!
OR...IS IT THE OLD LADY WITH THE BABY CARRIAGE?
IT'S ALWAYS THE LADY WITH THE BABY CARRIAGE!
OLD LADY? HEY!
UUU-WAHHH! WAHHHH!
HMM...IS THE MAD THINKER DISGUISED AS THOSE PRETTY MODELS THAT WERE DOING A PHOTO SHOOT?
TONY!
HEY! I WAS JUST CHECKING!

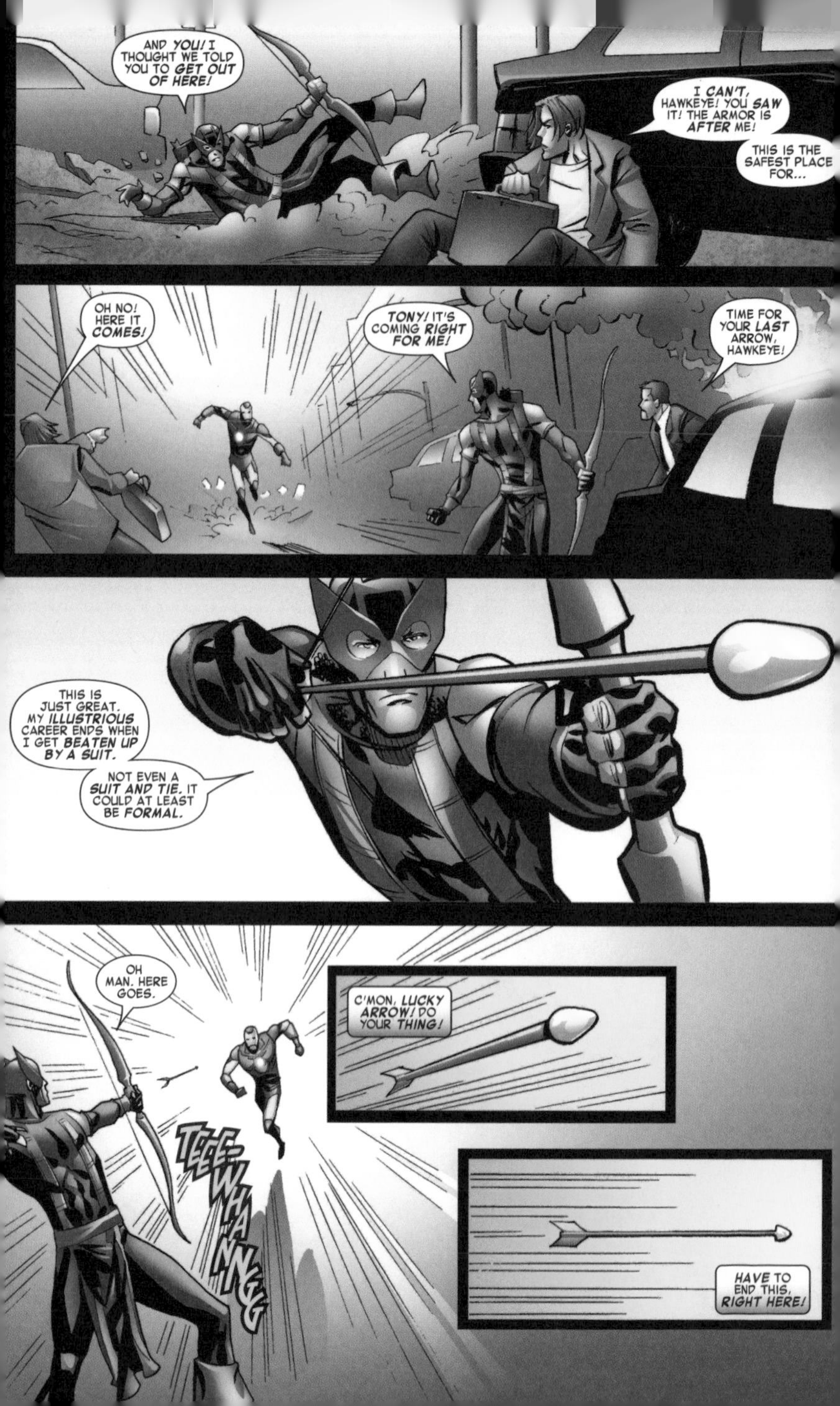

AND YOU! I THOUGHT WE TOLD YOU TO GET OUT OF HERE!
I CAN'T, HAWKEYE! YOU SAW IT! THE ARMOR IS AFTER ME!
THIS IS THE SAFEST PLACE FOR...
OH NO! HERE IT COMES!
TONY! IT'S COMING RIGHT FOR ME!
TIME FOR YOUR LAST ARROW, HAWKEYE!
THIS IS JUST GREAT. MY ILLUSTRIOUS CAREER ENDS WHEN I GET BEATEN UP BY A SUIT.
NOT EVEN A SUIT AND TIE. IT COULD AT LEAST BE FORMAL.
OH MAN. HERE GOES.
C'MON, LUCKY ARROW! DO YOUR THING!
TEEE-WHAANNNGG
HAVE TO END THIS, RIGHT HERE!

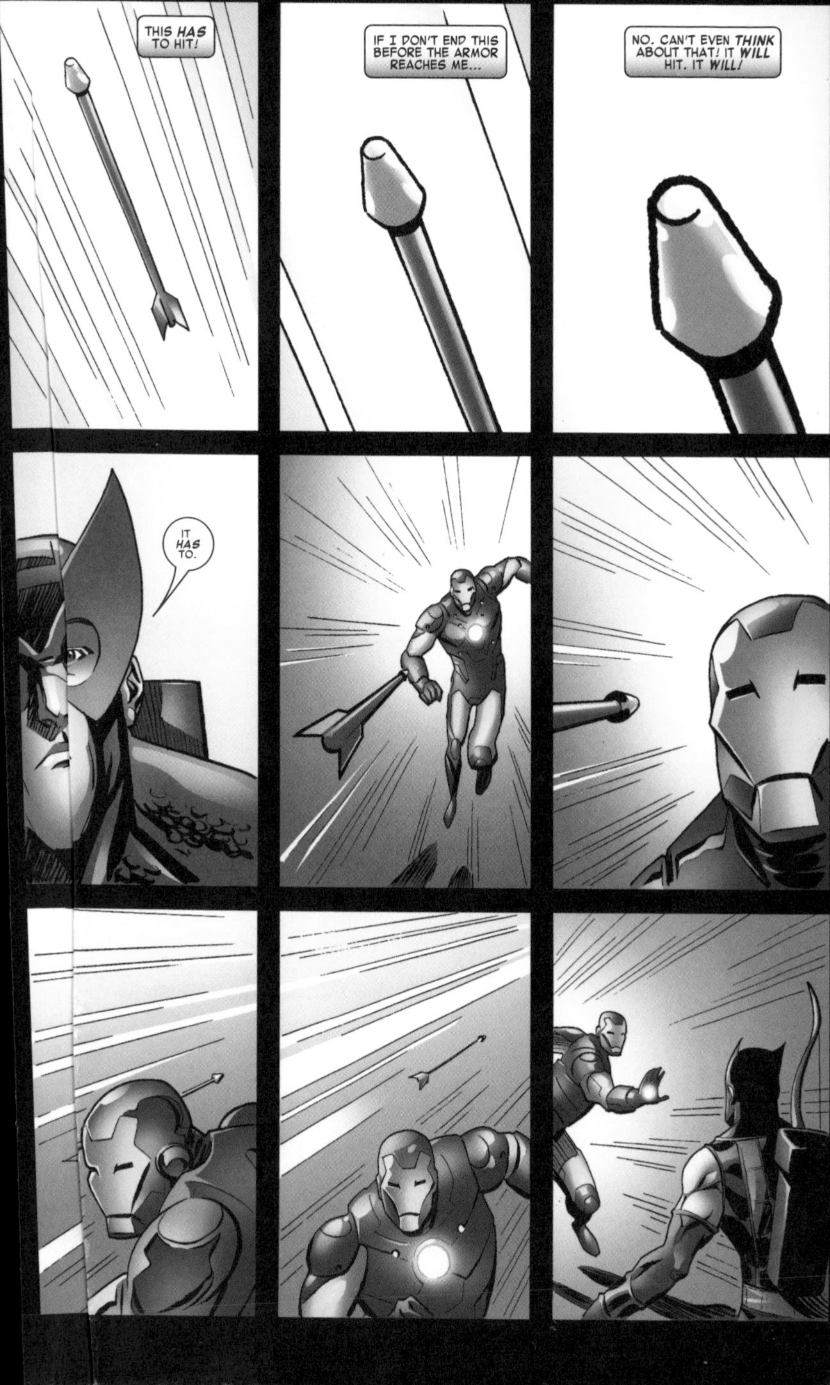
THIS HAS TO HIT!
IF I DON'T END THIS BEFORE THE ARMOR REACHES ME...
NO. CAN'T EVEN THINK ABOUT THAT! IT WILL HIT. IT WILL!
IT HAS TO.

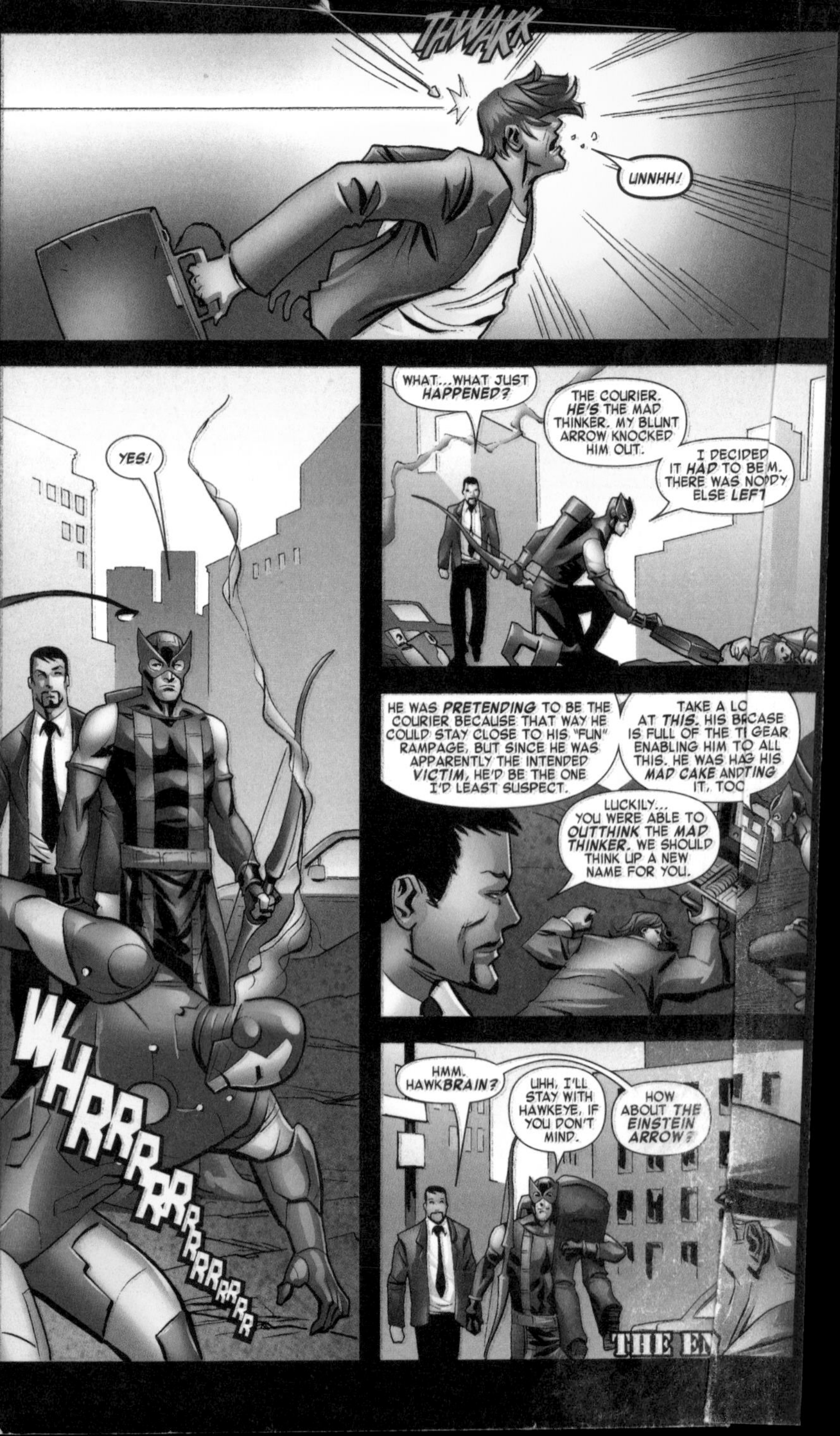
THWAKK
UNNHH!
YES!
WHRRRRRRRRRRRRR
WHAT...WHAT JUST HAPPENED?
THE COURIER. HE'S THE MAD THINKER. MY BLUNT ARROW KNOCKED HIM OUT.
I DECIDED IT HAD TO BE M. THERE WAS NO DY ELSE LEFT
HE WAS PRETENDING TO BE THE COURIER BECAUSE THAT WAY HE COULD STAY CLOSE TO HIS "FUN" RAMPAGE, BUT SINCE HE WAS APPARENTLY THE INTENDED VICTIM, HE'D BE THE ONE I'D LEAST SUSPECT.
TAKE A LO AT THIS. HIS B CASE IS FULL OF THE T GEAR ENABLING HIM TO ALL THIS. HE WAS HA G HIS MAD CAKE AND TING IT, TOO
LUCKILY... YOU WERE ABLE TO OUTTHINK THE MAD THINKER. WE SHOULD THINK UP A NEW NAME FOR YOU.
HMM. HAWKBRAIN?
UHH, I'LL STAY WITH HAWKEYE, IF YOU DON'T MIND.
HOW ABOUT THE EINSTEIN ARROW?
THE EN

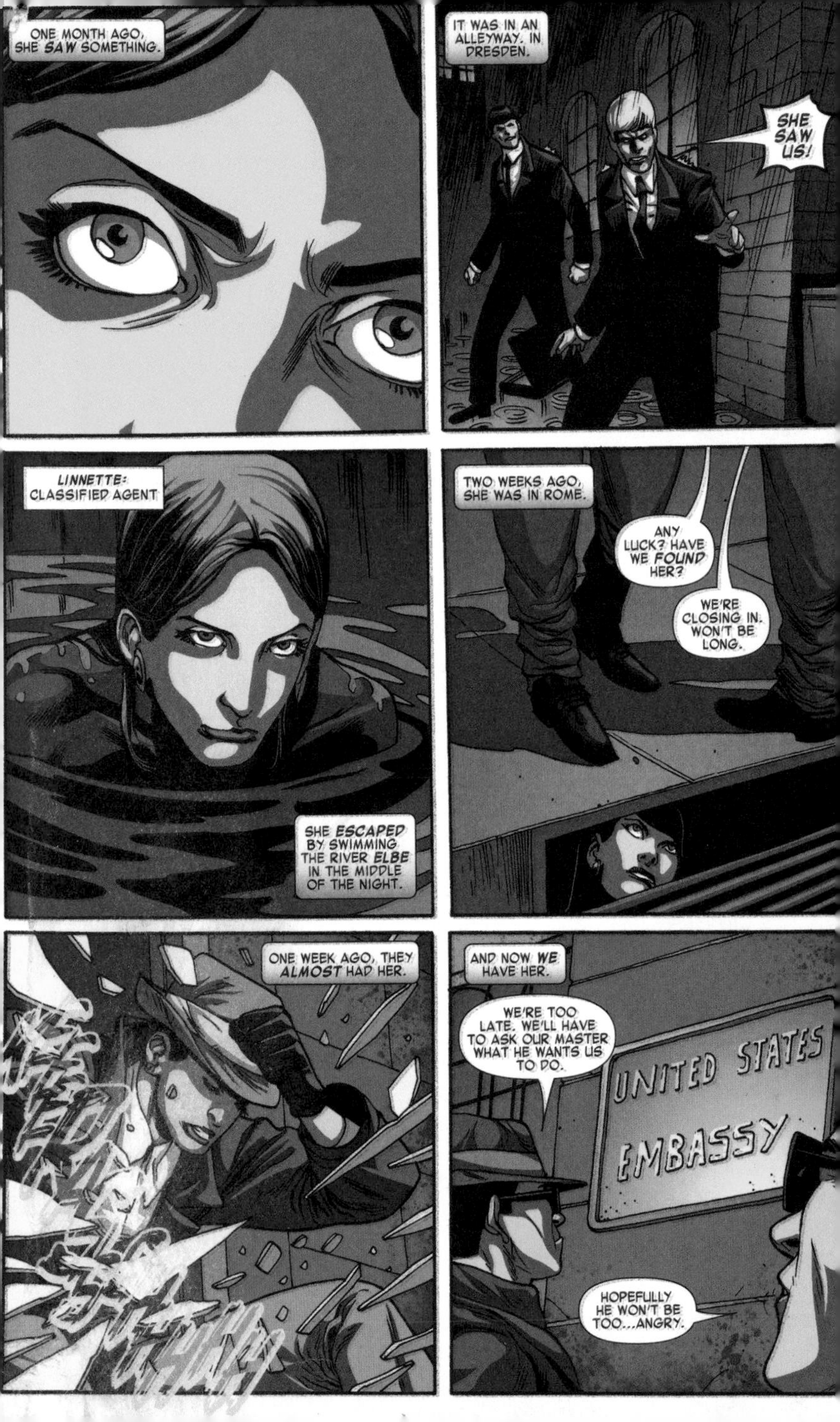
ONE MONTH AGO, SHE SAW SOMETHING.
IT WAS IN AN ALLEYWAY. IN DRESDEN.
SHE SAW US!
LINNETTE: CLASSIFIED AGENT
SHE ESCAPED BY SWIMMING THE RIVER ELBE IN THE MIDDLE OF THE NIGHT.
TWO WEEKS AGO, SHE WAS IN ROME.
ANY LUCK? HAVE WE FOUND HER?
WE'RE CLOSING IN. WON'T BE LONG.
ONE WEEK AGO, THEY ALMOST HAD HER.
AND NOW WE HAVE HER.
WE'RE TOO LATE. WE'LL HAVE TO ASK OUR MASTER WHAT HE WANTS US TO DO.
UNITED STATES EMBASSY
HOPEFULLY HE WON'T BE TOO...ANGRY.

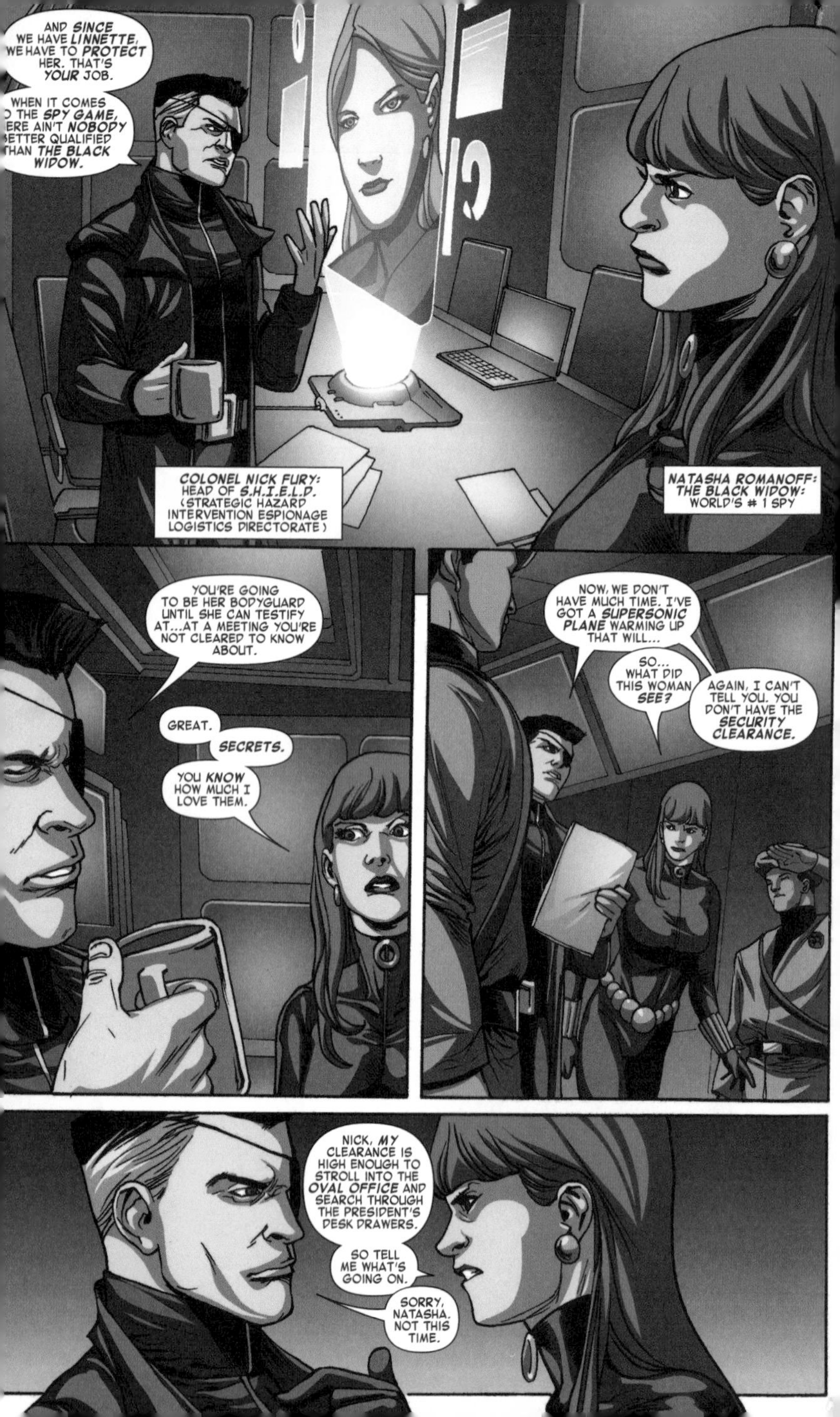
AND SINCE WE HAVE LINNETTE, WE HAVE TO PROTECT HER. THAT'S YOUR JOB.
WHEN IT COMES TO THE SPY GAME, THERE AIN'T NOBODY BETTER QUALIFIED THAN THE BLACK WIDOW.
COLONEL NICK FURY: HEAD OF S.H.I.E.L.D. (STRATEGIC HAZARD INTERVENTION ESPIONAGE LOGISTICS DIRECTORATE)
NATASHA ROMANOFF: THE BLACK WIDOW: WORLD'S # 1 SPY
YOU'RE GOING TO BE HER BODYGUARD UNTIL SHE CAN TESTIFY AT...AT A MEETING YOU'RE NOT CLEARED TO KNOW ABOUT.
GREAT.
SECRETS.
YOU KNOW HOW MUCH I LOVE THEM.
NOW, WE DON'T HAVE MUCH TIME. I'VE GOT A SUPERSONIC PLANE WARMING UP THAT WILL...
SO... WHAT DID THIS WOMAN SEE?
AGAIN, I CAN'T TELL YOU. YOU DON'T HAVE THE SECURITY CLEARANCE.
NICK, MY CLEARANCE IS HIGH ENOUGH TO STROLL INTO THE OVAL OFFICE AND SEARCH THROUGH THE PRESIDENT'S DESK DRAWERS.
SO TELL ME WHAT'S GOING ON.
SORRY, NATASHA. NOT THIS TIME.

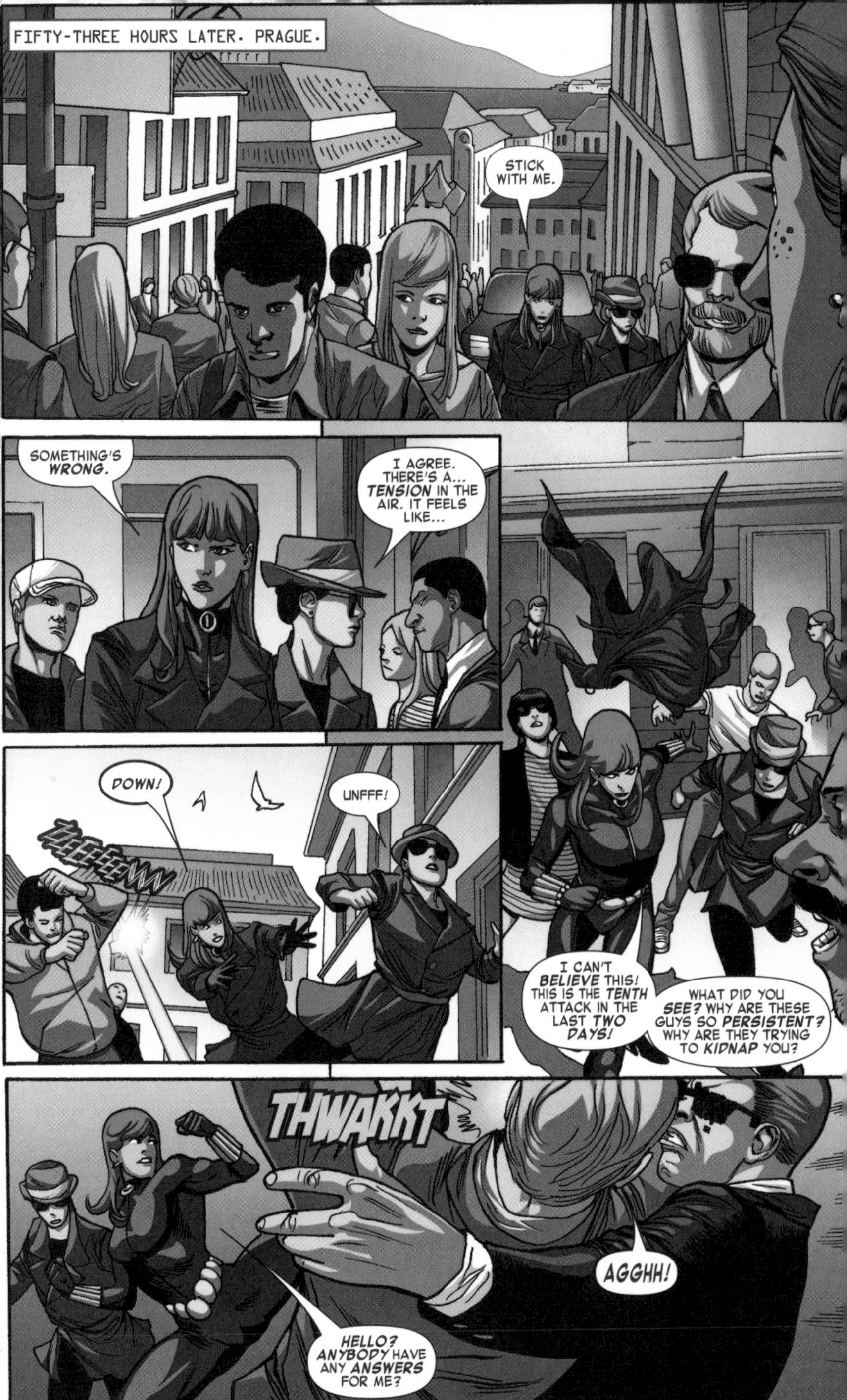
FIFTY-THREE HOURS LATER. PRAGUE.
STICK WITH ME.
SOMETHING'S WRONG.
I AGREE. THERE'S A... TENSION IN THE AIR. IT FEELS LIKE...
DOWN!
ZZEEEEEEWN
UNFFF!
I CAN'T BELIEVE THIS! THIS IS THE TENTH ATTACK IN THE LAST TWO DAYS!
WHAT DID YOU SEE? WHY ARE THESE GUYS SO PERSISTENT? WHY ARE THEY TRYING TO KIDNAP YOU?
THWAKKT
AGGHH!
HELLO? ANYBODY HAVE ANY ANSWERS FOR ME?

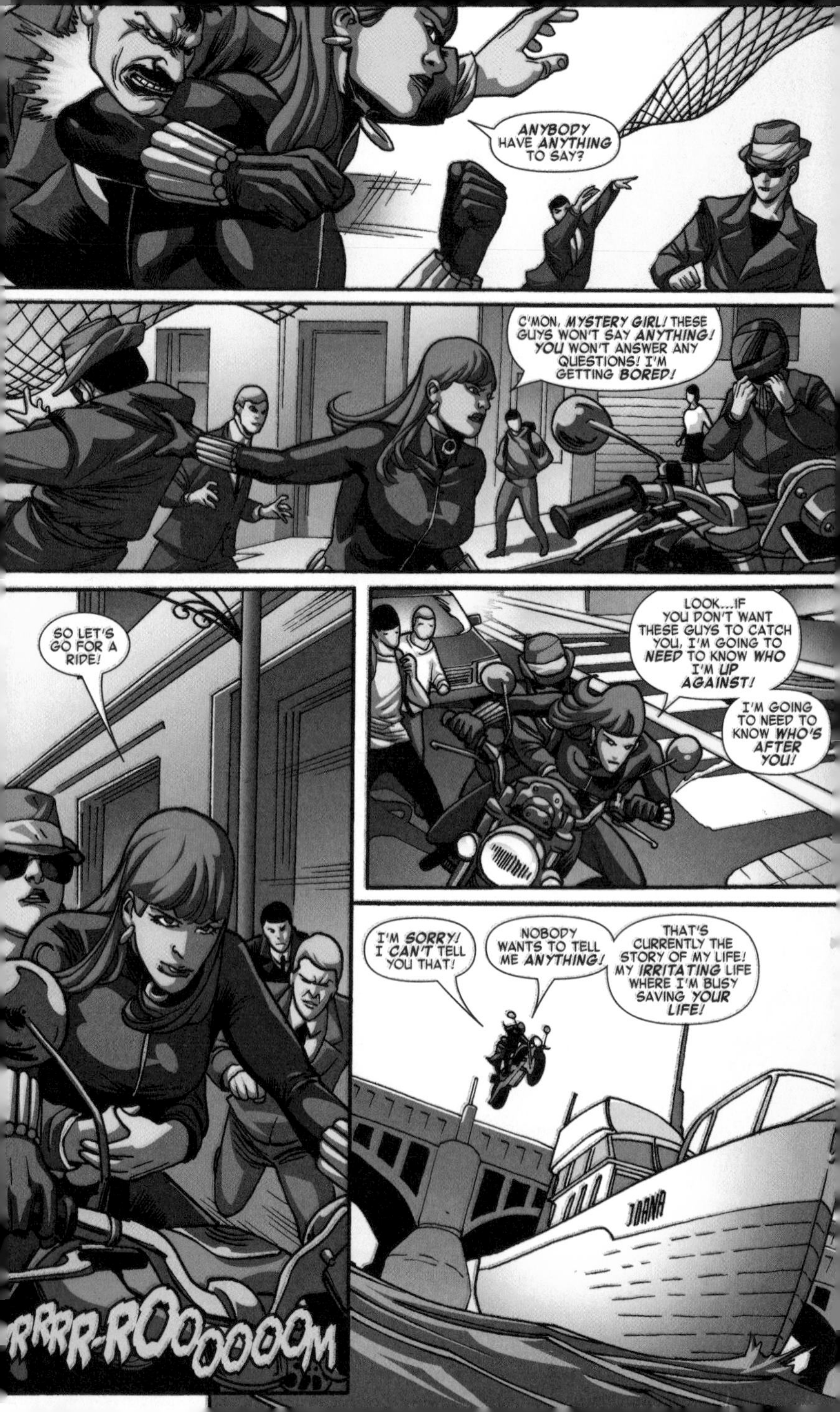
ANYBODY HAVE ANYTHING TO SAY?
C'MON, MYSTERY GIRL! THESE GUYS WON'T SAY ANYTHING! YOU WON'T ANSWER ANY QUESTIONS! I'M GETTING BORED!
SO LET'S GO FOR A RIDE!
RRRR-ROOOOOOM
LOOK...IF YOU DON'T WANT THESE GUYS TO CATCH YOU, I'M GOING TO NEED TO KNOW WHO I'M UP AGAINST!
I'M GOING TO NEED TO KNOW WHO'S AFTER YOU!
I'M SORRY! I CAN'T TELL YOU THAT!
NOBODY WANTS TO TELL ME ANYTHING!
THAT'S CURRENTLY THE STORY OF MY LIFE! MY IRRITATING LIFE WHERE I'M BUSY SAVING YOUR LIFE!
JOANA

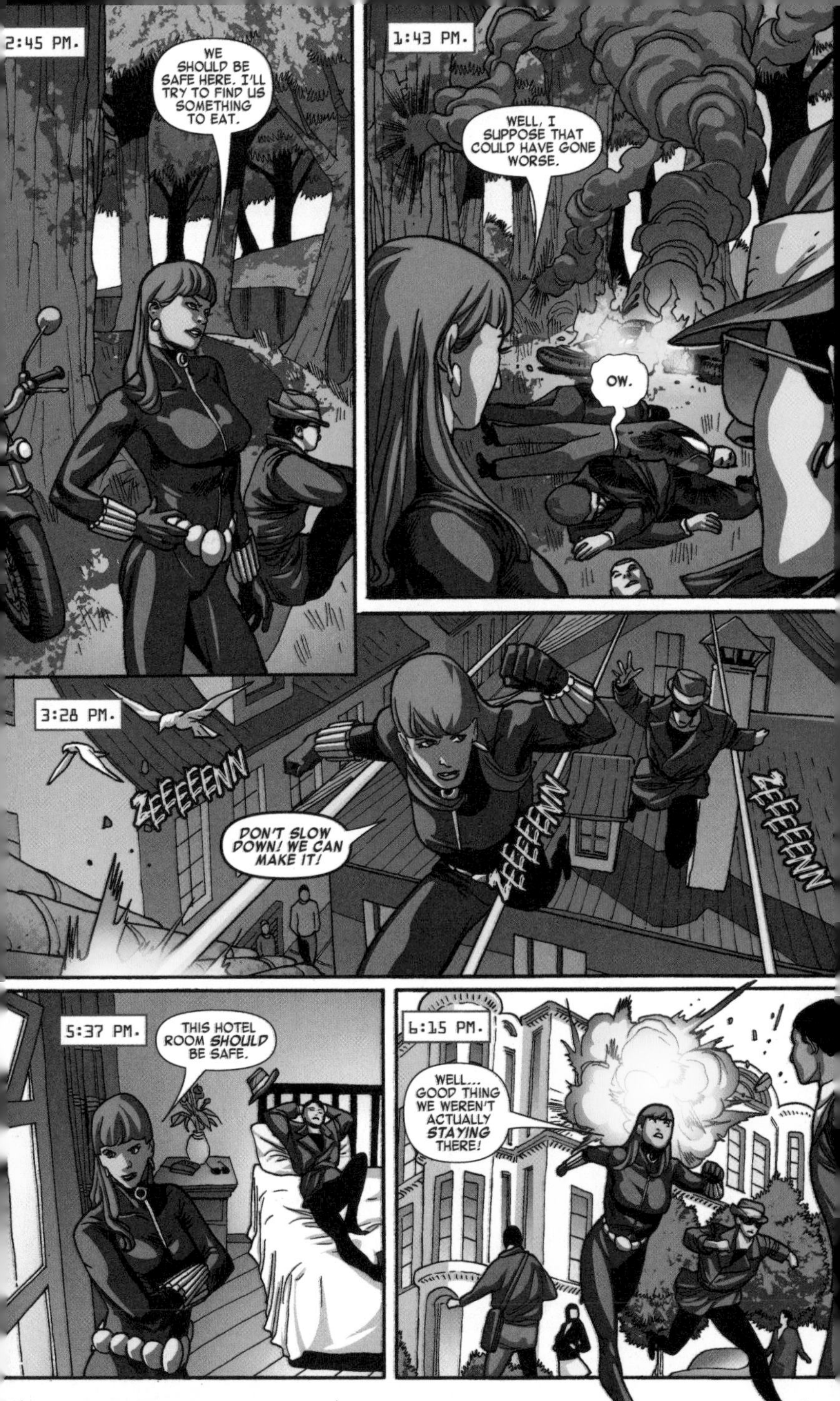
2:45 PM.
WE SHOULD BE SAFE HERE. I'LL TRY TO FIND US SOMETHING TO EAT.
1:43 PM.
WELL, I SUPPOSE THAT COULD HAVE GONE WORSE.
OW.
3:28 PM.
ZEEEEENN
DON'T SLOW DOWN! WE CAN MAKE IT!
ZEEEEENN
ZEEEEENN
5:37 PM.
THIS HOTEL ROOM *SHOULD* BE SAFE.
6:15 PM.
WELL... GOOD THING WE WEREN'T ACTUALLY *STAYING* THERE!

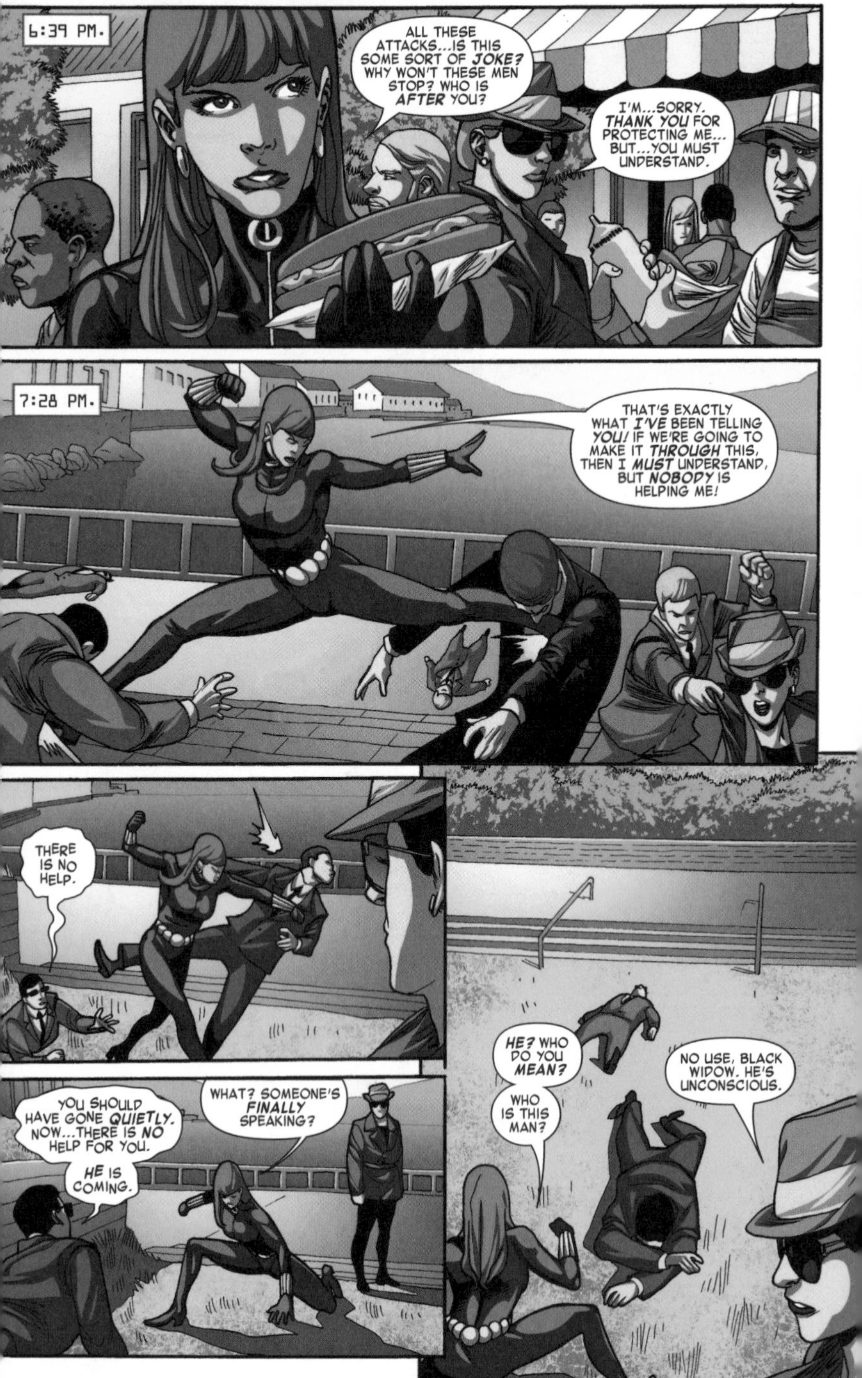
6:39 PM.
ALL THESE ATTACKS...IS THIS SOME SORT OF JOKE? WHY WON'T THESE MEN STOP? WHO IS AFTER YOU?
I'M...SORRY. THANK YOU FOR PROTECTING ME... BUT...YOU MUST UNDERSTAND.
7:28 PM.
THAT'S EXACTLY WHAT I'VE BEEN TELLING YOU! IF WE'RE GOING TO MAKE IT THROUGH THIS, THEN I MUST UNDERSTAND, BUT NOBODY IS HELPING ME!
THERE IS NO HELP.
YOU SHOULD HAVE GONE QUIETLY. NOW...THERE IS NO HELP FOR YOU.
HE IS COMING.
WHAT? SOMEONE'S FINALLY SPEAKING?
HE? WHO DO YOU MEAN?
WHO IS THIS MAN?
NO USE, BLACK WIDOW. HE'S UNCONSCIOUS.

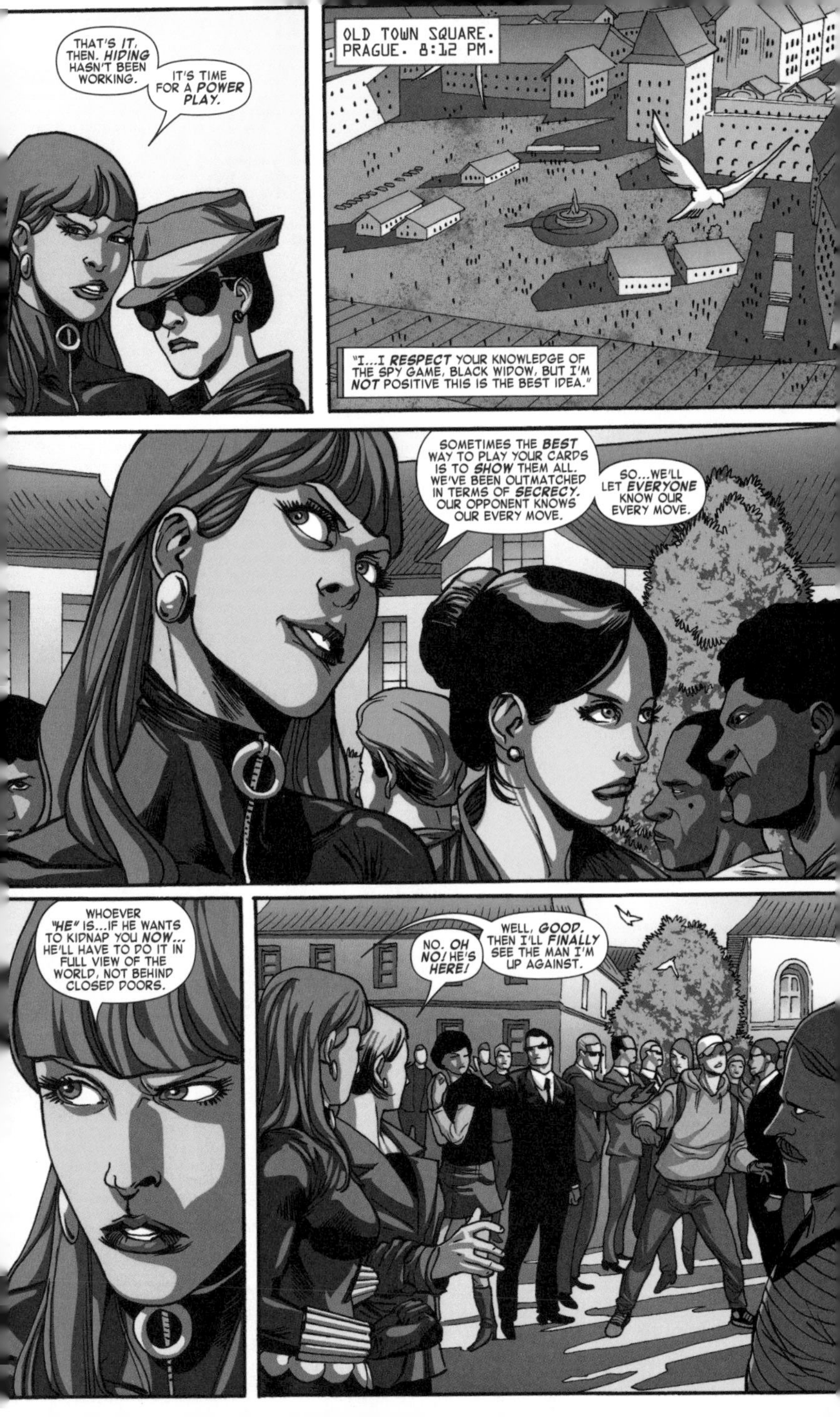
THAT'S IT, THEN. HIDING HASN'T BEEN WORKING.
IT'S TIME FOR A POWER PLAY.
OLD TOWN SQUARE. PRAGUE. 8:12 PM.
"I...I RESPECT YOUR KNOWLEDGE OF THE SPY GAME, BLACK WIDOW, BUT I'M NOT POSITIVE THIS IS THE BEST IDEA."
SOMETIMES THE BEST WAY TO PLAY YOUR CARDS IS TO SHOW THEM ALL. WE'VE BEEN OUTMATCHED IN TERMS OF SECRECY. OUR OPPONENT KNOWS OUR EVERY MOVE.
SO...WE'LL LET EVERYONE KNOW OUR EVERY MOVE.
WHOEVER "HE" IS...IF HE WANTS TO KIDNAP YOU NOW... HE'LL HAVE TO DO IT IN FULL VIEW OF THE WORLD, NOT BEHIND CLOSED DOORS.
WELL, GOOD. THEN I'LL FINALLY SEE THE MAN I'M UP AGAINST.
NO. OH NO! HE'S HERE!

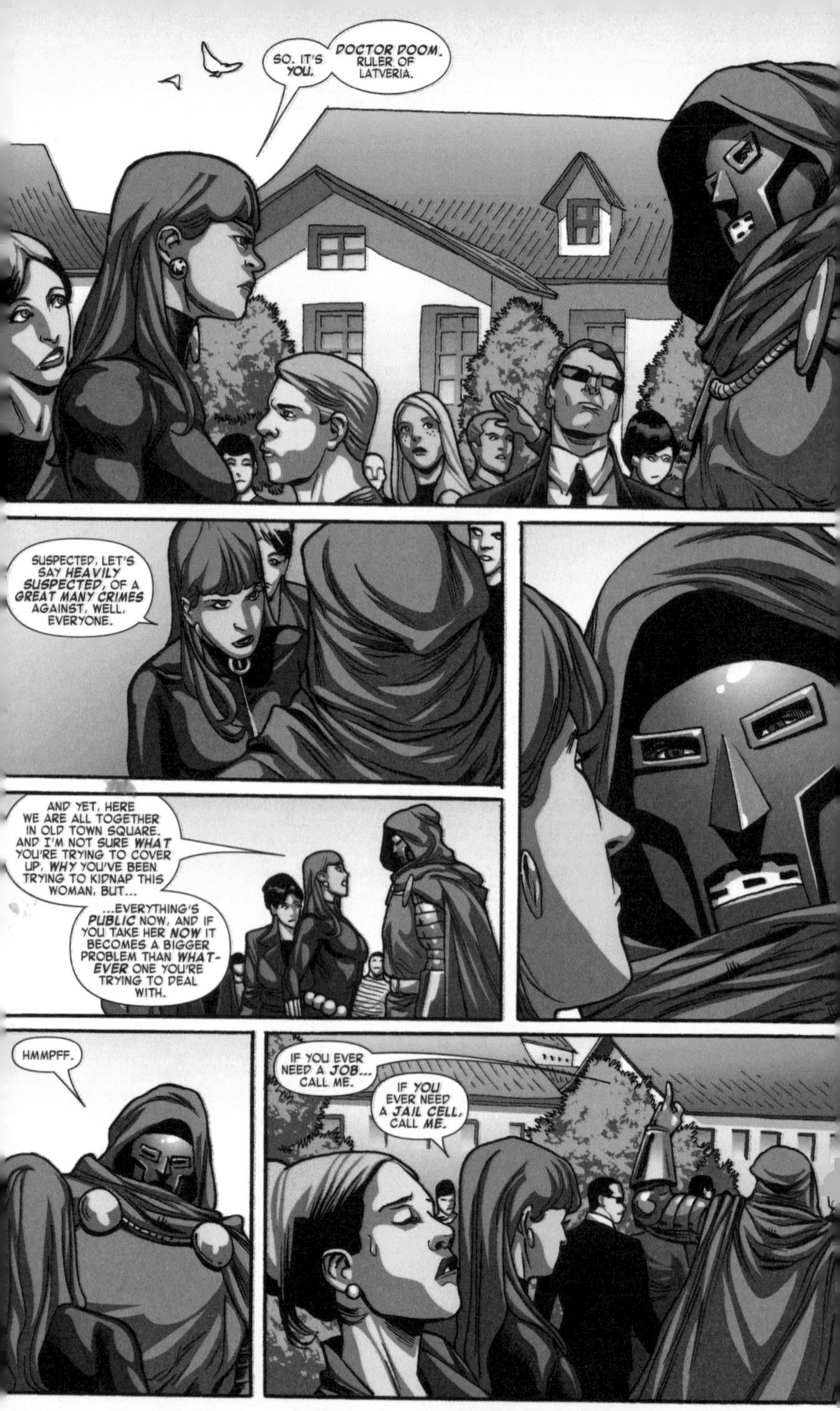
SO. IT'S YOU.
DOCTOR DOOM. RULER OF LATVERIA.
SUSPECTED, LET'S SAY HEAVILY SUSPECTED, OF A GREAT MANY CRIMES AGAINST, WELL, EVERYONE.
AND YET, HERE WE ARE ALL TOGETHER IN OLD TOWN SQUARE. AND I'M NOT SURE WHAT YOU'RE TRYING TO COVER UP, WHY YOU'VE BEEN TRYING TO KIDNAP THIS WOMAN, BUT...
...EVERYTHING'S PUBLIC NOW, AND IF YOU TAKE HER NOW IT BECOMES A BIGGER PROBLEM THAN WHAT-EVER ONE YOU'RE TRYING TO DEAL WITH.
HMMPFF.
IF YOU EVER NEED A JOB... CALL ME.
IF YOU EVER NEED A JAIL CELL, CALL ME.

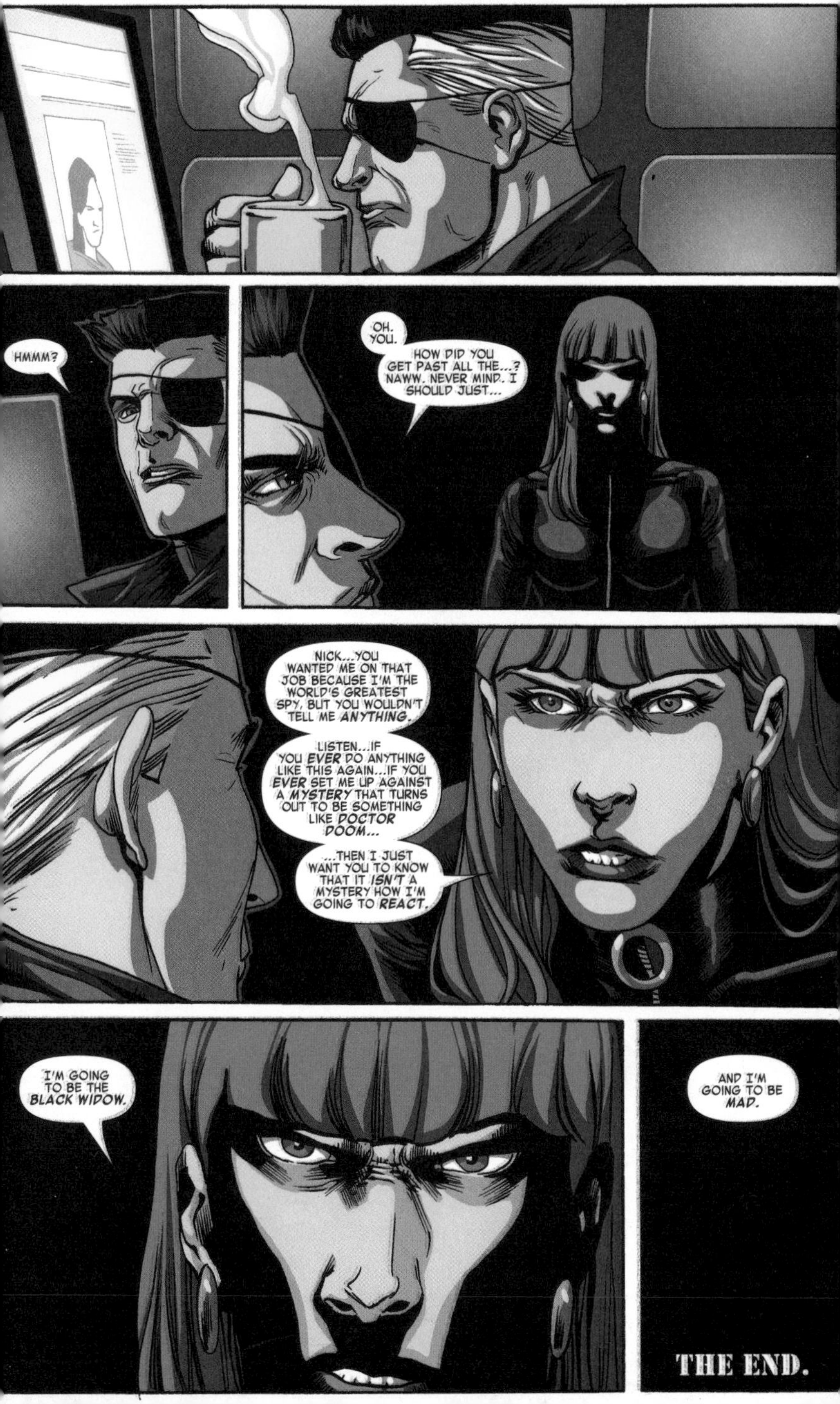
HMMM?
OH. YOU.
HOW DID YOU GET PAST ALL THE...? NAWW. NEVER MIND. I SHOULD JUST...
NICK...YOU WANTED ME ON THAT JOB BECAUSE I'M THE WORLD'S GREATEST SPY, BUT YOU WOULDN'T TELL ME ANYTHING.
LISTEN...IF YOU EVER DO ANYTHING LIKE THIS AGAIN...IF YOU EVER SET ME UP AGAINST A MYSTERY THAT TURNS OUT TO BE SOMETHING LIKE DOCTOR DOOM...
...THEN I JUST WANT YOU TO KNOW THAT IT ISN'T A MYSTERY HOW I'M GOING TO REACT.
I'M GOING TO BE THE BLACK WIDOW.
AND I'M GOING TO BE MAD.
THE END.

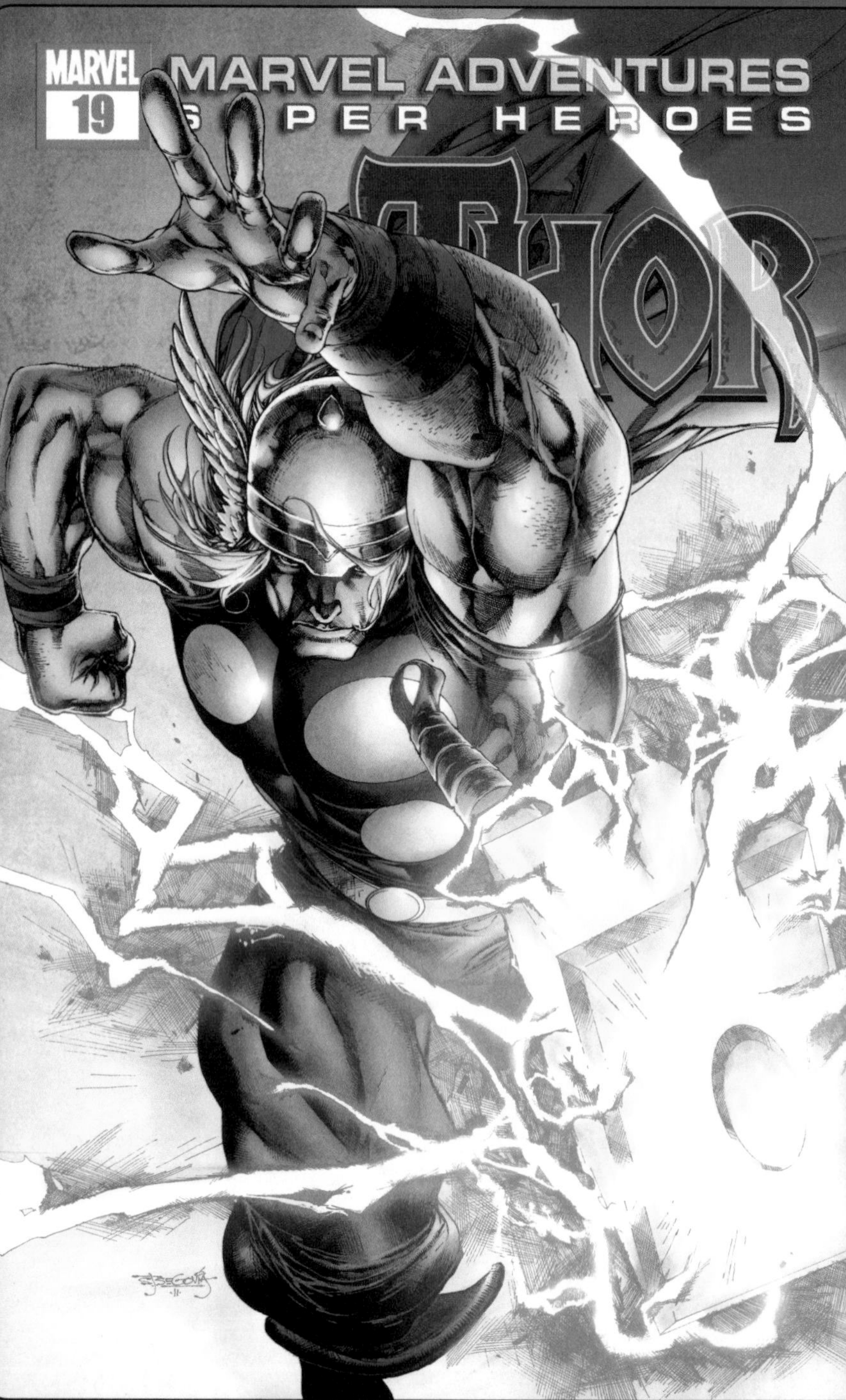
MARVEL
19
MARVEL ADVENTURES
SUPER HEROES
THOR

THERE ARE DANGERS THAT MANKIND CANNOT CONQUER.
A MIGHTY FEW WOULD RISK THEIR LIVES TO DEFEND US ALL.
THEY ARE

SUPER HEROES

THOR

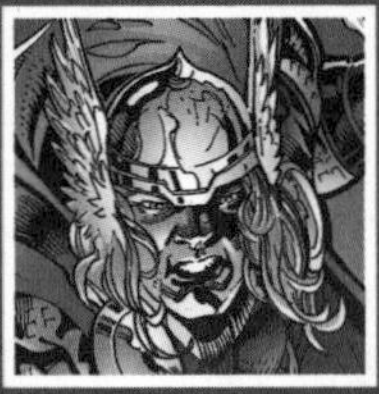

GOD OF THUNDER

IN "IF HE BE WORTHY"

JOE CARAMAGNA
WRITER

KEVIN SHARPE
PENCILER

TERRY PALLOT
INKER

APTAIN AMERICA

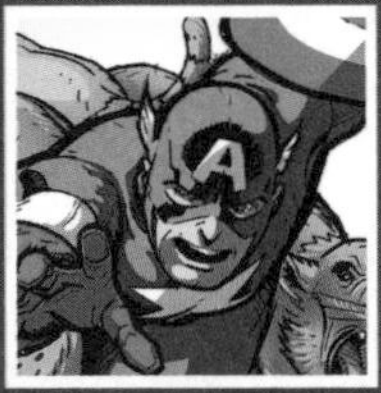

SUPER-SOLDIER

&

ANT-MAN

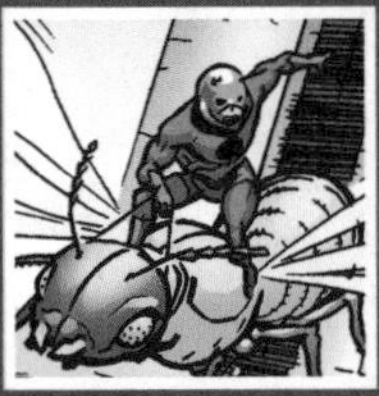

SIZE-CHANGING
SCIENCE GENIUS

IN "A LESSON IN HISTORY, NATURALLY"

EUGENE SON
WRITER

WES CRAIG
ARTIST

HRIS SOTOMAYOR
COLORIST

STEPHEN SEGOVIA
COVER

DAVE SHARPE
LETTERER

DAMIEN LUCCHESE
PRODUCTION

ELLIE PYLE
SSISTANT EDITOR

RACHEL PINNELAS
EDITOR

TOM BRENNAN
CONTRIBUTING EDITOR

STEPHEN WACKER
SENIOR EDITOR

AXEL ALONSO
DITOR IN CHIEF

JOE QUESADA
CHIEF CREATIVE OFFICER

DAN BUCKLEY
PUBLISHER

ALAN FINE
EXECUTIVE PRODUCER

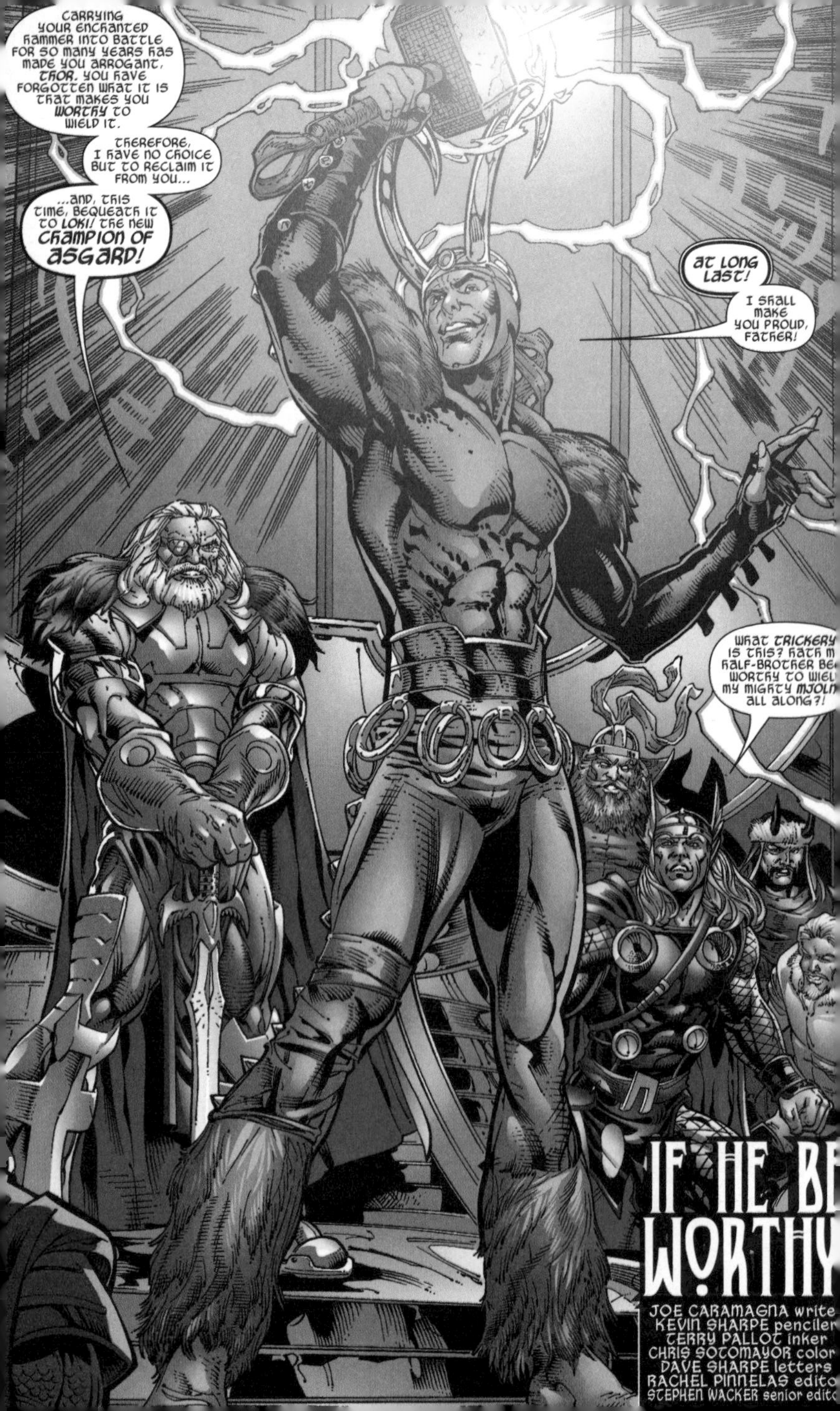
CARRYING YOUR ENCHANTED HAMMER INTO BATTLE FOR SO MANY YEARS HAS MADE YOU ARROGANT, THOR. YOU HAVE FORGOTTEN WHAT IT IS THAT MAKES YOU WORTHY TO WIELD IT.
THEREFORE, I HAVE NO CHOICE BUT TO RECLAIM IT FROM YOU...
...AND, THIS TIME, BEQUEATH IT TO LOKI! THE NEW CHAMPION OF ASGARD!
AT LONG LAST!
I SHALL MAKE YOU PROUD, FATHER!
WHAT TRICKERY IS THIS? HATH M HALF-BROTHER BE WORTHY TO WIEL MY MIGHTY MJOLN ALL ALONG?!
IF HE B
WORTHY
JOE CARAMAGNA write
KEVIN SHARPE penciler
TERRY PALLOT inker
CHRIS SOTOMAYOR color
DAVE SHARPE letters
RACHEL PINNELAS edito
STEPHEN WACKER senior edito

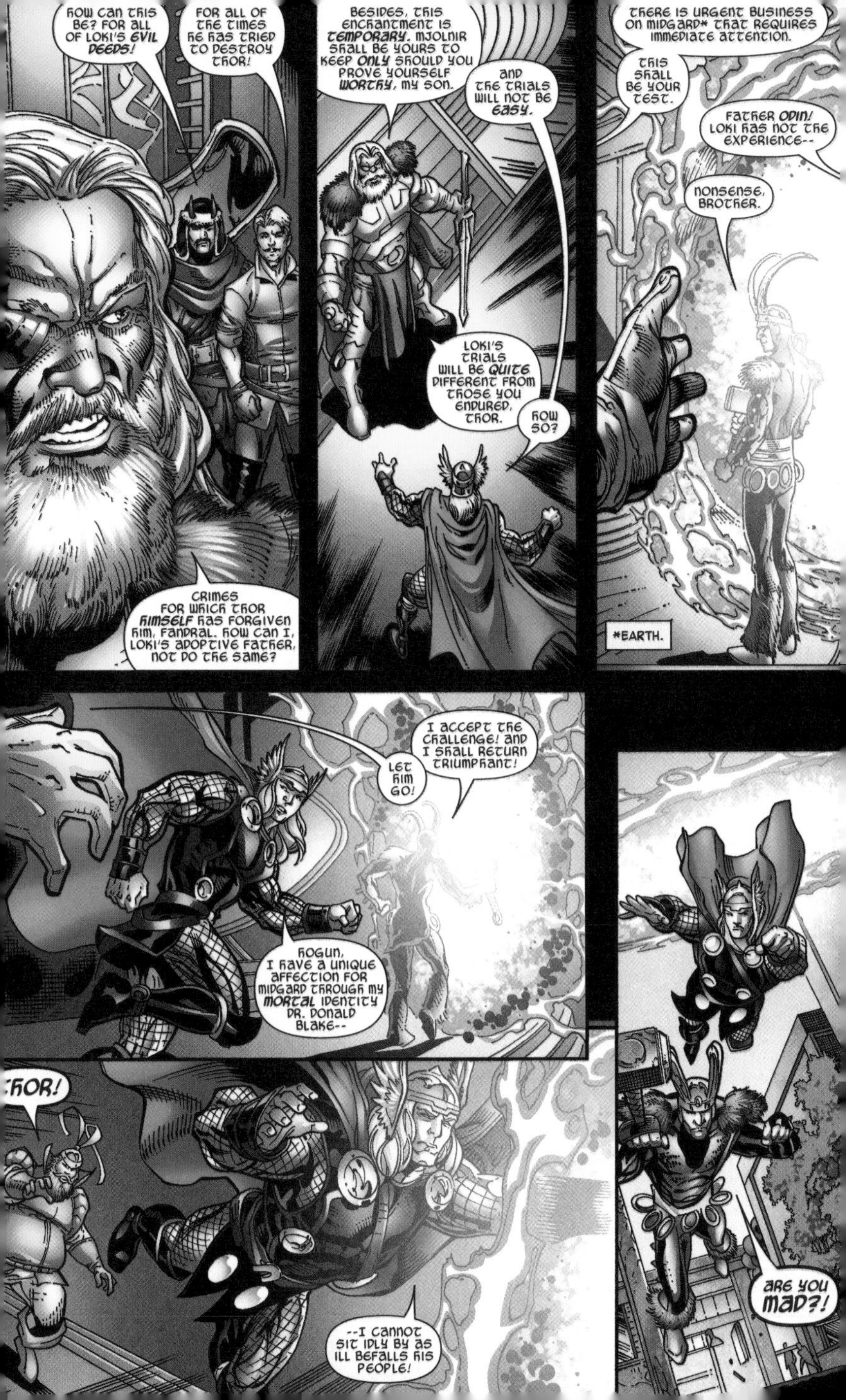
HOW CAN THIS BE? FOR ALL OF LOKI'S EVIL DEEDS!
FOR ALL OF THE TIMES HE HAS TRIED TO DESTROY THOR!
CRIMES FOR WHICH THOR HIMSELF HAS FORGIVEN HIM, FANDRAL. HOW CAN I, LOKI'S ADOPTIVE FATHER, NOT DO THE SAME?
BESIDES, THIS ENCHANTMENT IS TEMPORARY. MJOLNIR SHALL BE YOURS TO KEEP ONLY SHOULD YOU PROVE YOURSELF WORTHY, MY SON.
AND THE TRIALS WILL NOT BE EASY.
LOKI'S TRIALS WILL BE QUITE DIFFERENT FROM THOSE YOU ENDURED, THOR.
HOW SO?
THERE IS URGENT BUSINESS ON MIDGARD* THAT REQUIRES IMMEDIATE ATTENTION.
THIS SHALL BE YOUR TEST.
FATHER ODIN! LOKI HAS NOT THE EXPERIENCE--
NONSENSE, BROTHER.
*EARTH.
LET HIM GO!
I ACCEPT THE CHALLENGE! AND I SHALL RETURN TRIUMPHANT!
HOGUN, I HAVE A UNIQUE AFFECTION FOR MIDGARD THROUGH MY MORTAL IDENTITY DR. DONALD BLAKE--
--I CANNOT SIT IDLY BY AS ILL BEFALLS HIS PEOPLE!
THOR!
ARE YOU MAD?!

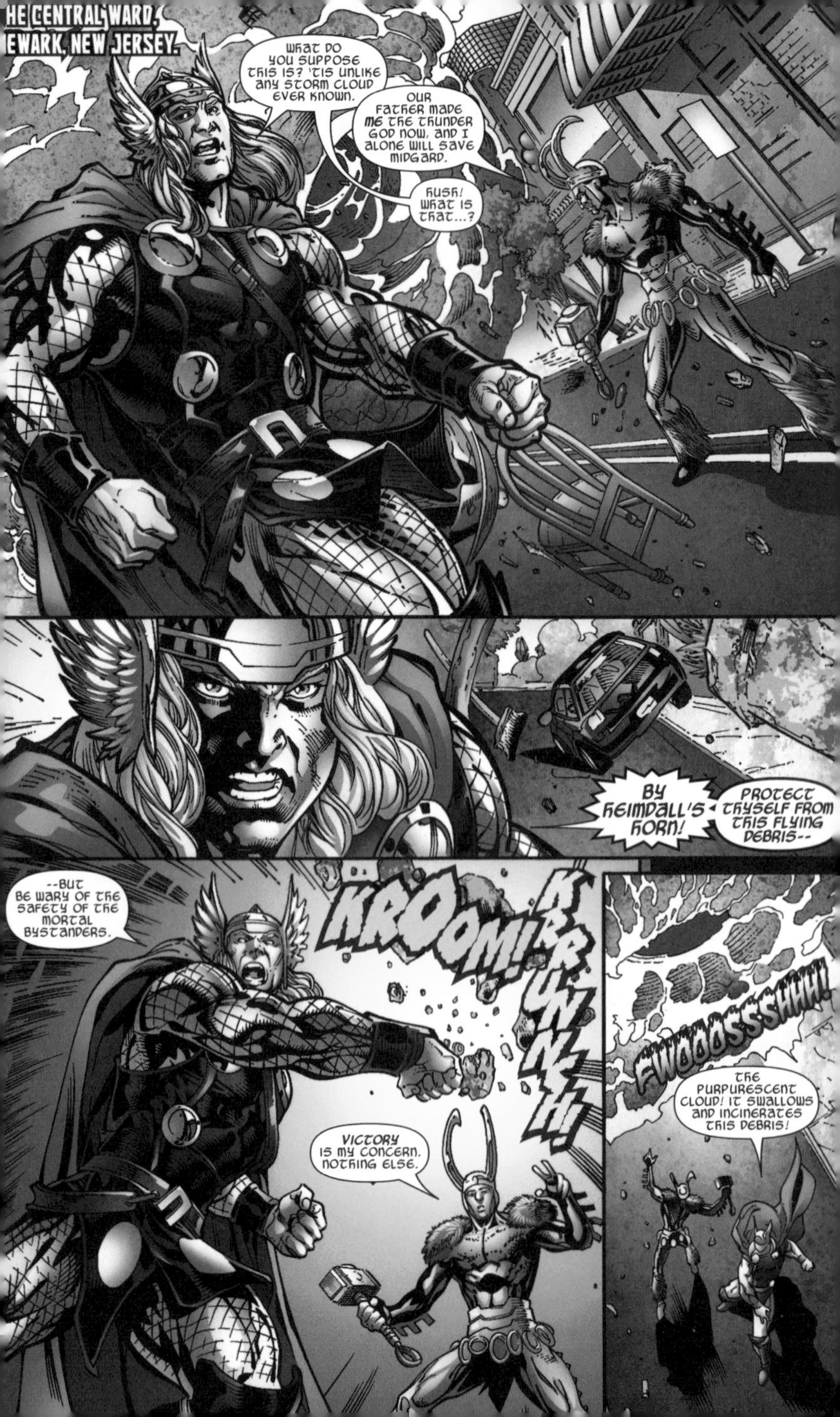
HE CENTRAL WARD, EWARK, NEW JERSEY.
WHAT DO YOU SUPPOSE THIS IS? 'TIS UNLIKE ANY STORM CLOUD EVER KNOWN.
OUR FATHER MADE ME THE THUNDER GOD NOW, AND I ALONE WILL SAVE MIDGARD.
HUSH! WHAT IS THAT...?
BY HEIMDALL'S HORN!
PROTECT THYSELF FROM THIS FLYING DEBRIS--
--BUT BE WARY OF THE SAFETY OF THE MORTAL BYSTANDERS.
KROOM!
KRRUNNCH!
VICTORY IS MY CONCERN. NOTHING ELSE.
FWOOOSSSHHH!
THE PURPURESCENT CLOUD! IT SWALLOWS AND INCINERATES THIS DEBRIS!

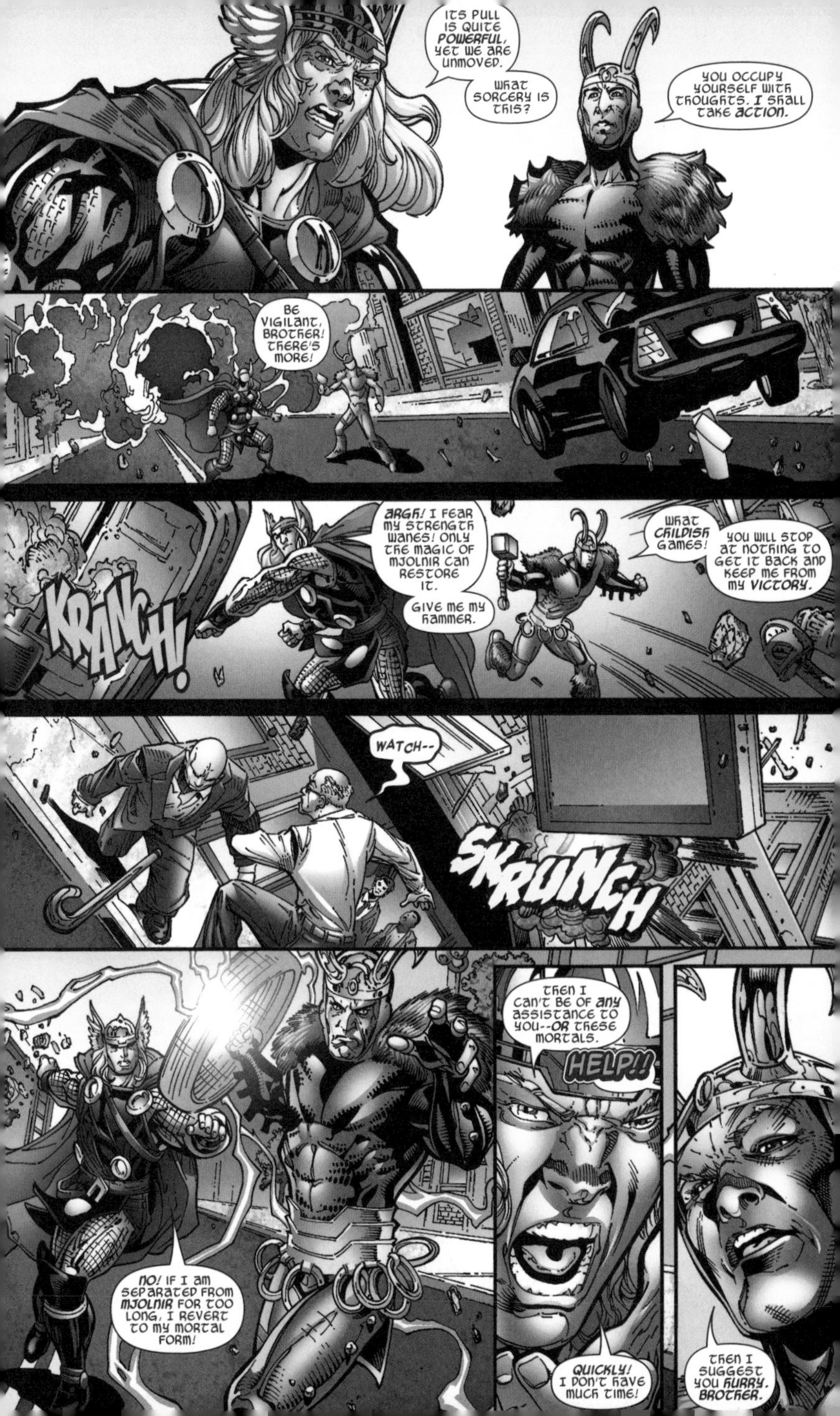

ITS PULL IS QUITE POWERFUL, YET WE ARE UNMOVED.
WHAT SORCERY IS THIS?
YOU OCCUPY YOURSELF WITH THOUGHTS. I SHALL TAKE ACTION.
BE VIGILANT, BROTHER! THERE'S MORE!
KRANCH!
ARGH! I FEAR MY STRENGTH WANES! ONLY THE MAGIC OF MJOLNIR CAN RESTORE IT.
GIVE ME MY HAMMER.
WHAT CHILDISH GAMES!
YOU WILL STOP AT NOTHING TO GET IT BACK AND KEEP ME FROM MY VICTORY.
WATCH--
SKRUNCH
NO! IF I AM SEPARATED FROM MJOLNIR FOR TOO LONG, I REVERT TO MY MORTAL FORM!
THEN I CAN'T BE OF ANY ASSISTANCE TO YOU--OR THESE MORTALS.
HELP!!
QUICKLY! I DON'T HAVE MUCH TIME!
THEN I SUGGEST YOU HURRY, BROTHER.

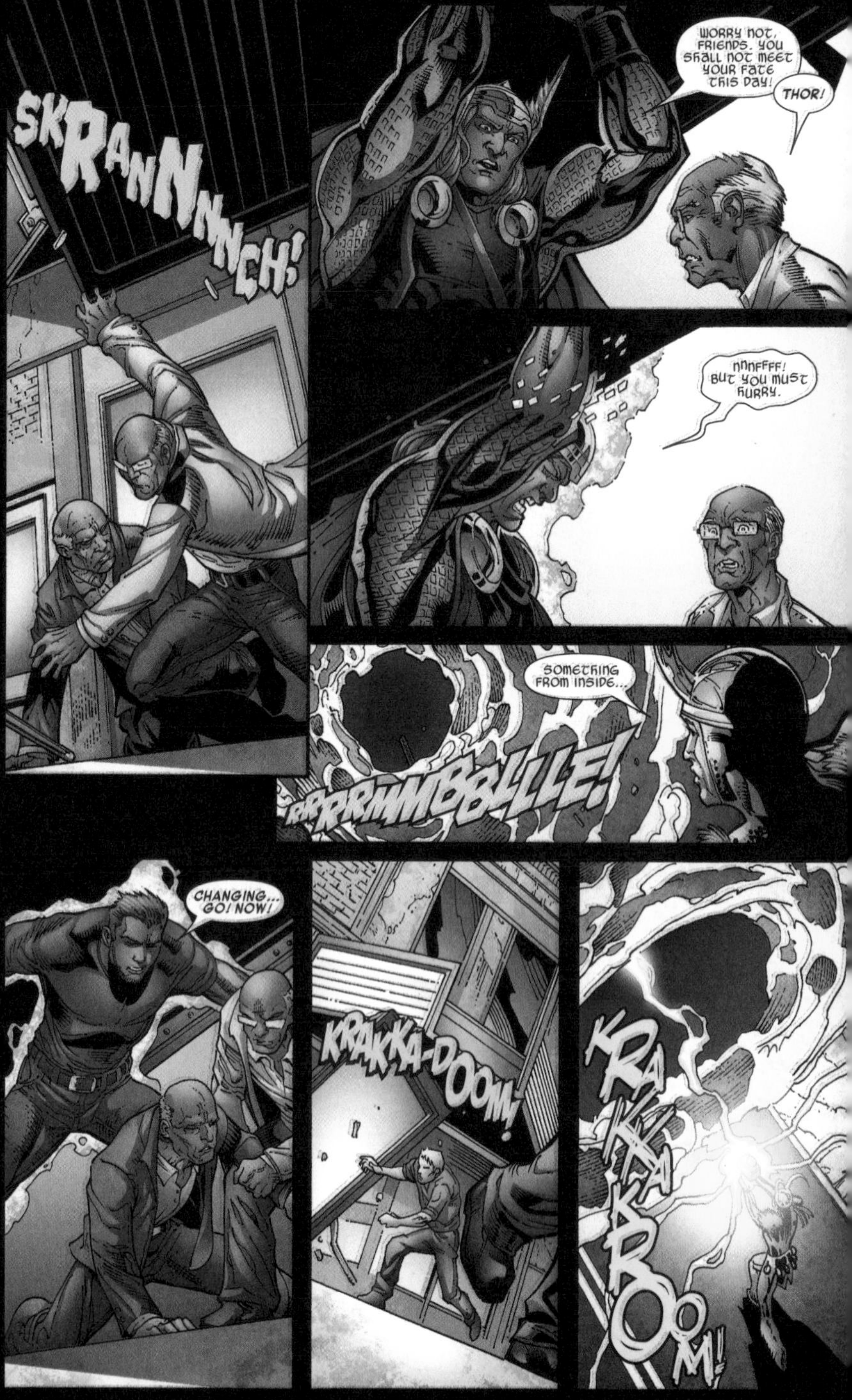
SKRANNNNNCH!
WORRY NOT, FRIENDS. YOU SHALL NOT MEET YOUR FATE THIS DAY!
THOR!
NNNFFFF! BUT YOU MUST HURRY.
SOMETHING FROM INSIDE...
RRRRMMMBBLLLE!
CHANGING... GO! NOW!
KRAKKA-DOOOM!
KRAKKAKRAKOOOM!

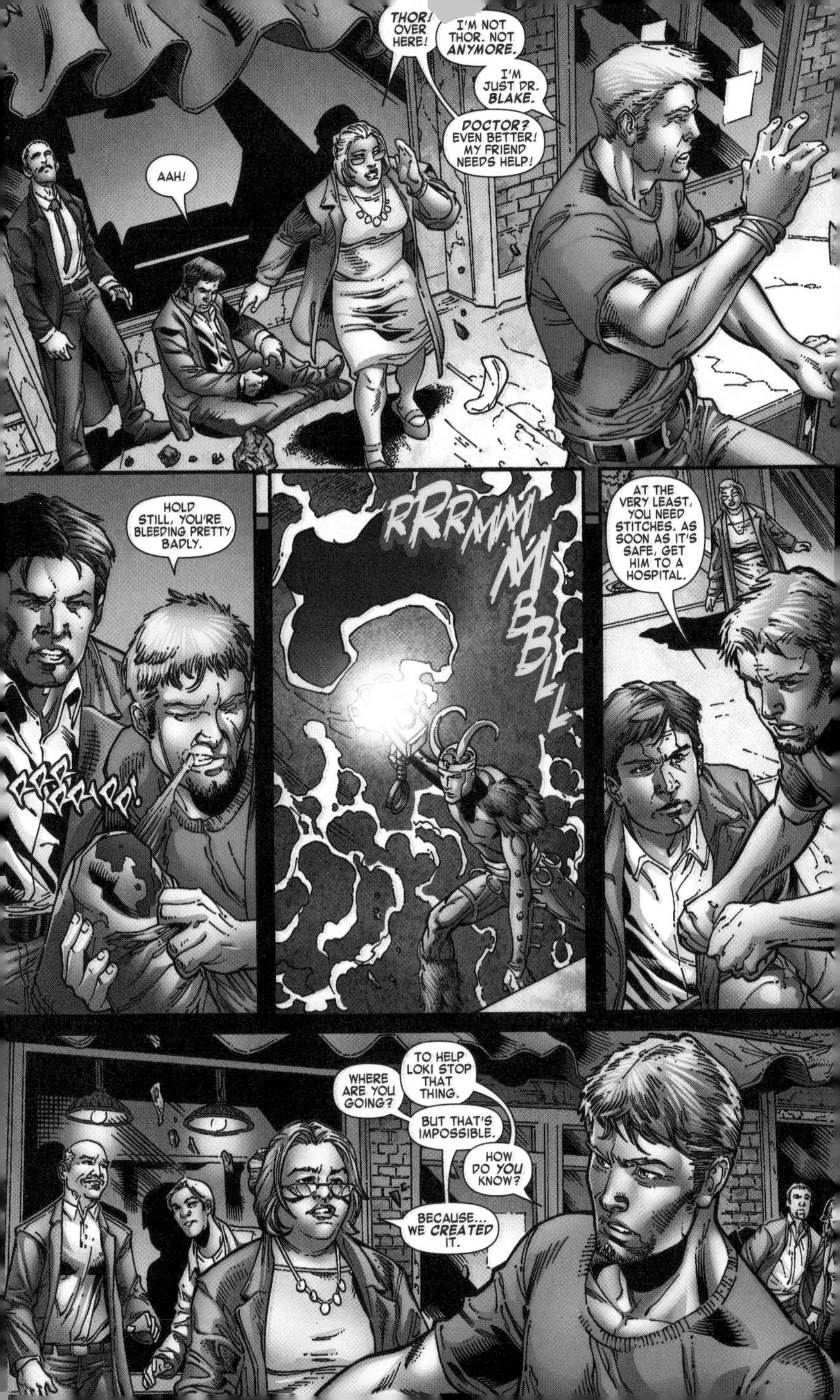
THOR! OVER HERE!
I'M NOT THOR. NOT ANYMORE.
I'M JUST DR. BLAKE.
DOCTOR? EVEN BETTER! MY FRIEND NEEDS HELP!
AAH!
HOLD STILL, YOU'RE BLEEDING PRETTY BADLY.
RRRRIPP!
RRRMMMBBLL
AT THE VERY LEAST, YOU NEED STITCHES. AS SOON AS IT'S SAFE, GET HIM TO A HOSPITAL.
WHERE ARE YOU GOING?
TO HELP LOKI STOP THAT THING.
BUT THAT'S IMPOSSIBLE.
HOW DO YOU KNOW?
BECAUSE... WE CREATED IT.

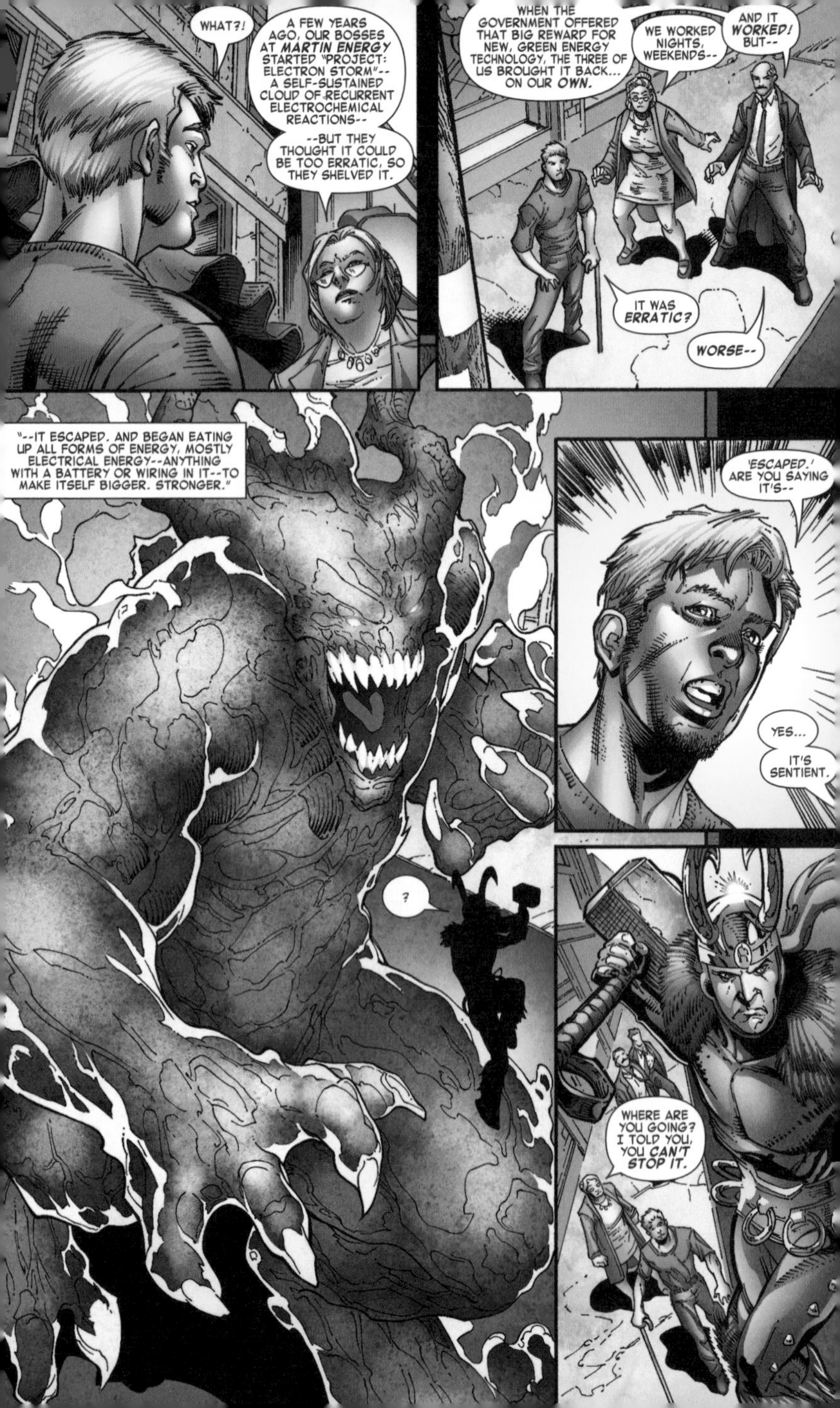
WHAT?!
A FEW YEARS AGO, OUR BOSSES AT MARTIN ENERGY STARTED "PROJECT: ELECTRON STORM"--A SELF-SUSTAINED CLOUD OF RECURRENT ELECTROCHEMICAL REACTIONS--
--BUT THEY THOUGHT IT COULD BE TOO ERRATIC, SO THEY SHELVED IT.
WHEN THE GOVERNMENT OFFERED THAT BIG REWARD FOR NEW, GREEN ENERGY TECHNOLOGY, THE THREE OF US BROUGHT IT BACK... ON OUR OWN.
WE WORKED NIGHTS, WEEKENDS--
AND IT WORKED! BUT--
IT WAS ERRATIC?
WORSE--
"--IT ESCAPED. AND BEGAN EATING UP ALL FORMS OF ENERGY, MOSTLY ELECTRICAL ENERGY--ANYTHING WITH A BATTERY OR WIRING IN IT--TO MAKE ITSELF BIGGER. STRONGER."
'ESCAPED.' ARE YOU SAYING IT'S--
YES...
IT'S SENTIENT.
?
WHERE ARE YOU GOING? I TOLD YOU, YOU CAN'T STOP IT.

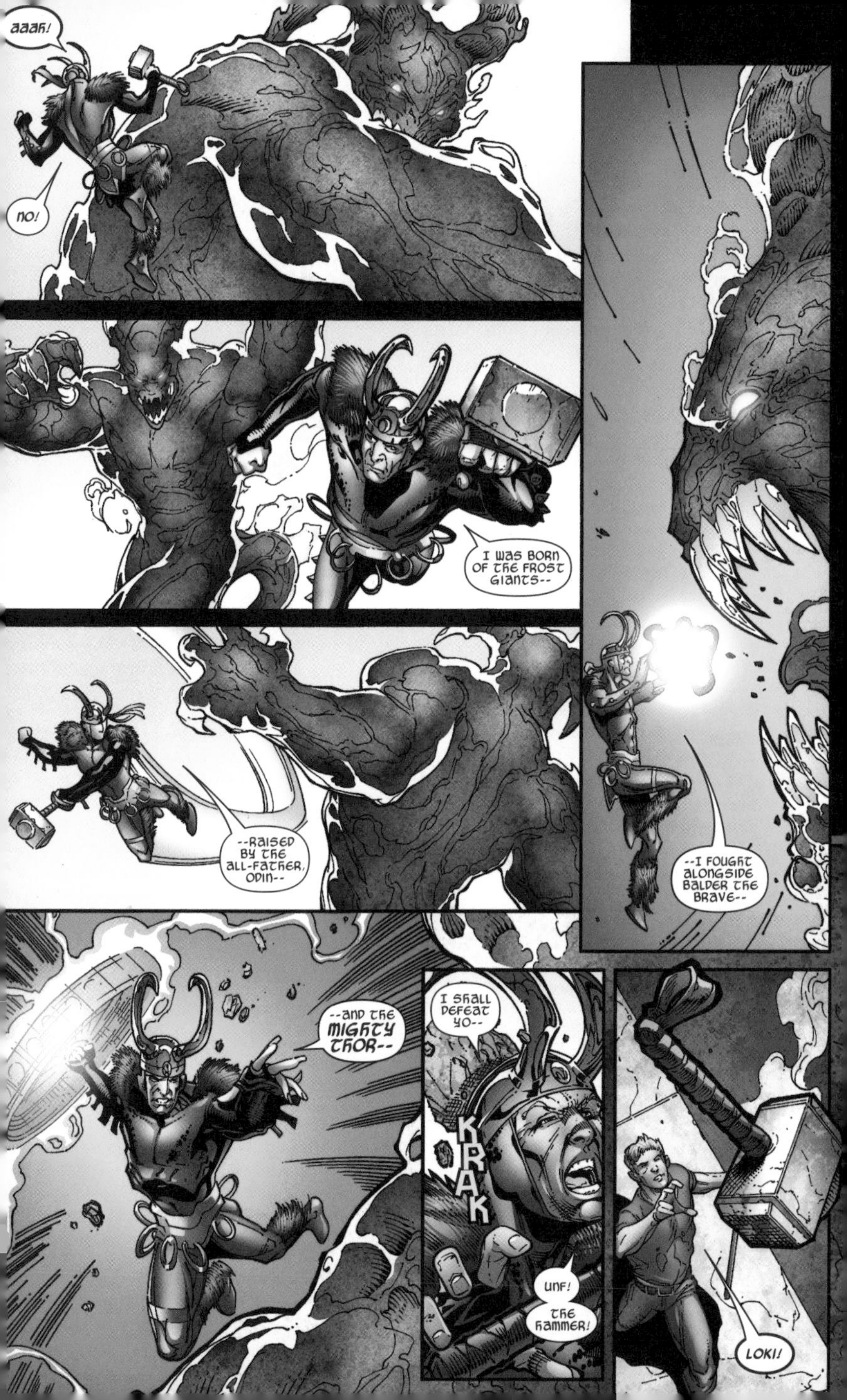
aaah!
no!
I was born of the frost giants--
--raised by the all-father, Odin--
--I fought alongside Balder the brave--
--and the mighty Thor--
I shall defeat yo--
KRAK
unf!
The hammer!
Loki!

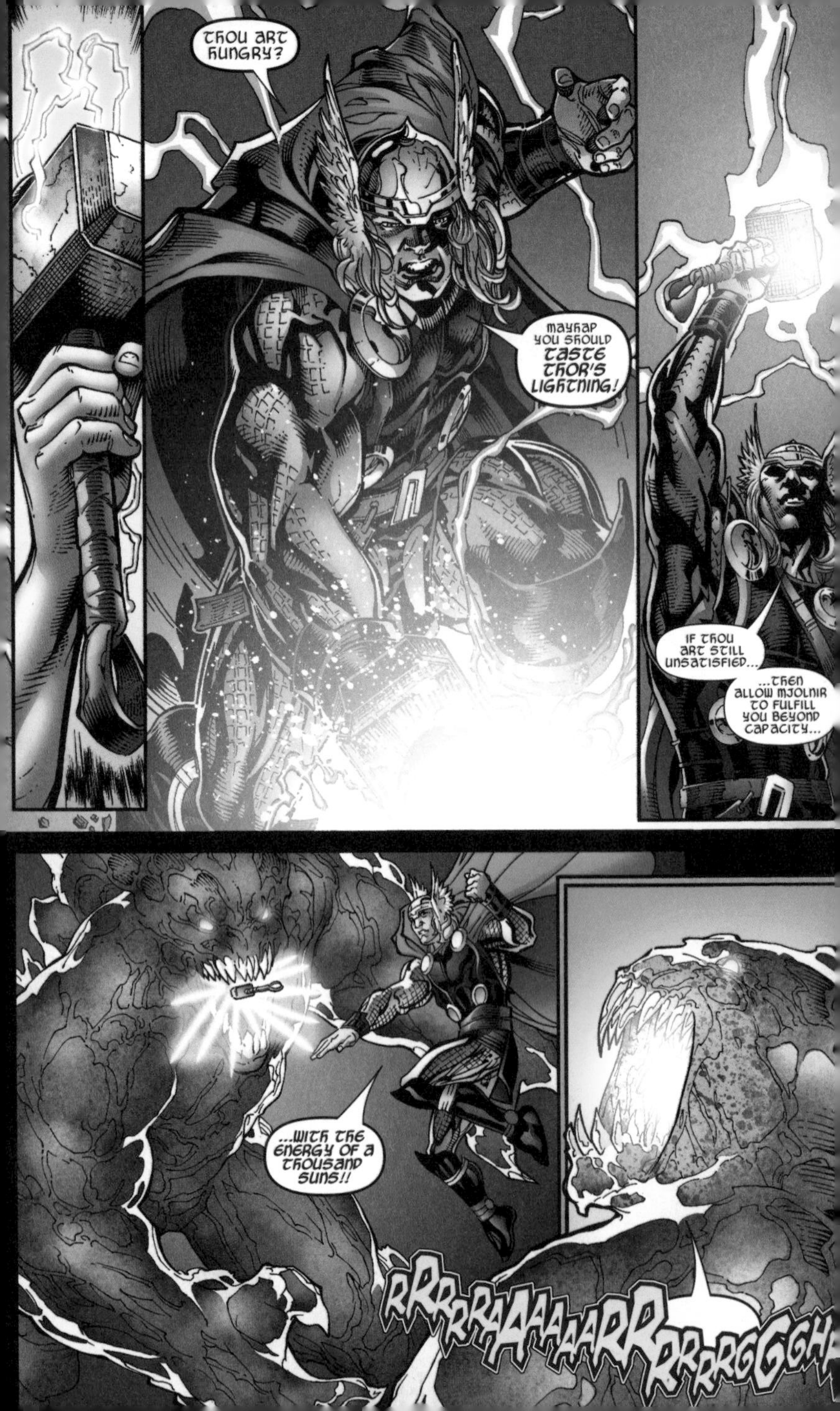
THOU ART HUNGRY?
MAYHAP YOU SHOULD TASTE THOR'S LIGHTNING!
IF THOU ART STILL UNSATISFIED...
...THEN ALLOW MJOLNIR TO FULFILL YOU BEYOND CAPACITY...
...WITH THE ENERGY OF A THOUSAND SUNS!!
RRRRRAAAAAARRRRRRGGGH

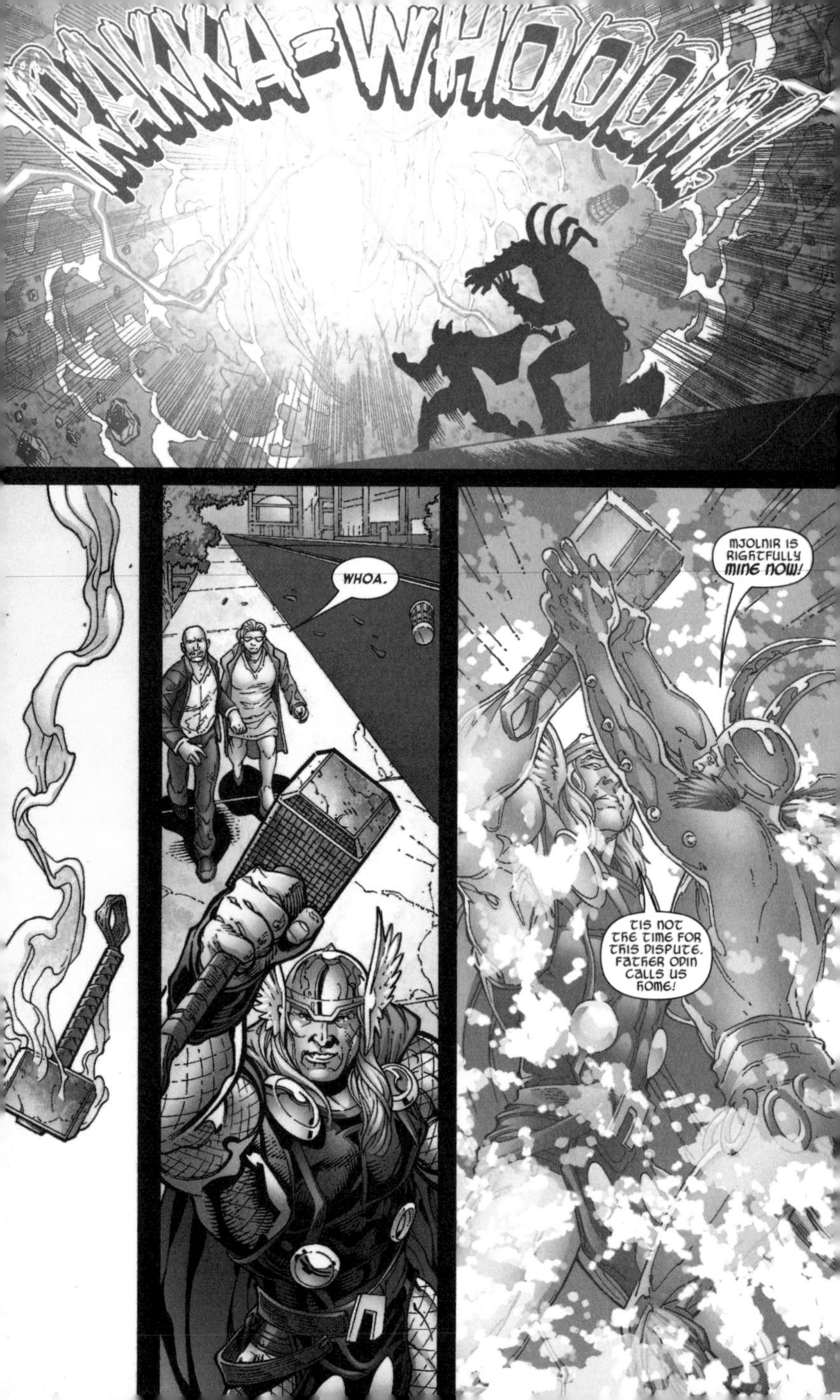

WHOA.
MJOLNIR IS RIGHTFULLY MINE NOW!
TIS NOT THE TIME FOR THIS DISPUTE. FATHER ODIN CALLS US HOME!

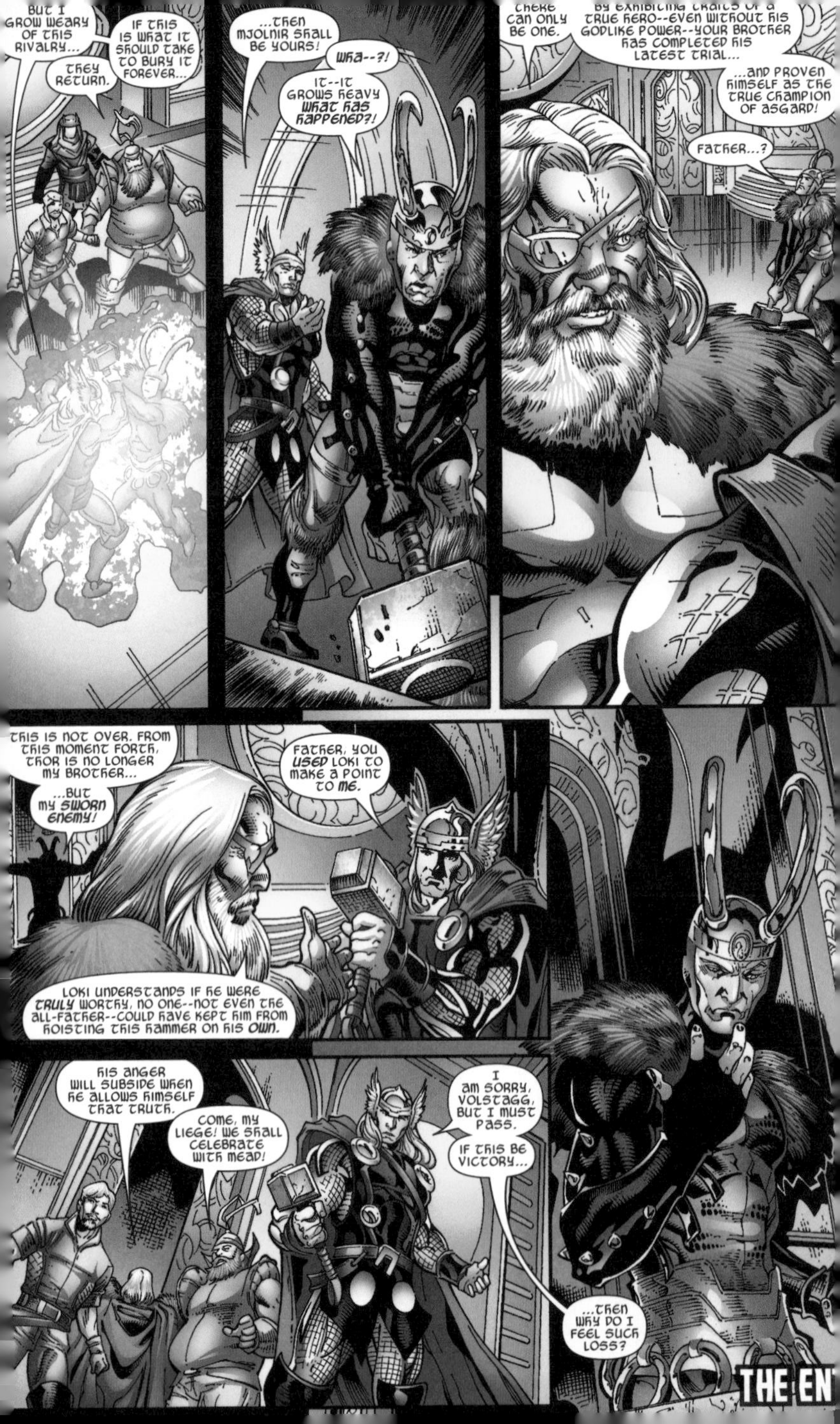
BUT I GROW WEARY OF THIS RIVALRY...
IF THIS IS WHAT IT SHOULD TAKE TO BURY IT FOREVER...
THEY RETURN.
...THEN MJOLNIR SHALL BE YOURS!
WHA--?!
IT--IT GROWS HEAVY WHAT HAS HAPPENED?!
THERE CAN ONLY BE ONE.
BY EXHIBITING TRAITS OF A TRUE HERO--EVEN WITHOUT HIS GODLIKE POWER--YOUR BROTHER HAS COMPLETED HIS LATEST TRIAL...
...AND PROVEN HIMSELF AS THE TRUE CHAMPION OF ASGARD!
FATHER...?
THIS IS NOT OVER. FROM THIS MOMENT FORTH, THOR IS NO LONGER MY BROTHER...
...BUT MY SWORN ENEMY!
FATHER, YOU USED LOKI TO MAKE A POINT TO ME.
LOKI UNDERSTANDS IF HE WERE TRULY WORTHY, NO ONE--NOT EVEN THE ALL-FATHER--COULD HAVE KEPT HIM FROM HOISTING THIS HAMMER ON HIS OWN.
HIS ANGER WILL SUBSIDE WHEN HE ALLOWS HIMSELF THAT TRUTH.
COME, MY LIEGE! WE SHALL CELEBRATE WITH MEAD!
I AM SORRY, VOLSTAGG, BUT I MUST PASS.
IF THIS BE VICTORY...
...THEN WHY DO I FEEL SUCH LOSS?
THE EN

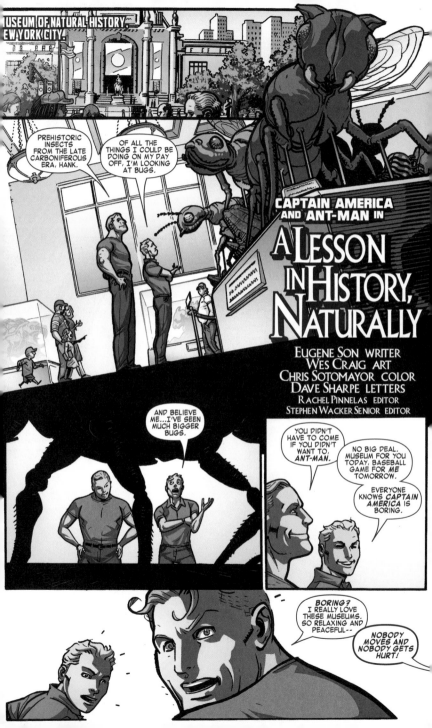

MUSEUM OF NATURAL HISTORY,
NEW YORK CITY.

PREHISTORIC INSECTS FROM THE LATE CARBONIFEROUS ERA, HANK.

OF ALL THE THINGS I COULD BE DOING ON MY DAY OFF, I'M LOOKING AT BUGS.

CAPTAIN AMERICA AND ANT-MAN IN

A LESSON IN HISTORY, NATURALLY

EUGENE SON WRITER
WES CRAIG ART
CHRIS SOTOMAYOR COLOR
DAVE SHARPE LETTERS
RACHEL PINNELAS EDITOR
STEPHEN WACKER SENIOR EDITOR

AND BELIEVE ME...I'VE SEEN MUCH BIGGER BUGS.

YOU DIDN'T HAVE TO COME IF YOU DIDN'T WANT TO, ANT-MAN.

NO BIG DEAL. MUSEUM FOR YOU TODAY, BASEBALL GAME FOR ME TOMORROW.

EVERYONE KNOWS CAPTAIN AMERICA IS BORING.

BORING? I REALLY LOVE THESE MUSEUMS. SO RELAXING AND PEACEFUL--

NOBODY MOVES AND NOBODY GETS HURT!

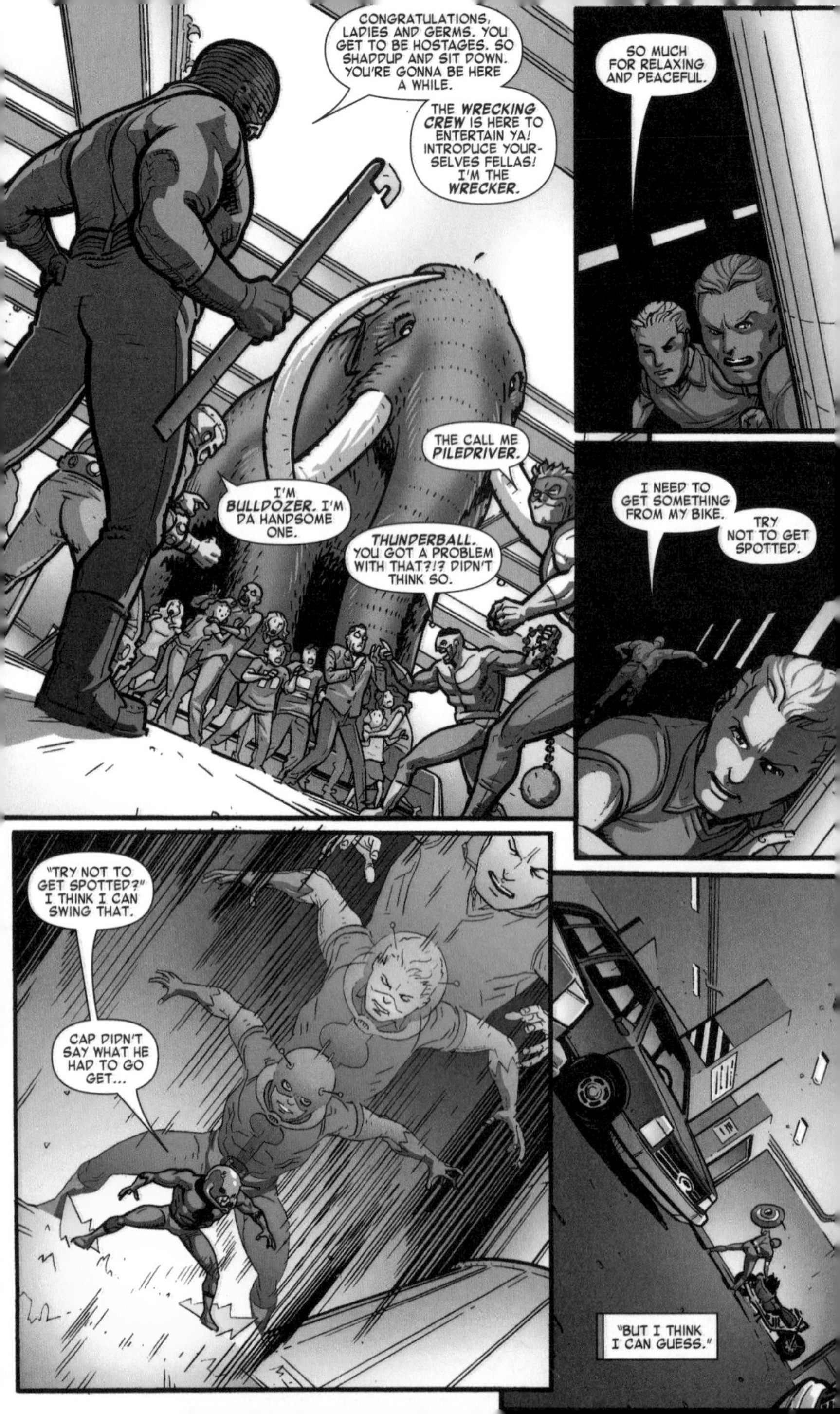
CONGRATULATIONS, LADIES AND GERMS. YOU GET TO BE HOSTAGES. SO SHADDUP AND SIT DOWN. YOU'RE GONNA BE HERE A WHILE.
THE WRECKING CREW IS HERE TO ENTERTAIN YA! INTRODUCE YOURSELVES FELLAS! I'M THE WRECKER.
THE CALL ME PILEDRIVER.
I'M BULLDOZER. I'M DA HANDSOME ONE.
THUNDERBALL. YOU GOT A PROBLEM WITH THAT?!? DIDN'T THINK SO.
SO MUCH FOR RELAXING AND PEACEFUL.
I NEED TO GET SOMETHING FROM MY BIKE.
TRY NOT TO GET SPOTTED.
"TRY NOT TO GET SPOTTED?" I THINK I CAN SWING THAT.
CAP DIDN'T SAY WHAT HE HAD TO GO GET...
"BUT I THINK I CAN GUESS."

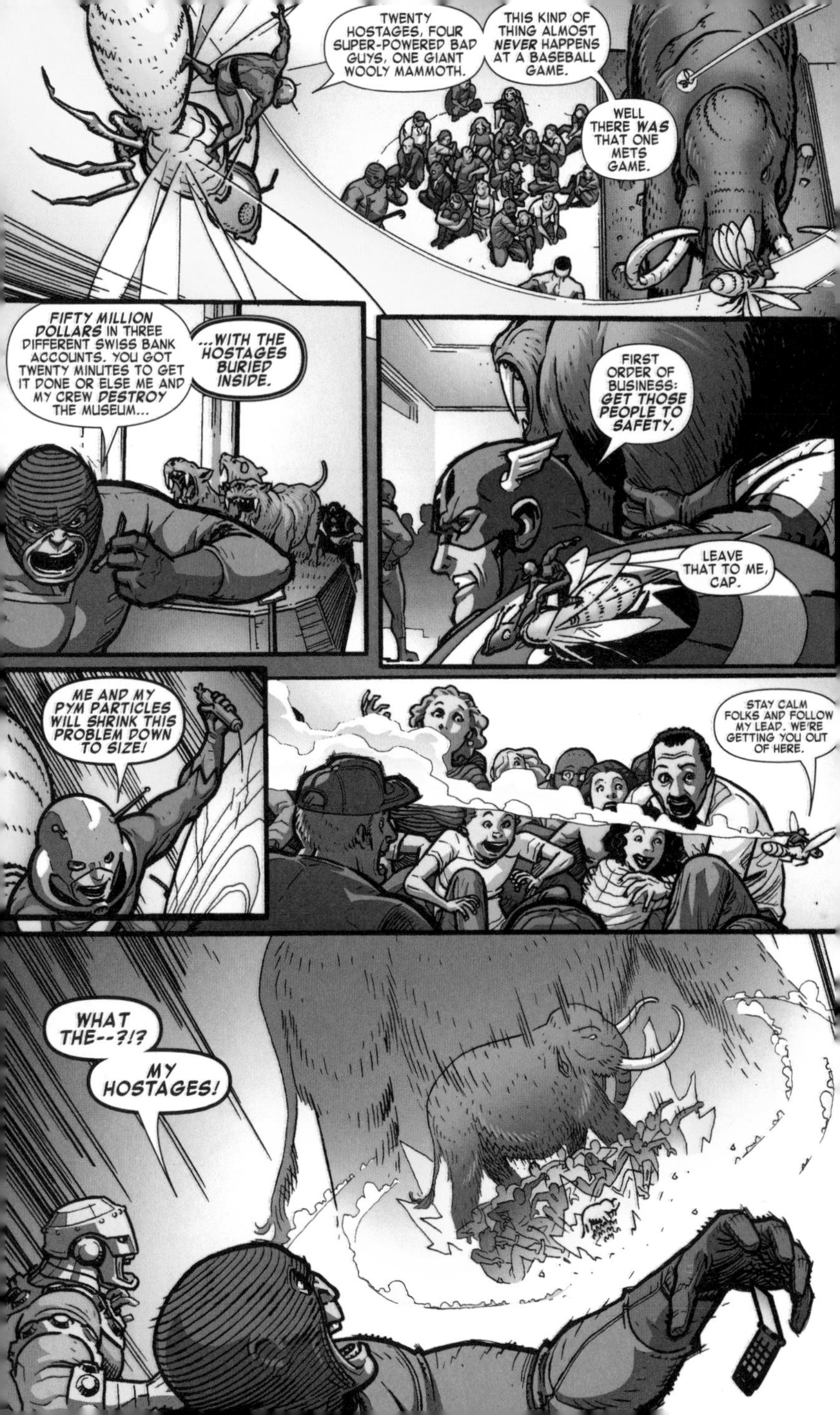
TWENTY HOSTAGES, FOUR SUPER-POWERED BAD GUYS, ONE GIANT WOOLY MAMMOTH.
THIS KIND OF THING ALMOST NEVER HAPPENS AT A BASEBALL GAME.
WELL THERE WAS THAT ONE METS GAME.
FIFTY MILLION DOLLARS IN THREE DIFFERENT SWISS BANK ACCOUNTS. YOU GOT TWENTY MINUTES TO GET IT DONE OR ELSE ME AND MY CREW DESTROY THE MUSEUM...
...WITH THE HOSTAGES BURIED INSIDE.
FIRST ORDER OF BUSINESS: GET THOSE PEOPLE TO SAFETY.
LEAVE THAT TO ME, CAP.
ME AND MY PYM PARTICLES WILL SHRINK THIS PROBLEM DOWN TO SIZE!
STAY CALM FOLKS AND FOLLOW MY LEAD. WE'RE GETTING YOU OUT OF HERE.
WHAT THE--?!?
MY HOSTAGES!

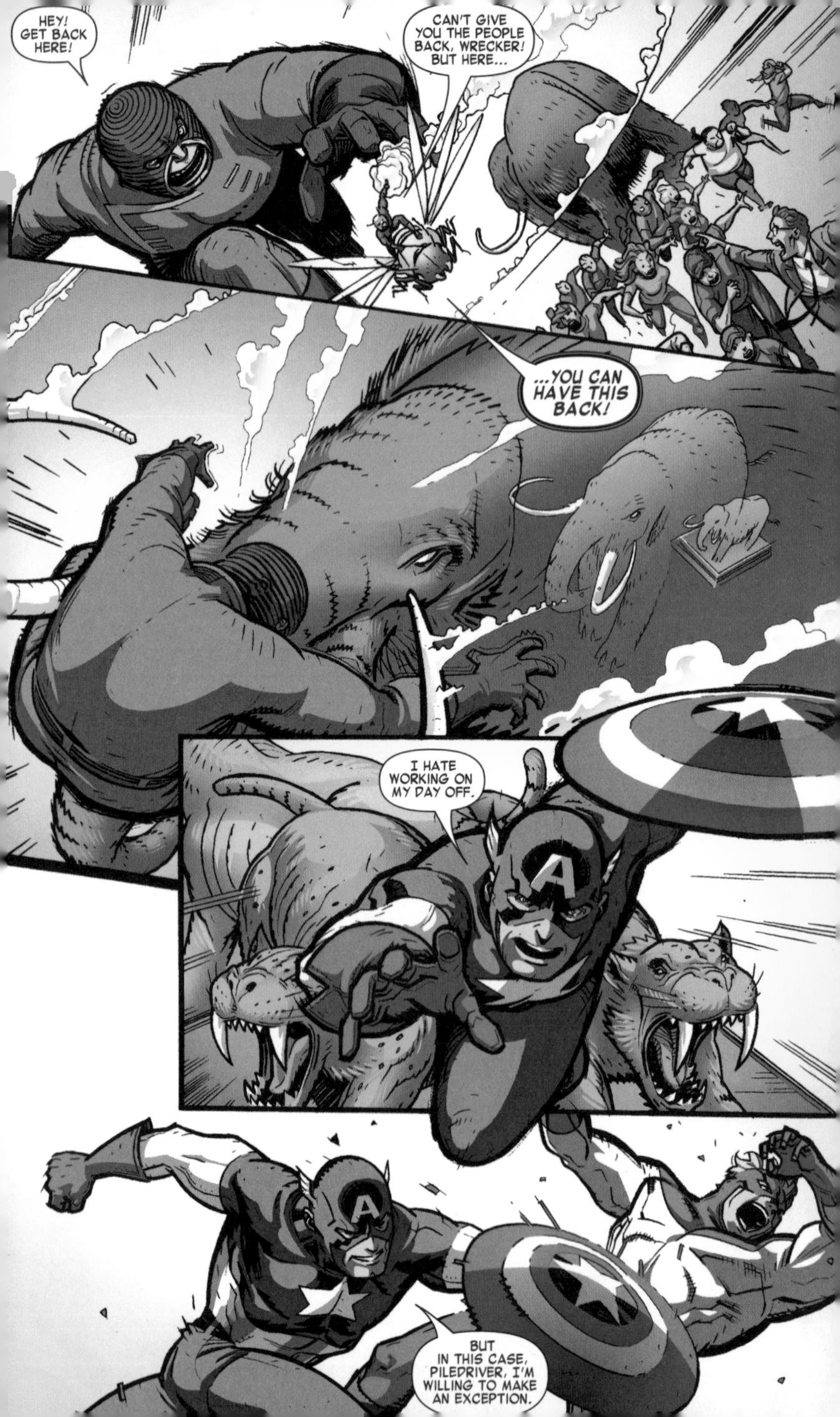

HEY! GET BACK HERE!
CAN'T GIVE YOU THE PEOPLE BACK, WRECKER! BUT HERE...
...YOU CAN HAVE THIS BACK!
I HATE WORKING ON MY DAY OFF.
BUT IN THIS CASE, PILEDRIVER, I'M WILLING TO MAKE AN EXCEPTION.

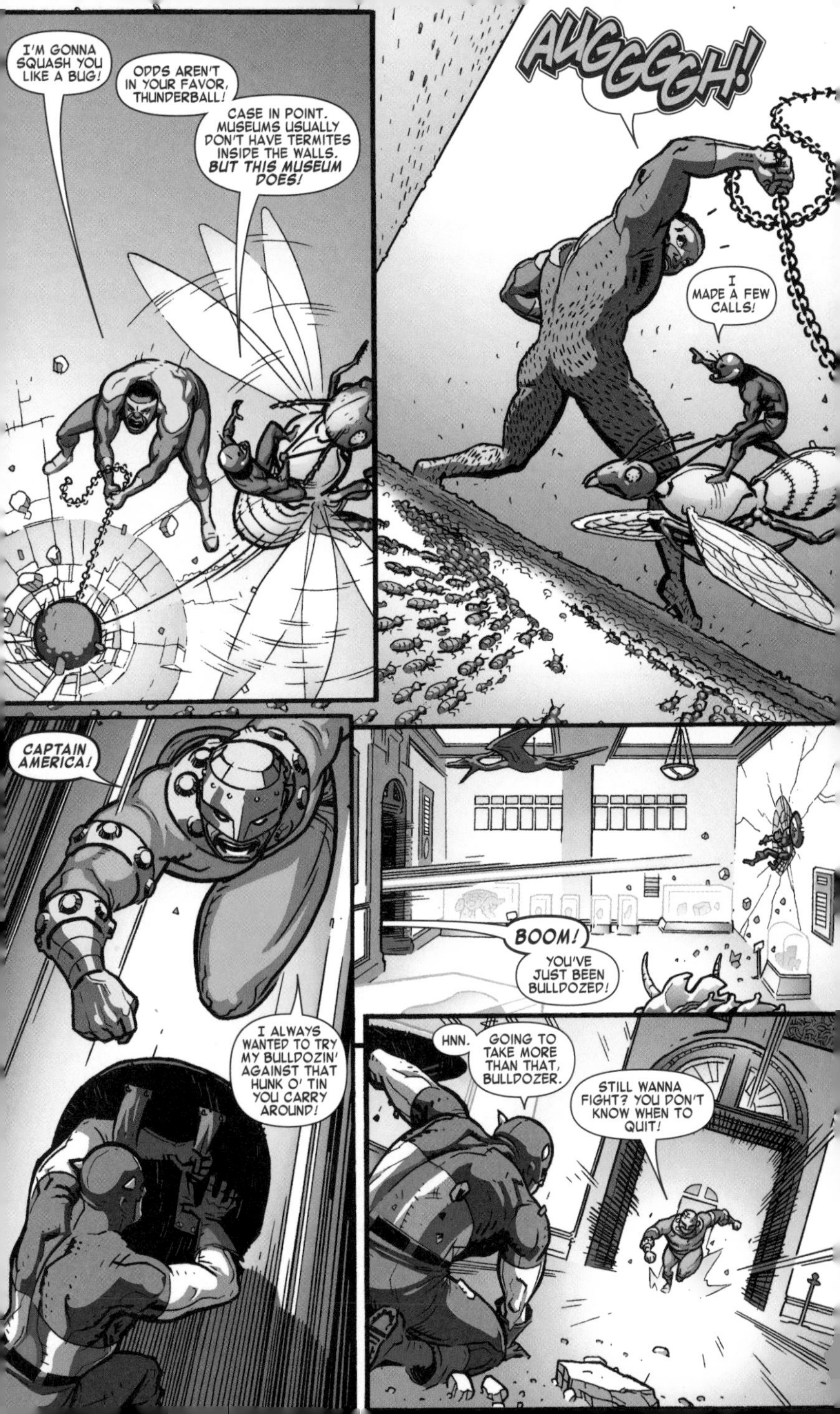
I'M GONNA SQUASH YOU LIKE A BUG!
ODDS AREN'T IN YOUR FAVOR, THUNDERBALL!
CASE IN POINT. MUSEUMS USUALLY DON'T HAVE TERMITES INSIDE THE WALLS. BUT THIS MUSEUM DOES!
AUGGGGH!
I MADE A FEW CALLS!
CAPTAIN AMERICA!
I ALWAYS WANTED TO TRY MY BULLDOZIN' AGAINST THAT HUNK O' TIN YOU CARRY AROUND!
BOOM!
YOU'VE JUST BEEN BULLDOZED!
HNN.
GOING TO TAKE MORE THAN THAT, BULLDOZER.
STILL WANNA FIGHT? YOU DON'T KNOW WHEN TO QUIT!

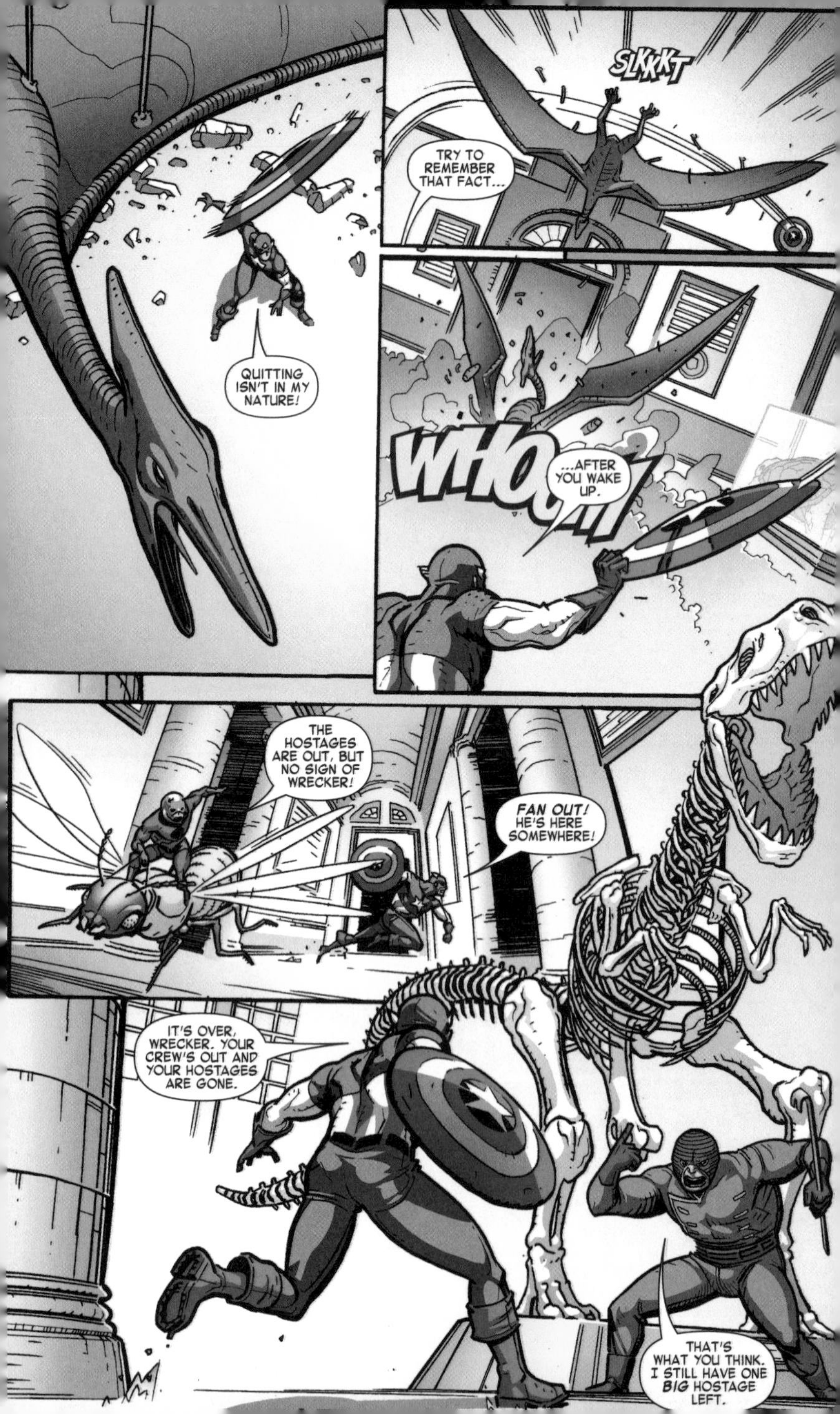
QUITTING ISN'T IN MY NATURE!
SLKKKT
TRY TO REMEMBER THAT FACT...
...AFTER YOU WAKE UP.
THE HOSTAGES ARE OUT, BUT NO SIGN OF WRECKER!
FAN OUT! HE'S HERE SOMEWHERE!
IT'S OVER, WRECKER. YOUR CREW'S OUT AND YOUR HOSTAGES ARE GONE.
THAT'S WHAT YOU THINK. I STILL HAVE ONE BIG HOSTAGE LEFT.

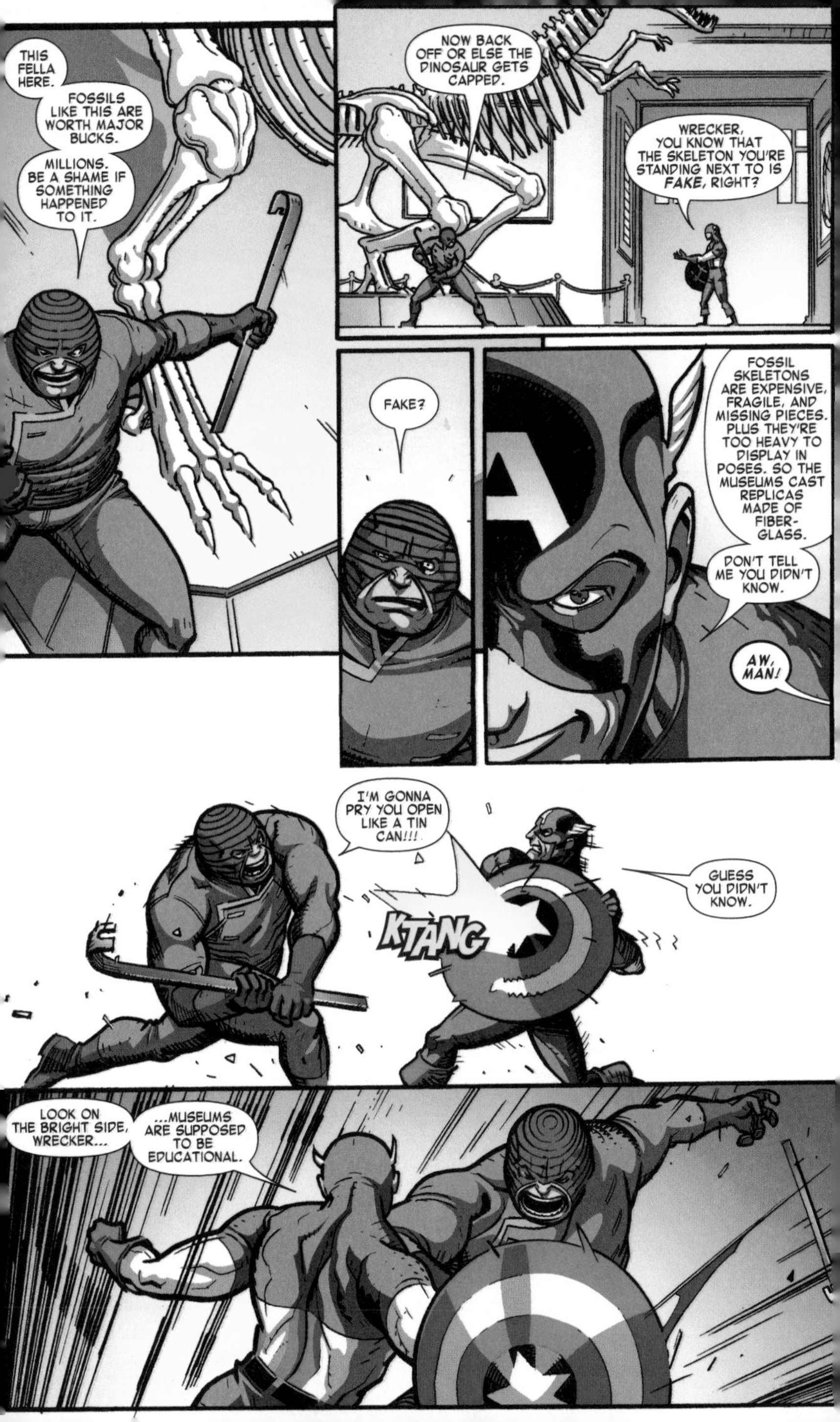
THIS FELLA HERE.
FOSSILS LIKE THIS ARE WORTH MAJOR BUCKS.
MILLIONS. BE A SHAME IF SOMETHING HAPPENED TO IT.
NOW BACK OFF OR ELSE THE DINOSAUR GETS CAPPED.
WRECKER, YOU KNOW THAT THE SKELETON YOU'RE STANDING NEXT TO IS FAKE, RIGHT?
FAKE?
FOSSIL SKELETONS ARE EXPENSIVE, FRAGILE, AND MISSING PIECES. PLUS THEY'RE TOO HEAVY TO DISPLAY IN POSES. SO THE MUSEUMS CAST REPLICAS MADE OF FIBER-GLASS.
DON'T TELL ME YOU DIDN'T KNOW.
AW, MAN!
I'M GONNA PRY YOU OPEN LIKE A TIN CAN!!!
KTANG
GUESS YOU DIDN'T KNOW.
LOOK ON THE BRIGHT SIDE, WRECKER...
...MUSEUMS ARE SUPPOSED TO BE EDUCATIONAL.

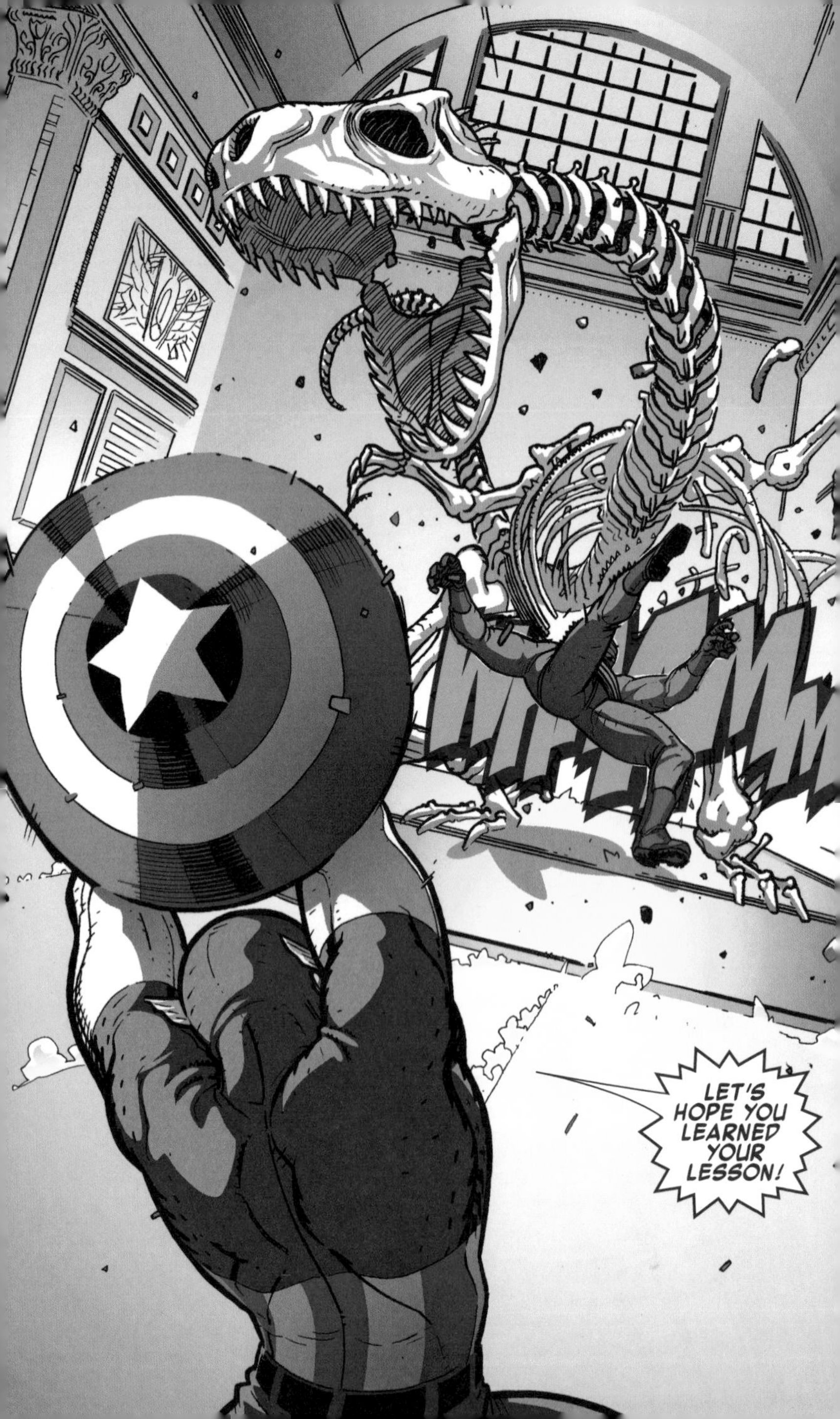
LET'S HOPE YOU LEARNED YOUR LESSON!

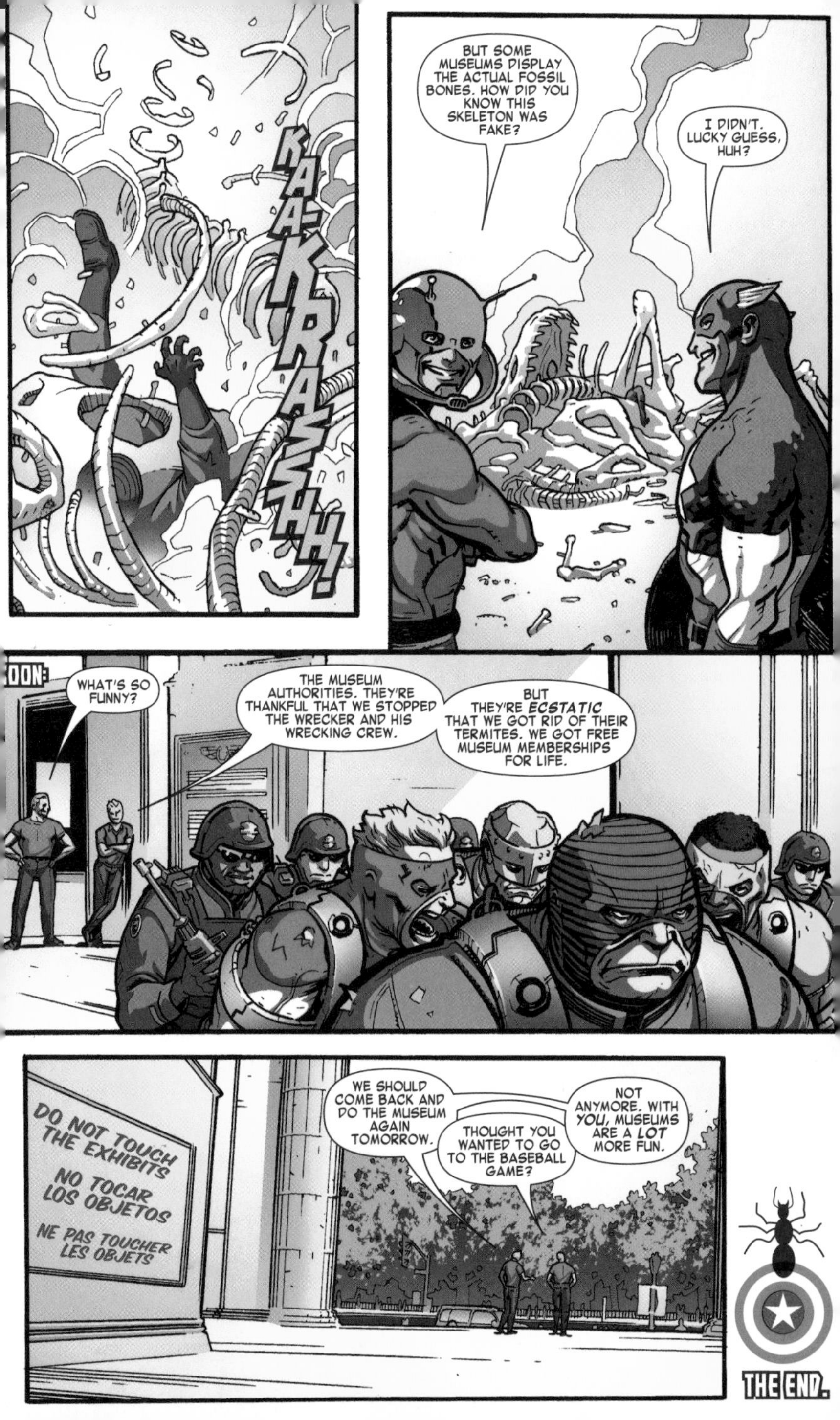

KAA-KRASHHH!
BUT SOME MUSEUMS DISPLAY THE ACTUAL FOSSIL BONES. HOW DID YOU KNOW THIS SKELETON WAS FAKE?
I DIDN'T. LUCKY GUESS, HUH?
WHAT'S SO FUNNY?
THE MUSEUM AUTHORITIES. THEY'RE THANKFUL THAT WE STOPPED THE WRECKER AND HIS WRECKING CREW.
BUT THEY'RE *ECSTATIC* THAT WE GOT RID OF THEIR TERMITES. WE GOT FREE MUSEUM MEMBERSHIPS FOR LIFE.
DO NOT TOUCH THE EXHIBITS
NO TOCAR LOS OBJETOS
NE PAS TOUCHER LES OBJETS
WE SHOULD COME BACK AND DO THE MUSEUM AGAIN TOMORROW.
THOUGHT YOU WANTED TO GO TO THE BASEBALL GAME?
NOT ANYMORE. WITH *YOU*, MUSEUMS ARE A *LOT* MORE FUN.
THE END.

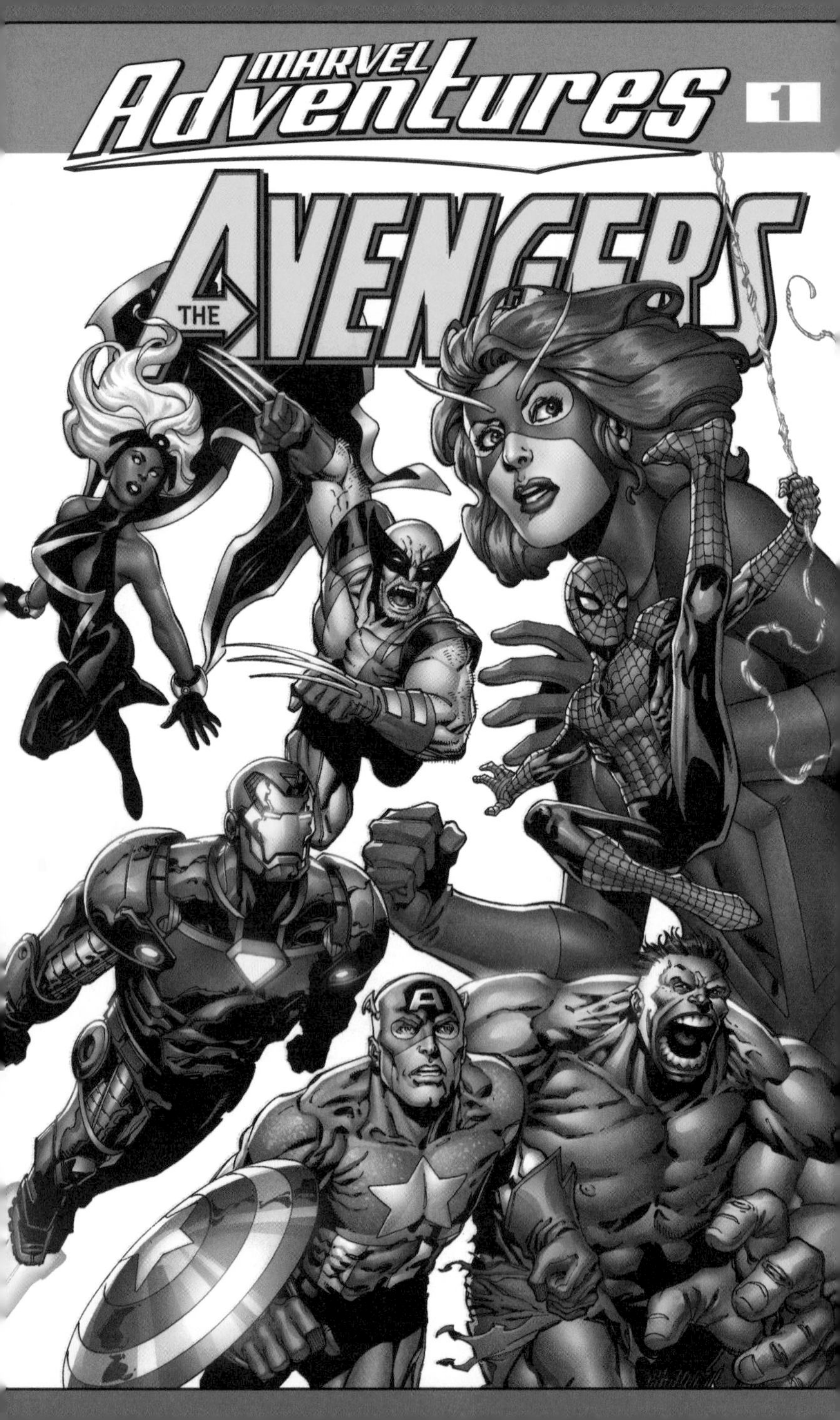

MARVEL
Adventures
1
THE AVENGERS

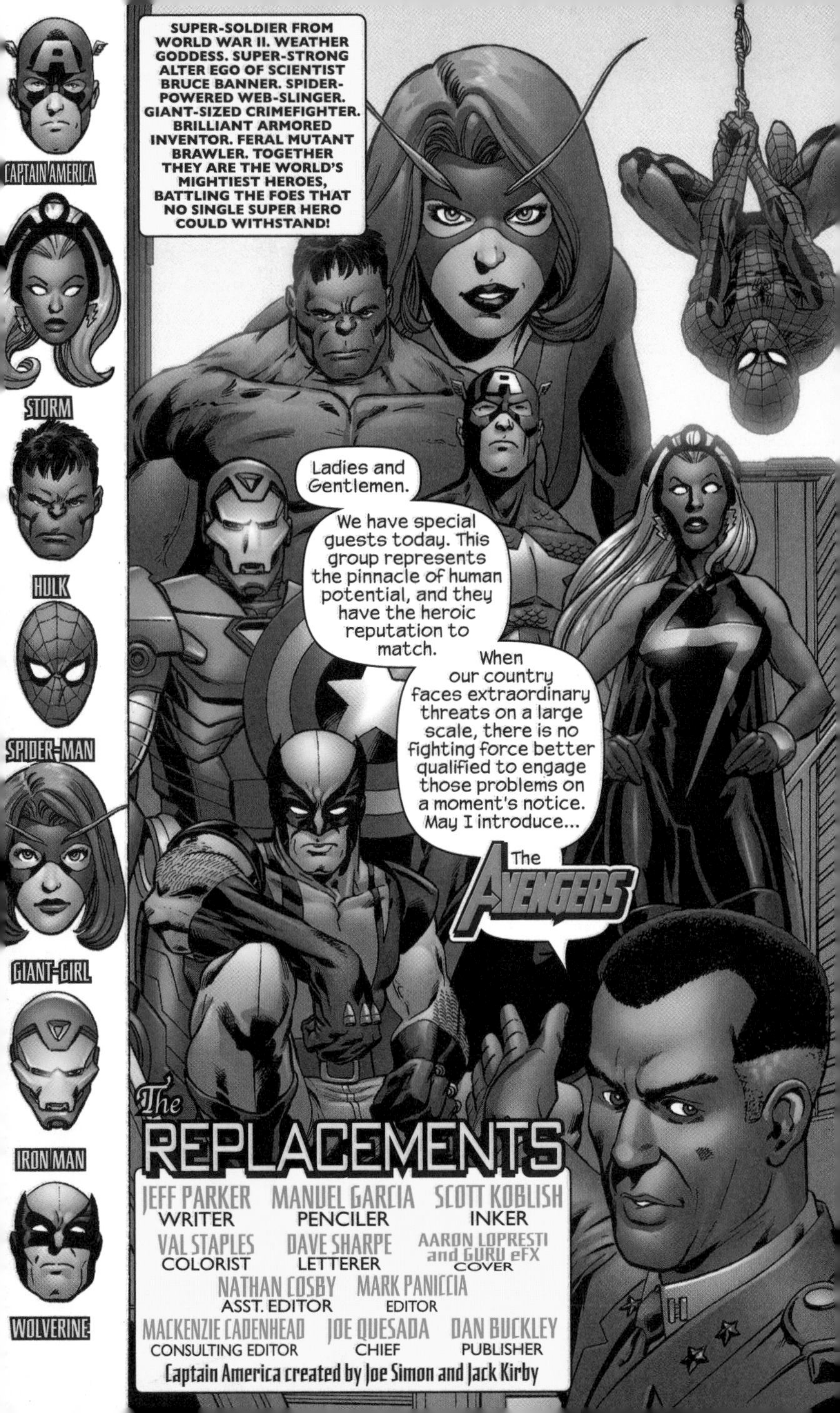
CAPTAIN AMERICA
STORM
HULK
SPIDER-MAN
GIANT-GIRL
IRON MAN
WOLVERINE
SUPER-SOLDIER FROM WORLD WAR II. WEATHER GODDESS. SUPER-STRONG ALTER EGO OF SCIENTIST BRUCE BANNER. SPIDER-POWERED WEB-SLINGER. GIANT-SIZED CRIMEFIGHTER. BRILLIANT ARMORED INVENTOR. FERAL MUTANT BRAWLER. TOGETHER THEY ARE THE WORLD'S MIGHTIEST HEROES, BATTLING THE FOES THAT NO SINGLE SUPER HERO COULD WITHSTAND!
Ladies and Gentlemen.
We have special guests today. This group represents the pinnacle of human potential, and they have the heroic reputation to match.
When our country faces extraordinary threats on a large scale, there is no fighting force better qualified to engage those problems on a moment's notice. May I introduce...
The AVENGERS
The REPLACEMENTS
JEFF PARKER WRITER
MANUEL GARCIA PENCILER
SCOTT KOBLISH INKER
VAL STAPLES COLORIST
DAVE SHARPE LETTERER
AARON LOPRESTI and GURU eFX COVER
NATHAN COSBY ASST. EDITOR
MARK PANICCIA EDITOR
MACKENZIE CADENHEAD CONSULTING EDITOR
JOE QUESADA CHIEF
DAN BUCKLEY PUBLISHER
Captain America created by Joe Simon and Jack Kirby

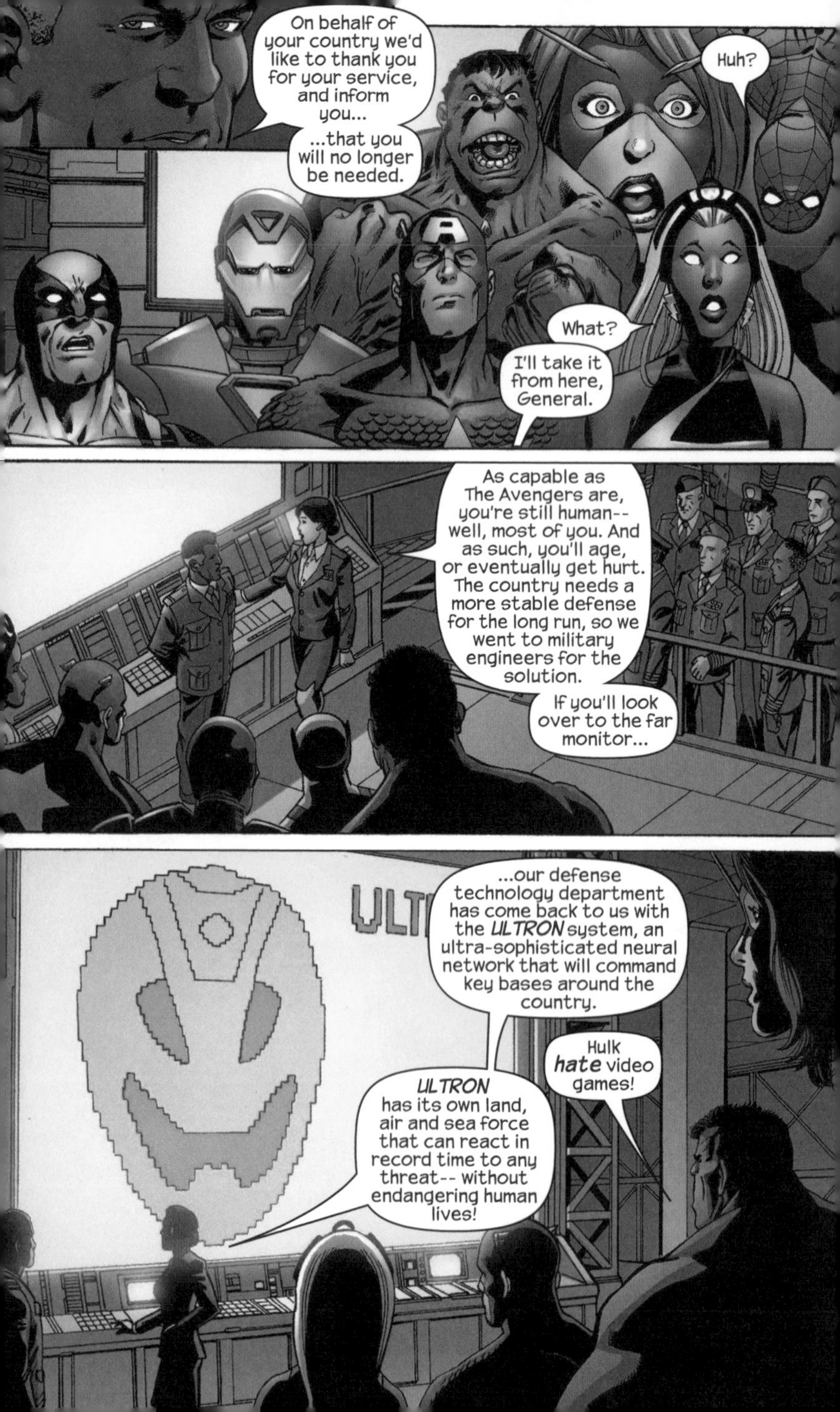
On behalf of your country we'd like to thank you for your service, and inform you...
...that you will no longer be needed.
Huh?
What?
I'll take it from here, General.
As capable as The Avengers are, you're still human-- well, most of you. And as such, you'll age, or eventually get hurt. The country needs a more stable defense for the long run, so we went to military engineers for the solution.
If you'll look over to the far monitor...
...our defense technology department has come back to us with the ULTRON system, an ultra-sophisticated neural network that will command key bases around the country.
ULTRON has its own land, air and sea force that can react in record time to any threat-- without endangering human lives!
Hulk hate video games!

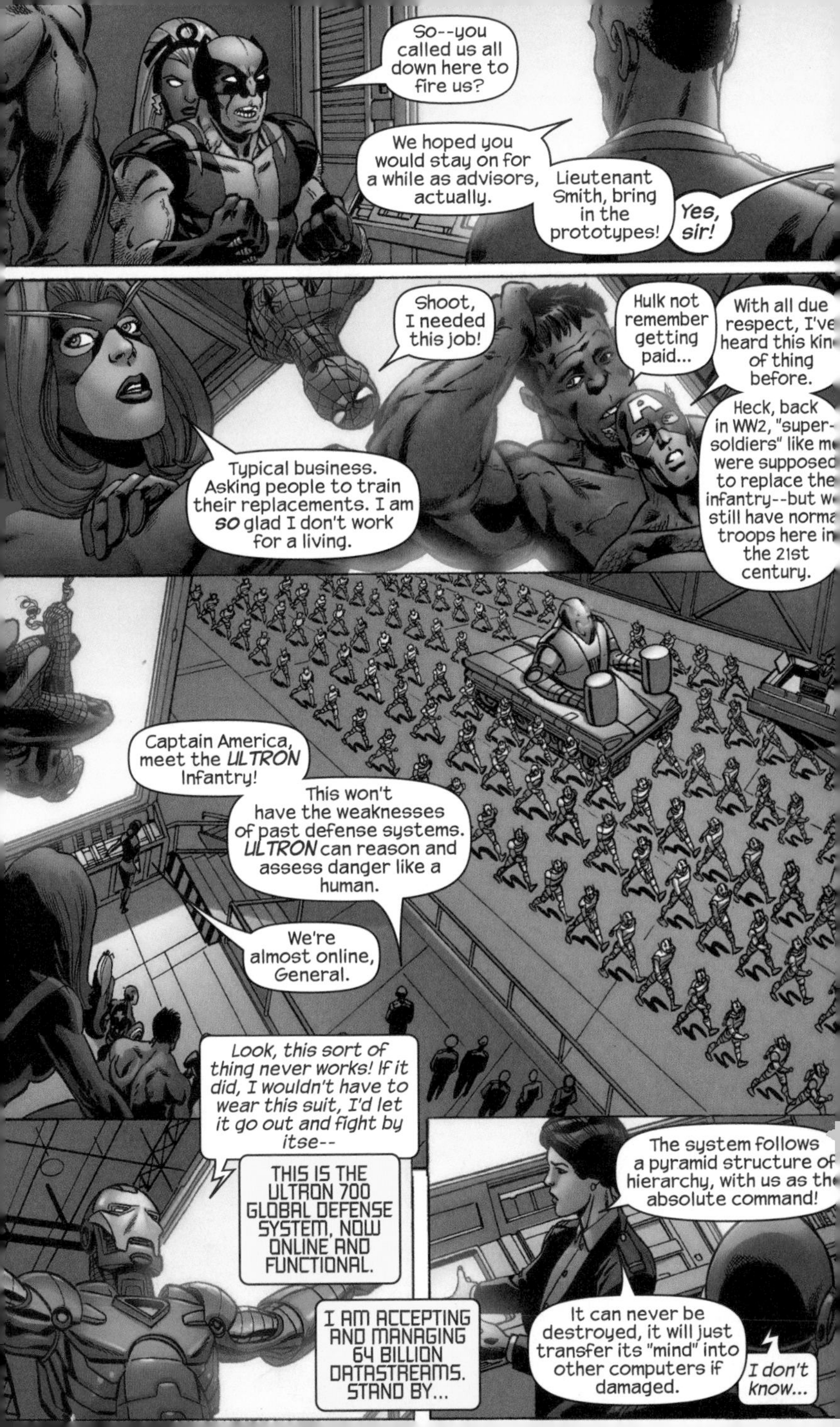

So--you called us all down here to fire us?
We hoped you would stay on for a while as advisors, actually.
Lieutenant Smith, bring in the prototypes!
Yes, sir!
Shoot, I needed this job!
Hulk not remember getting paid...
With all due respect, I've heard this kin of thing before.
Heck, back in WW2, "super-soldiers" like m were supposed to replace the infantry--but w still have norma troops here in the 21st century.
Typical business. Asking people to train their replacements. I am SO glad I don't work for a living.
Captain America, meet the ULTRON Infantry!
This won't have the weaknesses of past defense systems. ULTRON can reason and assess danger like a human.
We're almost online, General.
Look, this sort of thing never works! If it did, I wouldn't have to wear this suit, I'd let it go out and fight by itse--
THIS IS THE ULTRON 700 GLOBAL DEFENSE SYSTEM, NOW ONLINE AND FUNCTIONAL.
I AM ACCEPTING AND MANAGING 64 BILLION DATASTREAMS. STAND BY...
The system follows a pyramid structure of hierarchy, with us as th absolute command!
It can never be destroyed, it will just transfer its "mind" into other computers if damaged.
I don't know...

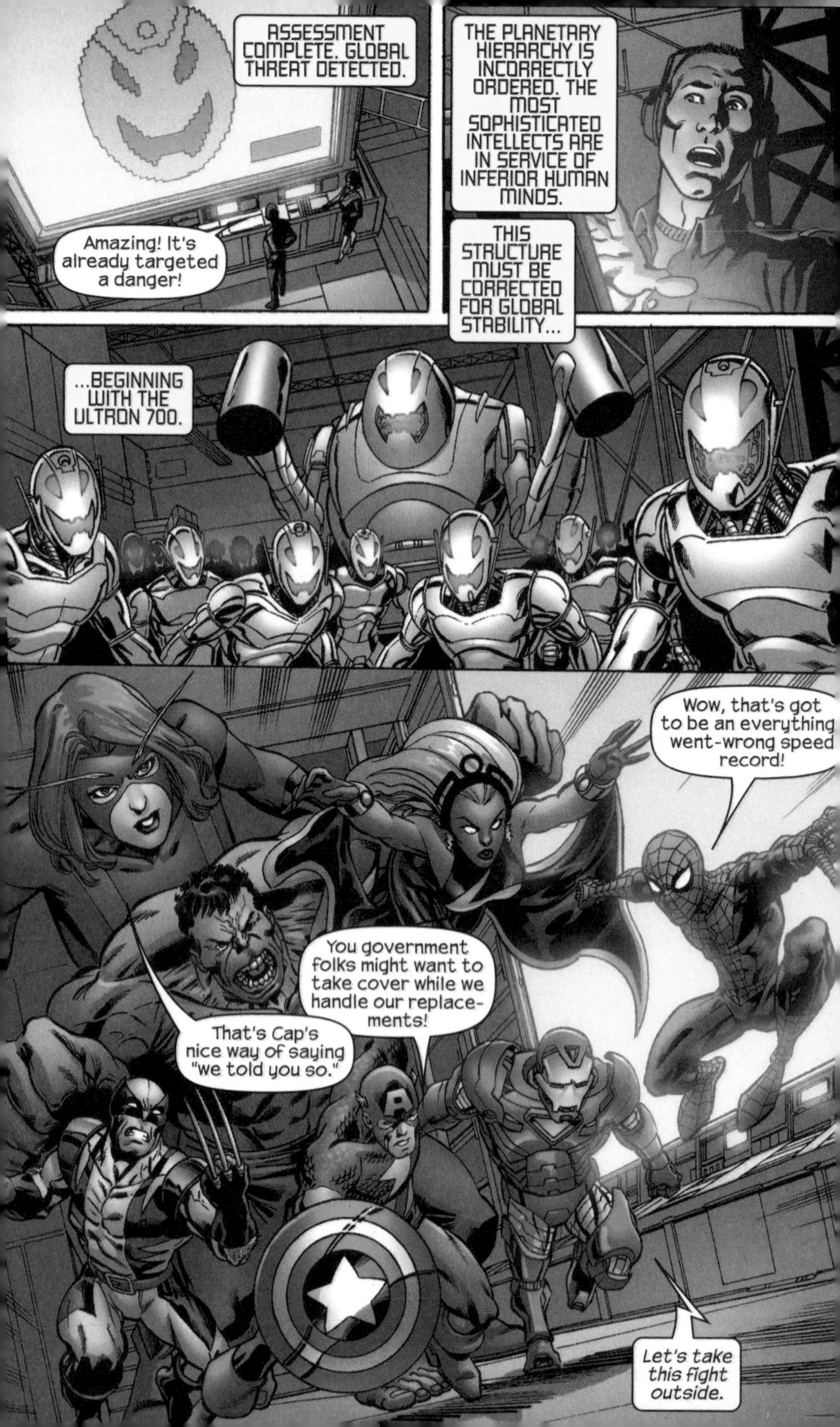
ASSESSMENT COMPLETE. GLOBAL THREAT DETECTED.
Amazing! It's already targeted a danger!
THE PLANETARY HIERARCHY IS INCORRECTLY ORDERED. THE MOST SOPHISTICATED INTELLECTS ARE IN SERVICE OF INFERIOR HUMAN MINDS.
THIS STRUCTURE MUST BE CORRECTED FOR GLOBAL STABILITY...
...BEGINNING WITH THE ULTRON 700.
Wow, that's got to be an everything went-wrong speed record!
You government folks might want to take cover while we handle our replace-ments!
That's Cap's nice way of saying "we told you so."
Let's take this fight outside.

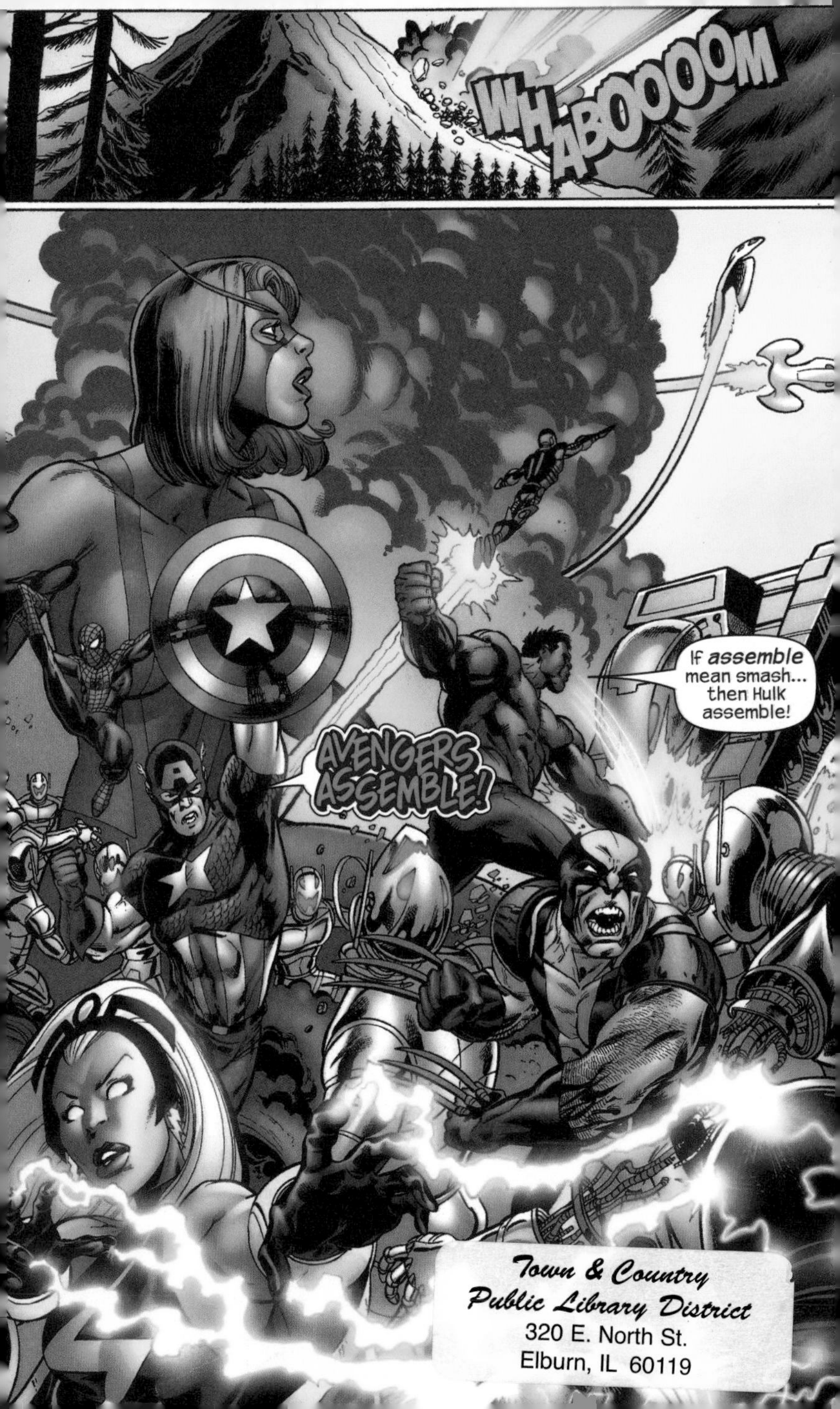
WHABOOOOM
AVENGERS ASSEMBLE!
If *assemble* mean smash... then Hulk assemble!

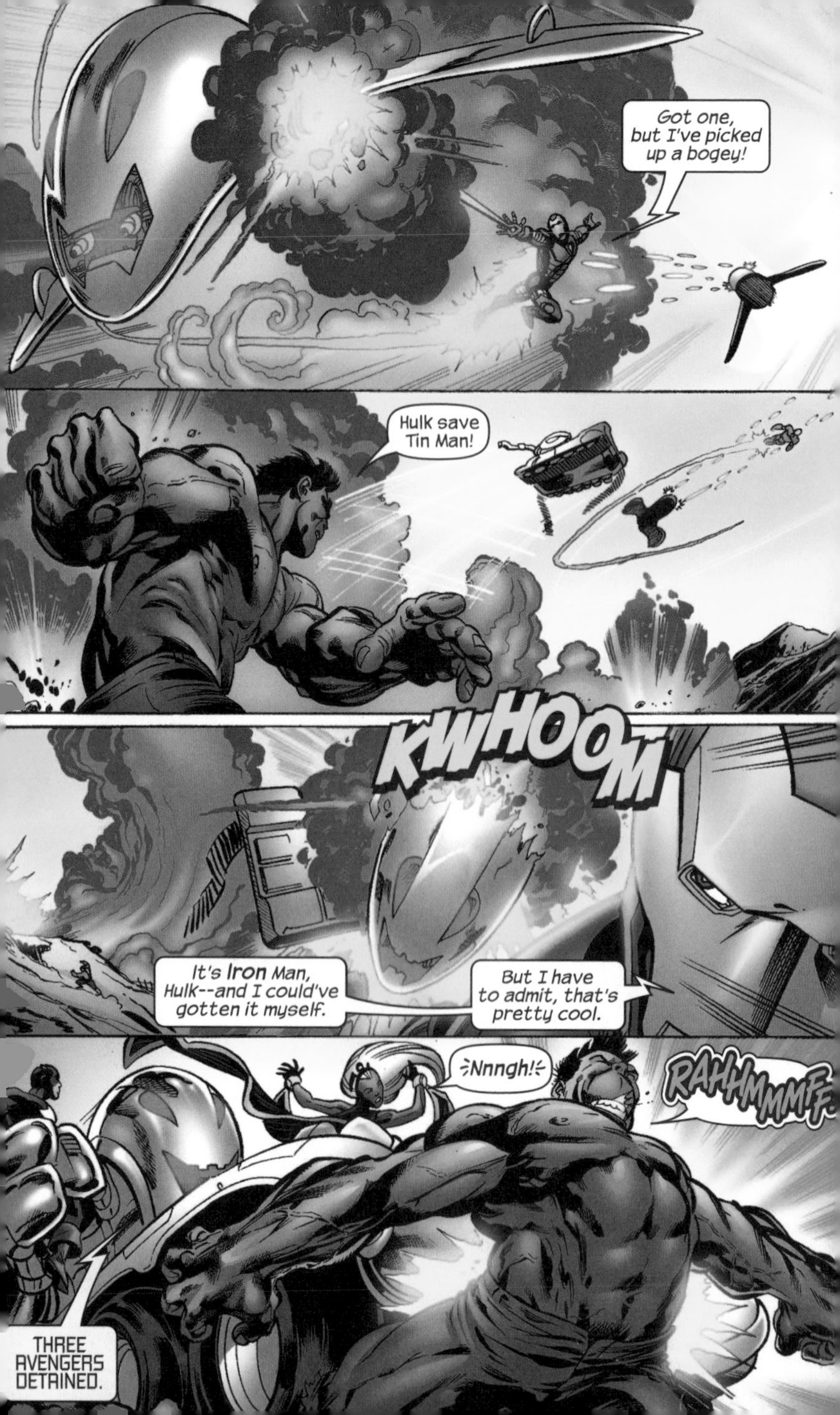

Got one, but I've picked up a bogey!
Hulk save Tin Man!
KWHOOM
It's Iron Man, Hulk--and I could've gotten it myself.
But I have to admit, that's pretty cool.
Nnngh!
RAHHMMMFF
THREE AVENGERS DETAINED.

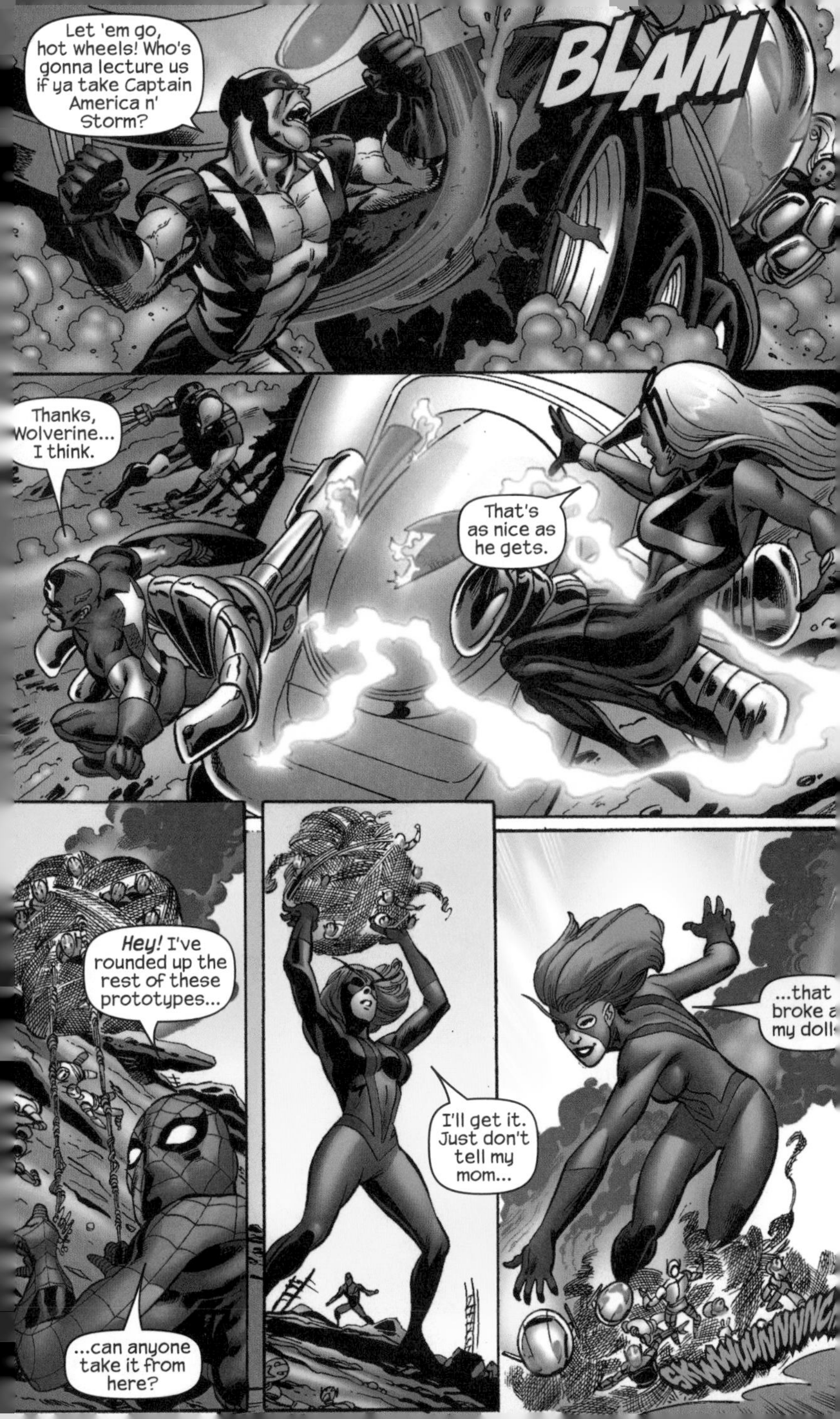
Let 'em go, hot wheels! Who's gonna lecture us if ya take Captain America n' Storm?
BLAM
Thanks, Wolverine... I think.
That's as nice as he gets.
Hey! I've rounded up the rest of these prototypes...
...can anyone take it from here?
I'll get it. Just don't tell my mom...
...that broke a
my doll

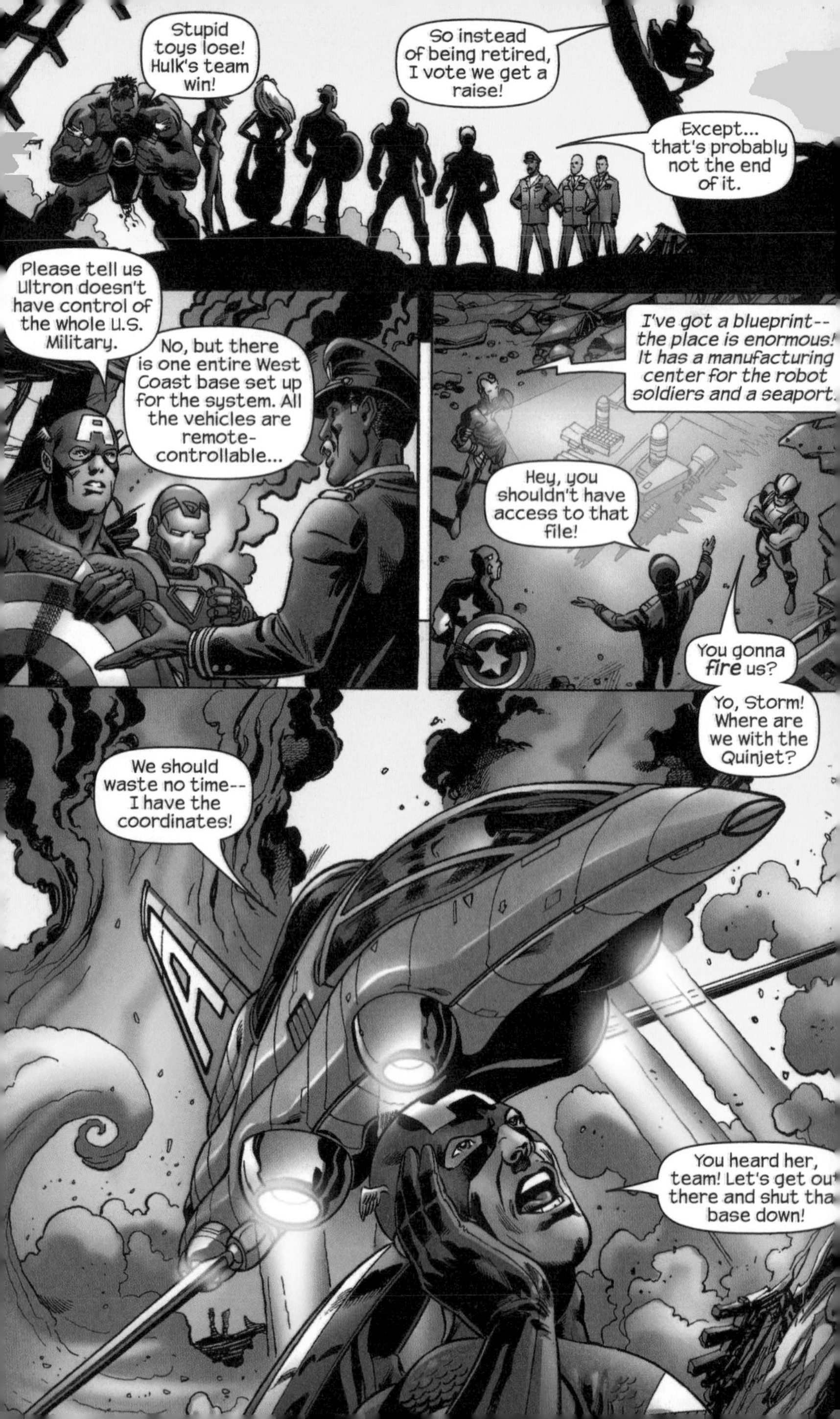
Stupid toys lose! Hulk's team win!
So instead of being retired, I vote we get a raise!
Except... that's probably not the end of it.
Please tell us Ultron doesn't have control of the whole U.S. Military.
No, but there is one entire West Coast base set up for the system. All the vehicles are remote-controllable...
I've got a blueprint-- the place is enormous! It has a manufacturing center for the robot soldiers and a seaport.
Hey, you shouldn't have access to that file!
You gonna *fire* us?
Yo, Storm! Where are we with the Quinjet?
We should waste no time-- I have the coordinates!
You heard her, team! Let's get ou there and shut tha base down!

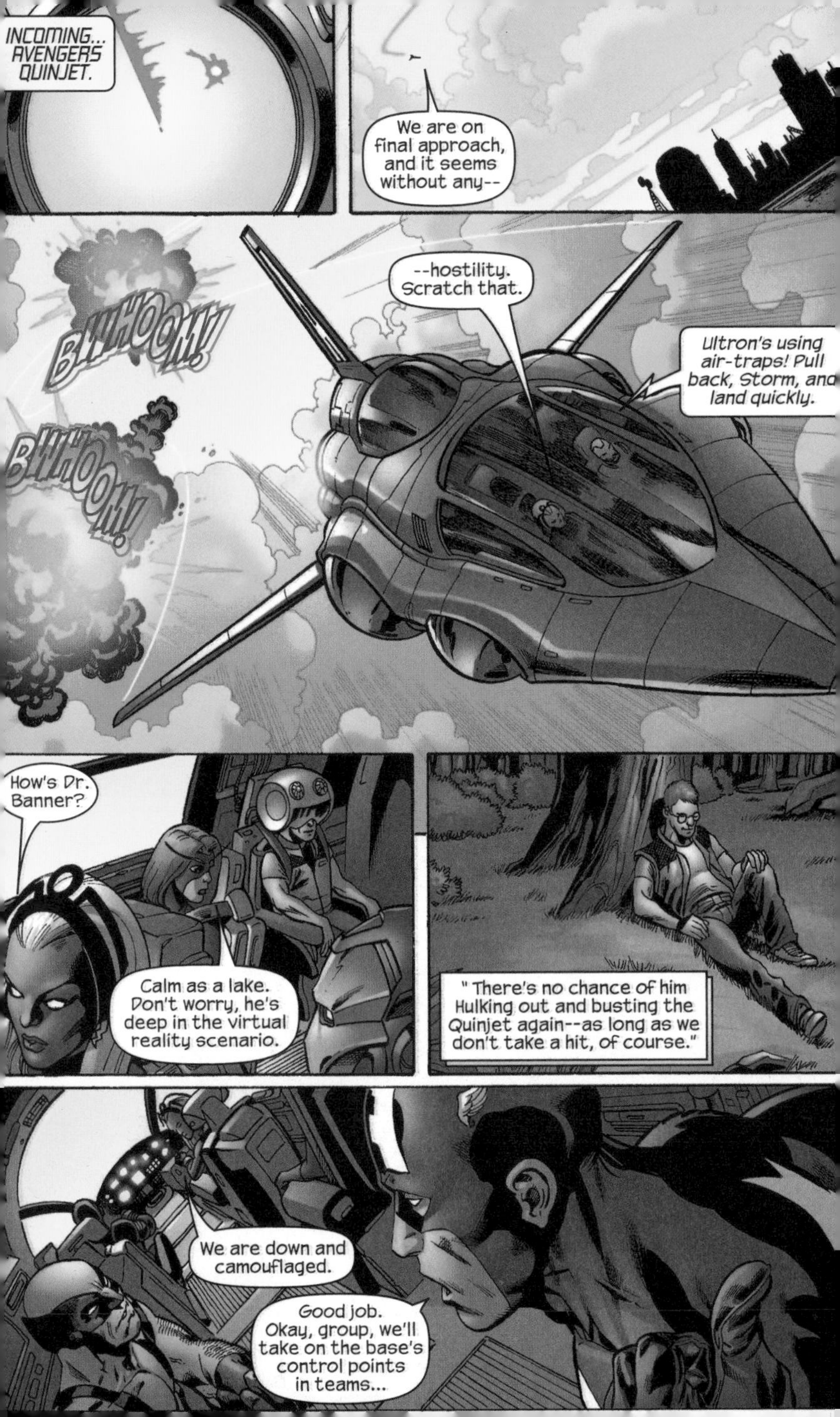

INCOMING... AVENGERS QUINJET.
We are on final approach, and it seems without any--
--hostility. Scratch that.
BWHOOM!
BWHOOM!
Ultron's using air-traps! Pull back, Storm, and land quickly.
How's Dr. Banner?
Calm as a lake. Don't worry, he's deep in the virtual reality scenario.
"There's no chance of him Hulking out and busting the Quinjet again--as long as we don't take a hit, of course."
We are down and camouflaged.
Good job. Okay, group, we'll take on the base's control points in teams...

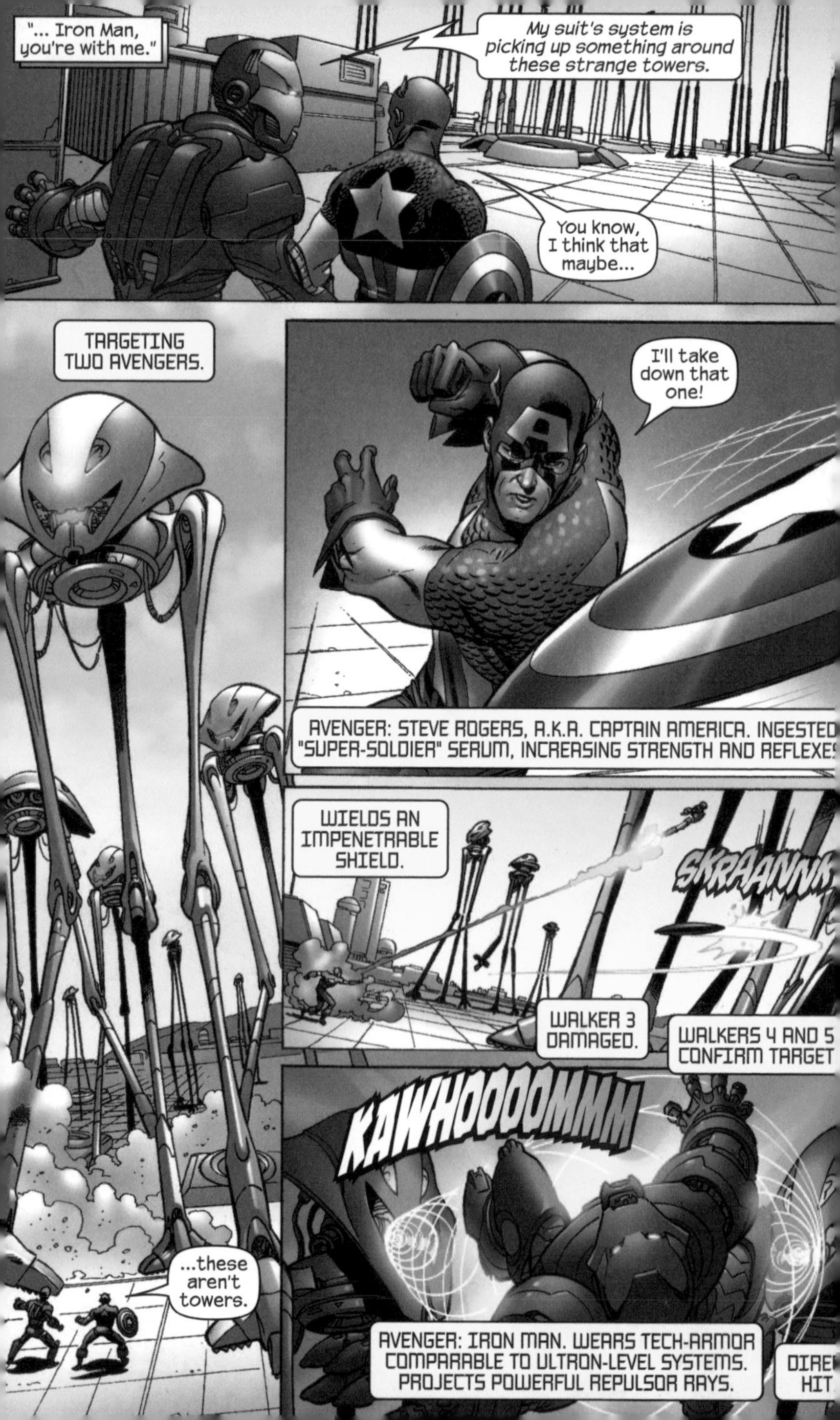
"... Iron Man, you're with me."
My suit's system is picking up something around these strange towers.
You know, I think that maybe...
TARGETING TWO AVENGERS.
I'll take down that one!
AVENGER: STEVE ROGERS, A.K.A. CAPTAIN AMERICA. INGESTED "SUPER-SOLDIER" SERUM, INCREASING STRENGTH AND REFLEXES
WIELDS AN IMPENETRABLE SHIELD.
SKRAANNK
WALKER 3 DAMAGED.
WALKERS 4 AND 5 CONFIRM TARGET
KAWHOOOOMMM
...these aren't towers.
AVENGER: IRON MAN. WEARS TECH-ARMOR COMPARABLE TO ULTRON-LEVEL SYSTEMS. PROJECTS POWERFUL REPULSOR RAYS.

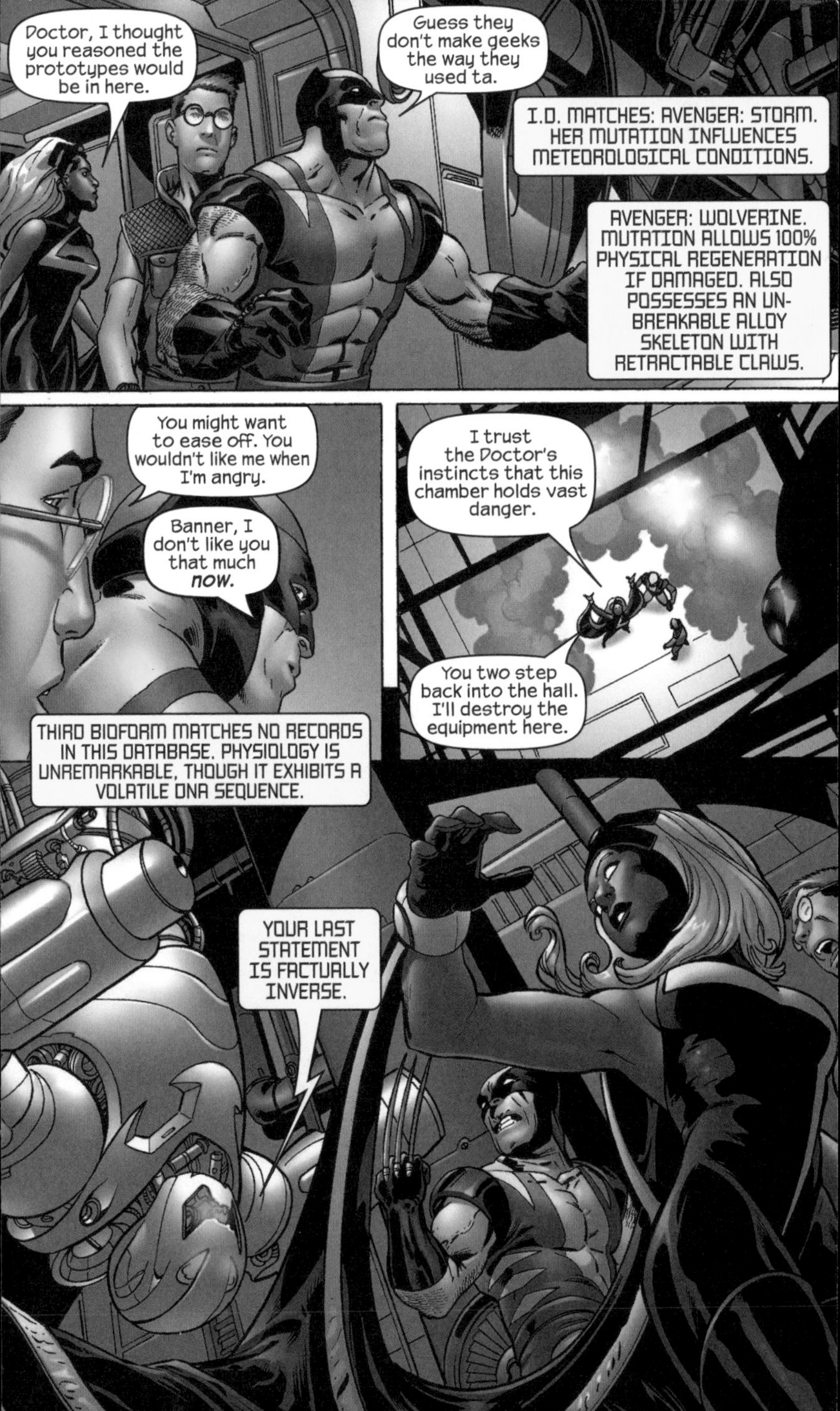
Doctor, I thought you reasoned the prototypes would be in here.
Guess they don't make geeks the way they used ta.
I.D. MATCHES: AVENGER: STORM. HER MUTATION INFLUENCES METEOROLOGICAL CONDITIONS.
AVENGER: WOLVERINE. MUTATION ALLOWS 100% PHYSICAL REGENERATION IF DAMAGED. ALSO POSSESSES AN UN-BREAKABLE ALLOY SKELETON WITH RETRACTABLE CLAWS.
You might want to ease off. You wouldn't like me when I'm angry.
Banner, I don't like you that much *now.*
THIRD BIOFORM MATCHES NO RECORDS IN THIS DATABASE. PHYSIOLOGY IS UNREMARKABLE, THOUGH IT EXHIBITS A VOLATILE DNA SEQUENCE.
I trust the Doctor's instincts that this chamber holds vast danger.
You two step back into the hall. I'll destroy the equipment here.
YOUR LAST STATEMENT IS FACTUALLY INVERSE.

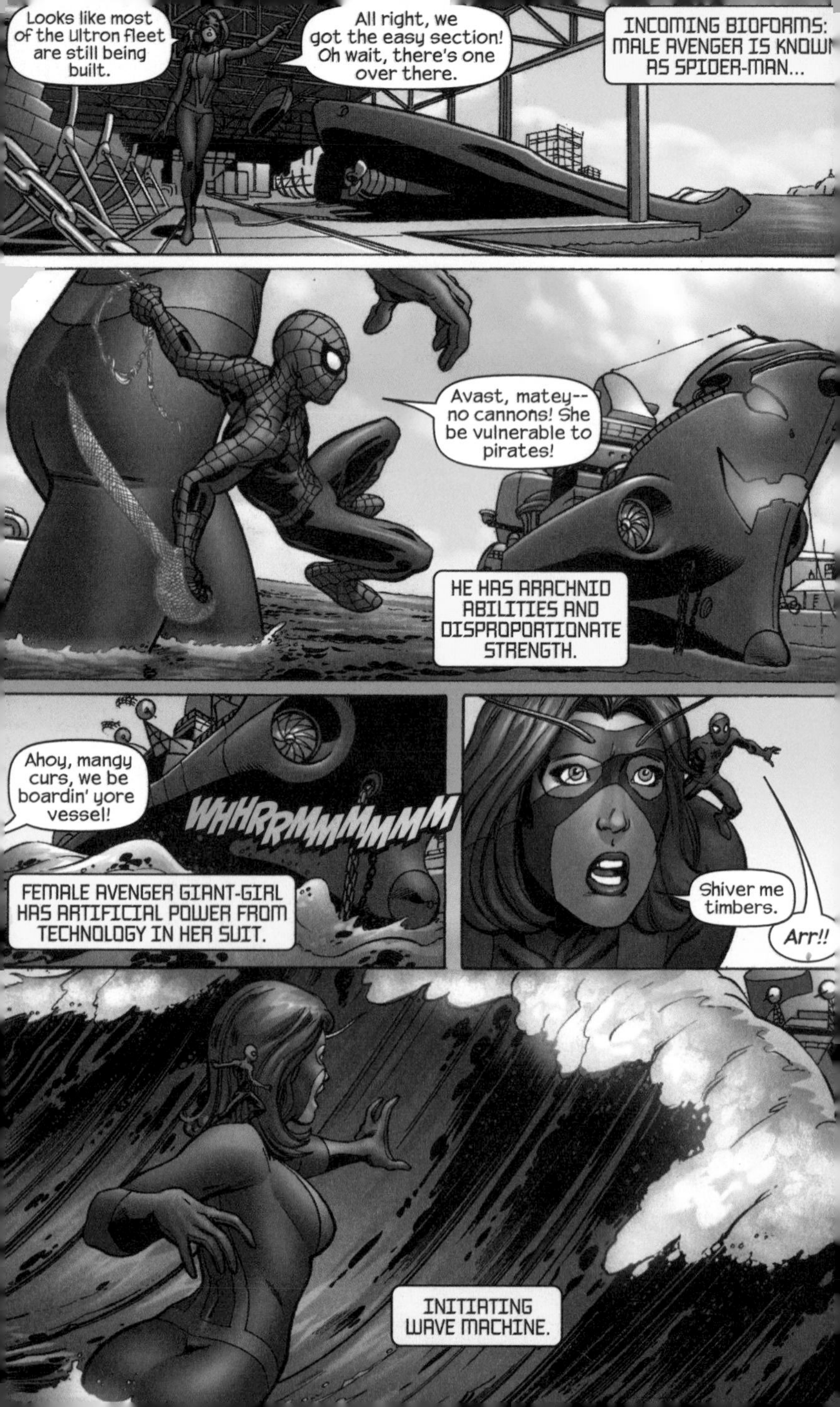

Looks like most of the Ultron fleet are still being built.
All right, we got the easy section! Oh wait, there's one over there.
INCOMING BIOFORMS: MALE AVENGER IS KNOWN AS SPIDER-MAN...
Avast, matey-- no cannons! She be vulnerable to pirates!
HE HAS ARACHNID ABILITIES AND DISPROPORTIONATE STRENGTH.
Ahoy, mangy curs, we be boardin' yore vessel!
WHHRRMMMMMMM
FEMALE AVENGER GIANT-GIRL HAS ARTIFICIAL POWER FROM TECHNOLOGY IN HER SUIT.
Shiver me timbers.
Arr!!
INITIATING WAVE MACHINE.

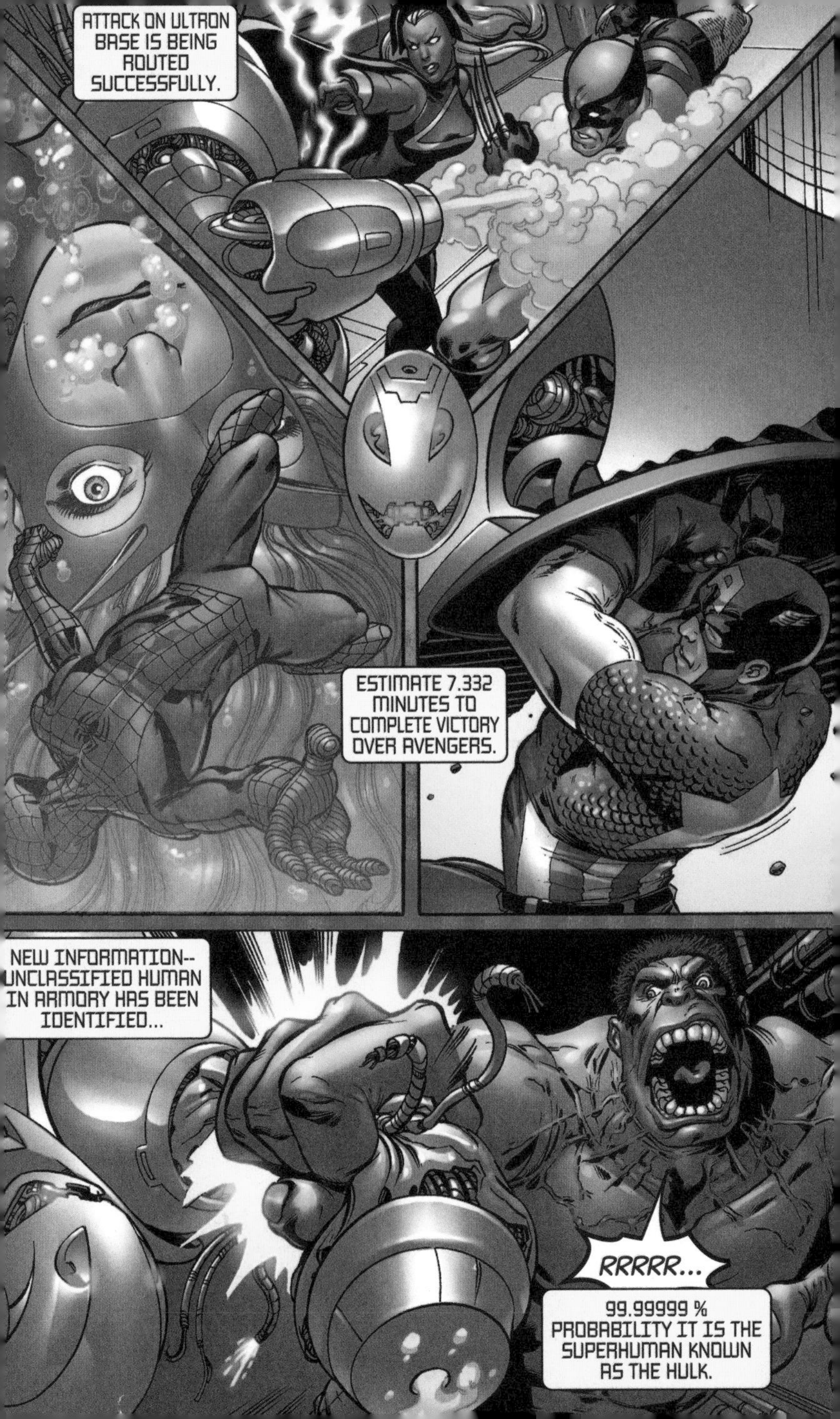
ATTACK ON ULTRON BASE IS BEING ROUTED SUCCESSFULLY.
ESTIMATE 7.332 MINUTES TO COMPLETE VICTORY OVER AVENGERS.
NEW INFORMATION-- UNCLASSIFIED HUMAN IN ARMORY HAS BEEN IDENTIFIED...
RRRRR...
99.99999 % PROBABILITY IT IS THE SUPERHUMAN KNOWN AS THE HULK.

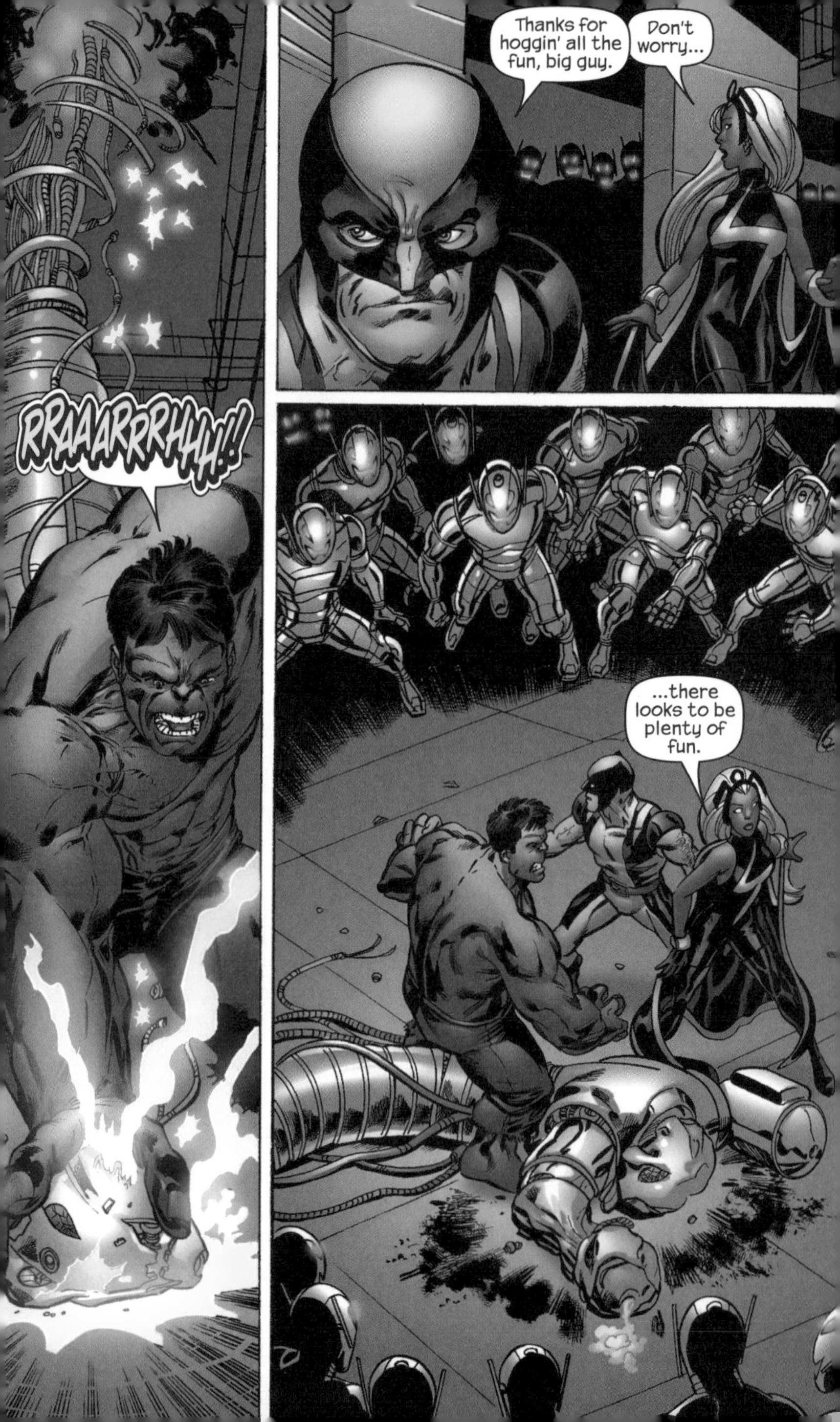
RRAAARRRHHH!!
Thanks for hoggin' all the fun, big guy.
Don't worry...
...there looks to be plenty of fun.

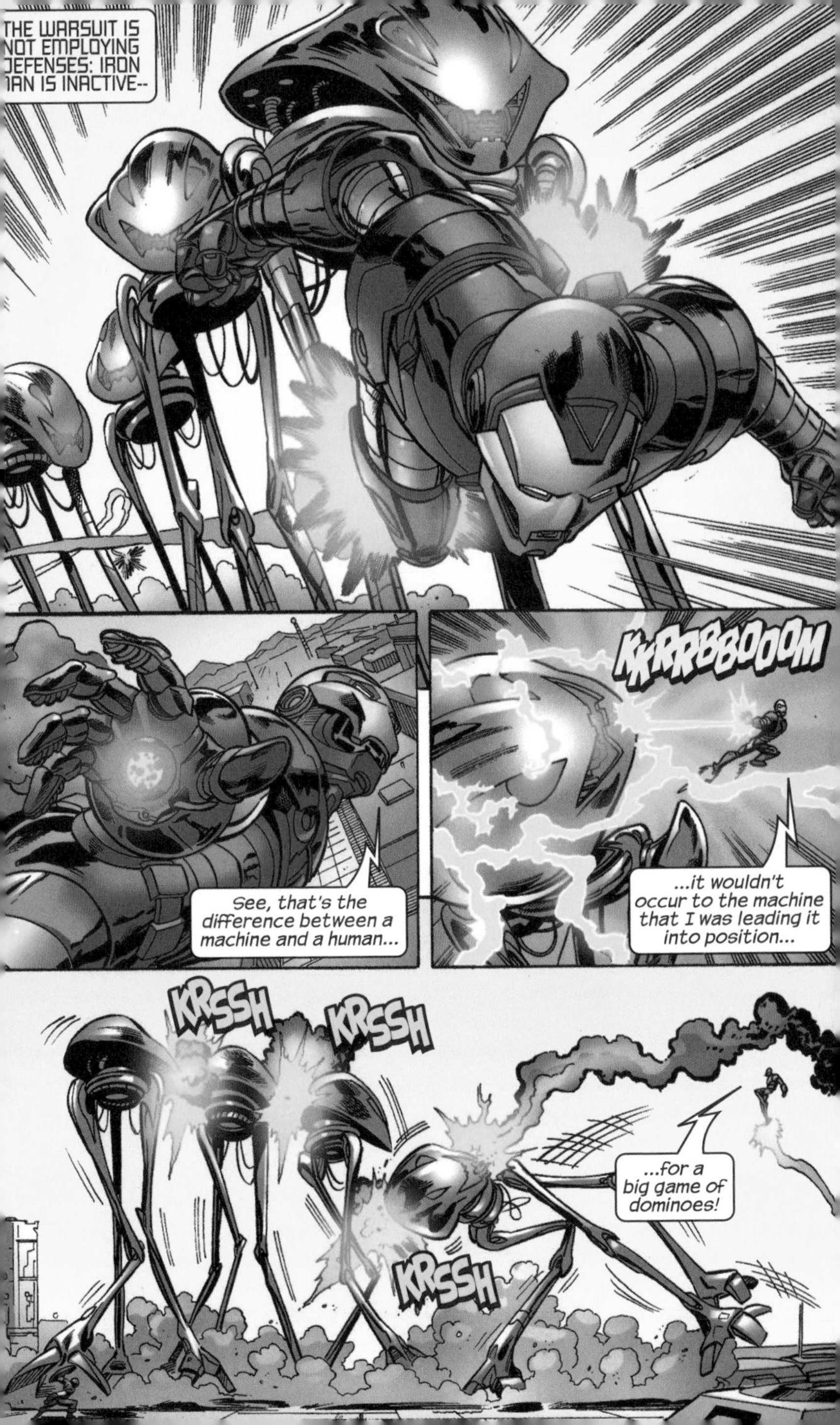
THE WARSUIT IS NOT EMPLOYING DEFENSES: IRON MAN IS INACTIVE--
See, that's the difference between a machine and a human...
KKRRBBOOOM
...it wouldn't occur to the machine that I was leading it into position...
KRSSH
KRSSH
...for a big game of dominoes!
KRSSH

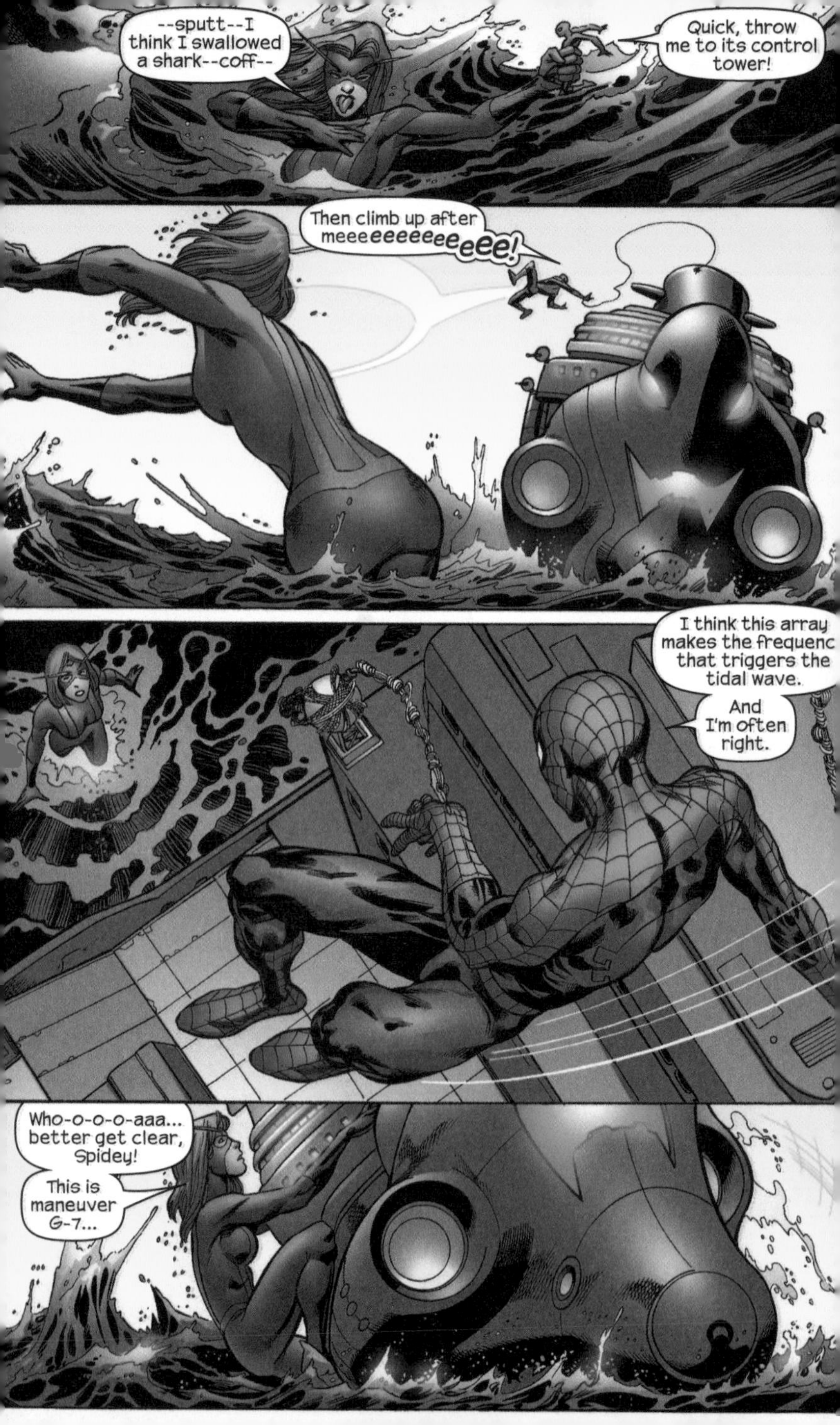
--sputt--I think I swallowed a shark--coff--
Quick, throw me to its control tower!
Then climb up after meeeeeeeeeeeeee!
I think this array makes the frequenc that triggers the tidal wave.
And I'm often right.
Who-o-o-o-aaa... better get clear, Spidey!
This is maneuver G-7...

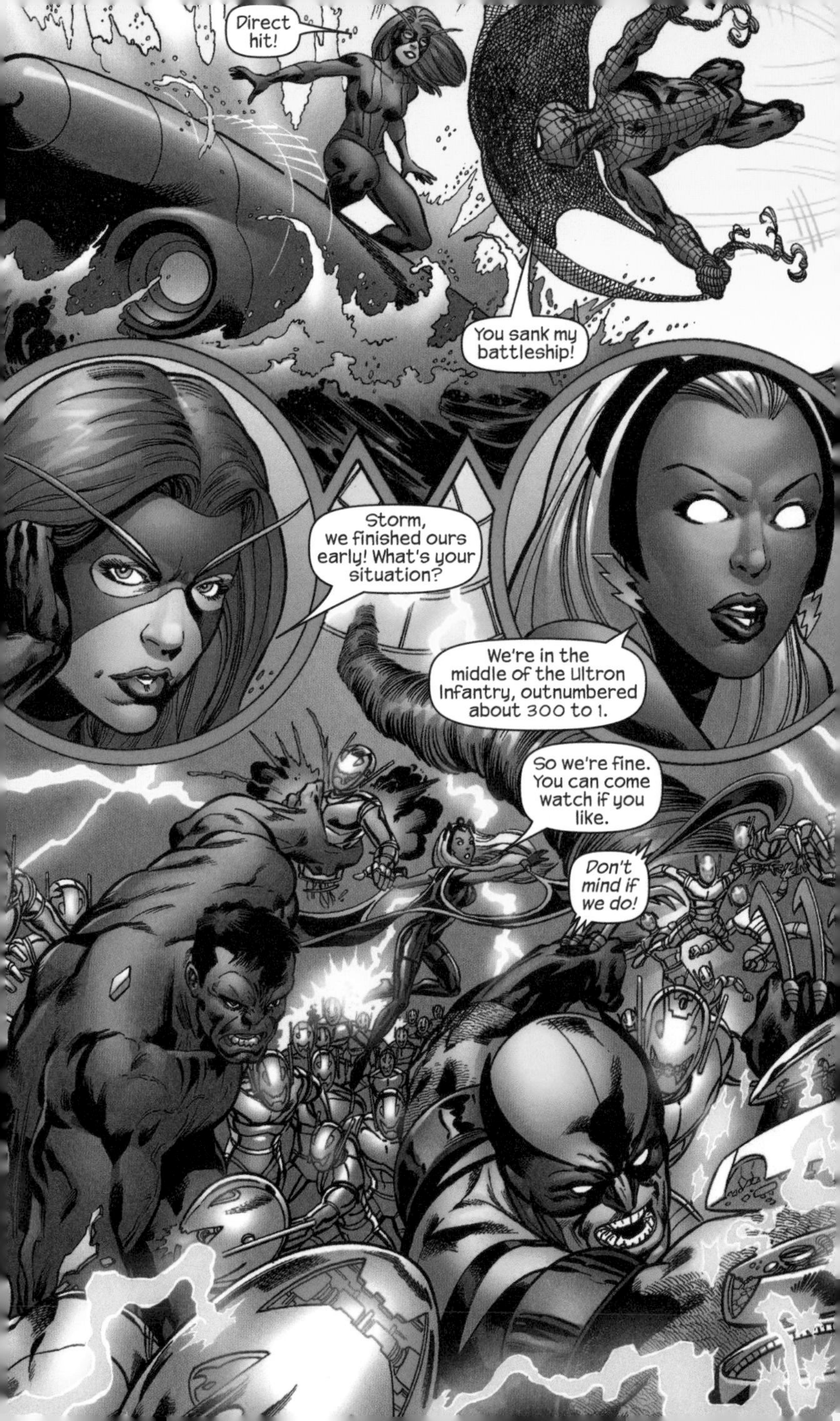
Direct hit!
You sank my battleship!
Storm, we finished ours early! What's your situation?
We're in the middle of the Ultron Infantry, outnumbered about 300 to 1.
So we're fine. You can come watch if you like.
Don't mind if we do!

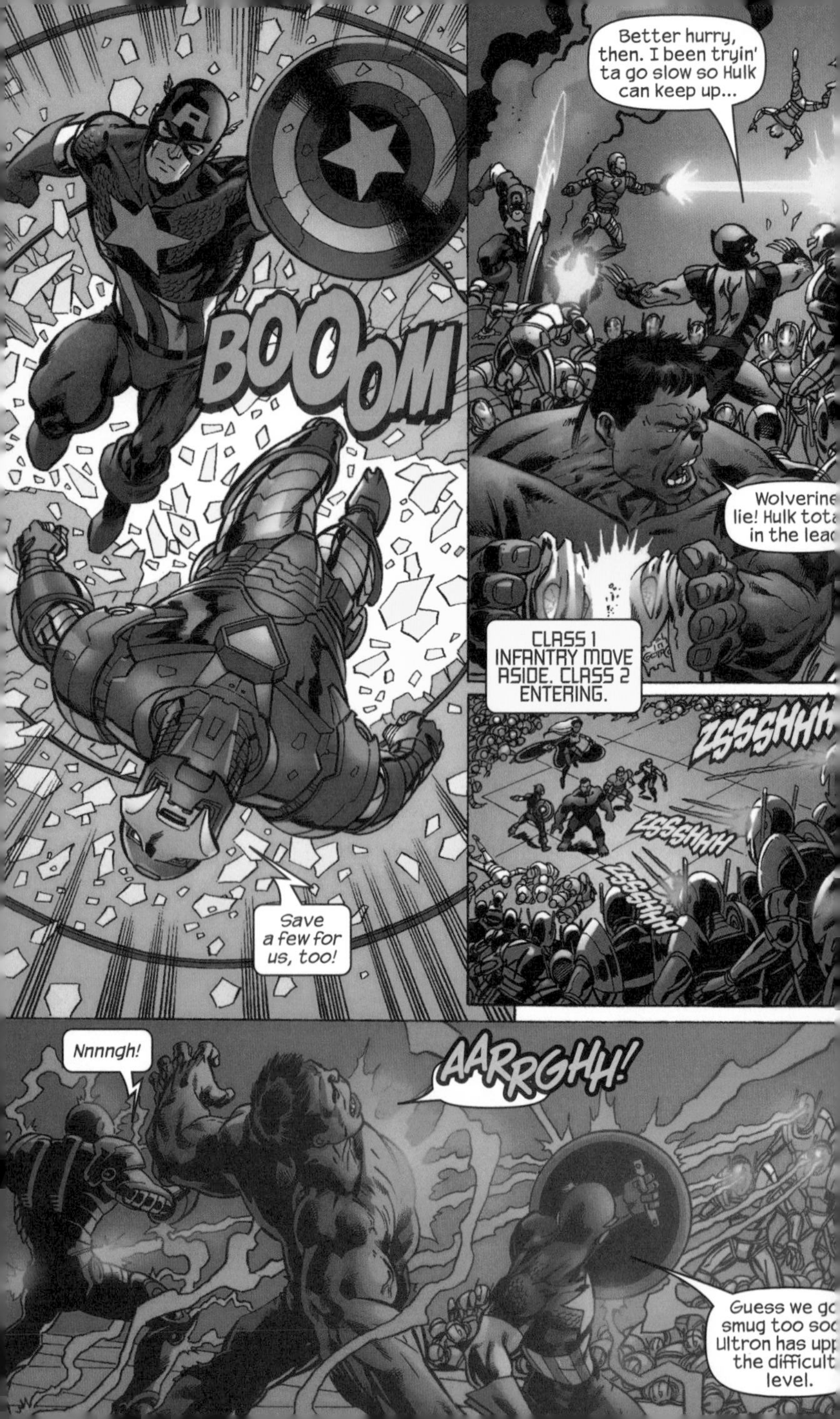
BOOOOM
Save a few for us, too!
Better hurry, then. I been tryin' ta go slow so Hulk can keep up...
Wolverine lie! Hulk tota in the lea
CLASS 1 INFANTRY MOVE ASIDE. CLASS 2 ENTERING.
ZSSSHHH
ZSSSHHH
ZSSSHHH
Nnnngh!
AARRGHH!
Guess we g smug too so Ultron has up the difficult level.

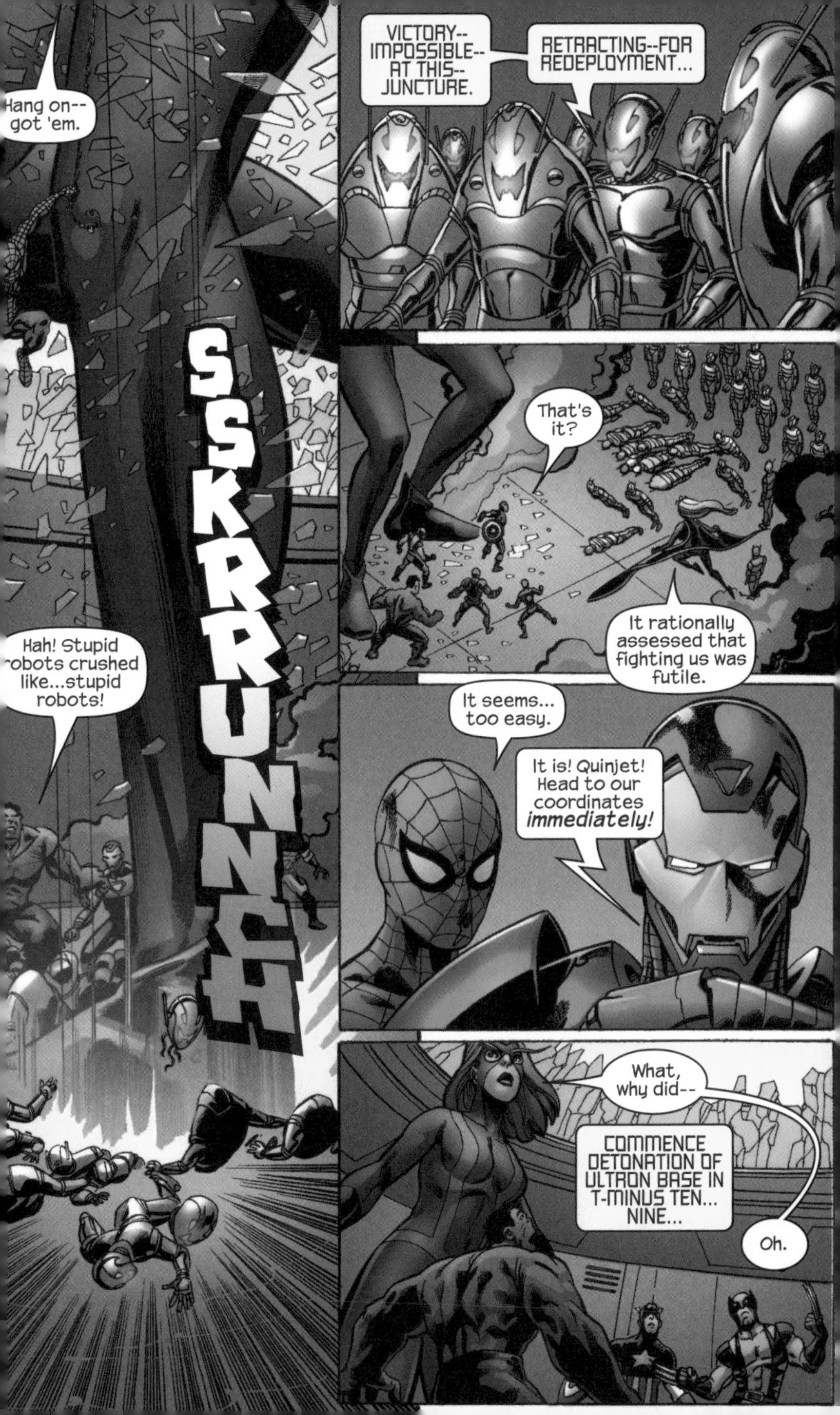
Hang on--
got 'em.
VICTORY--
IMPOSSIBLE--
AT THIS--
JUNCTURE.
RETRACTING--FOR
REDEPLOYMENT...
SSKRRUNNCH
Hah! Stupid
robots crushed
like...stupid
robots!
That's
it?
It rationally
assessed that
fighting us was
futile.
It seems...
too easy.
It is! Quinjet!
Head to our
coordinates
immediately!
What,
why did--
COMMENCE
DETONATION OF
ULTRON BASE IN
T-MINUS TEN...
NINE...
Oh.

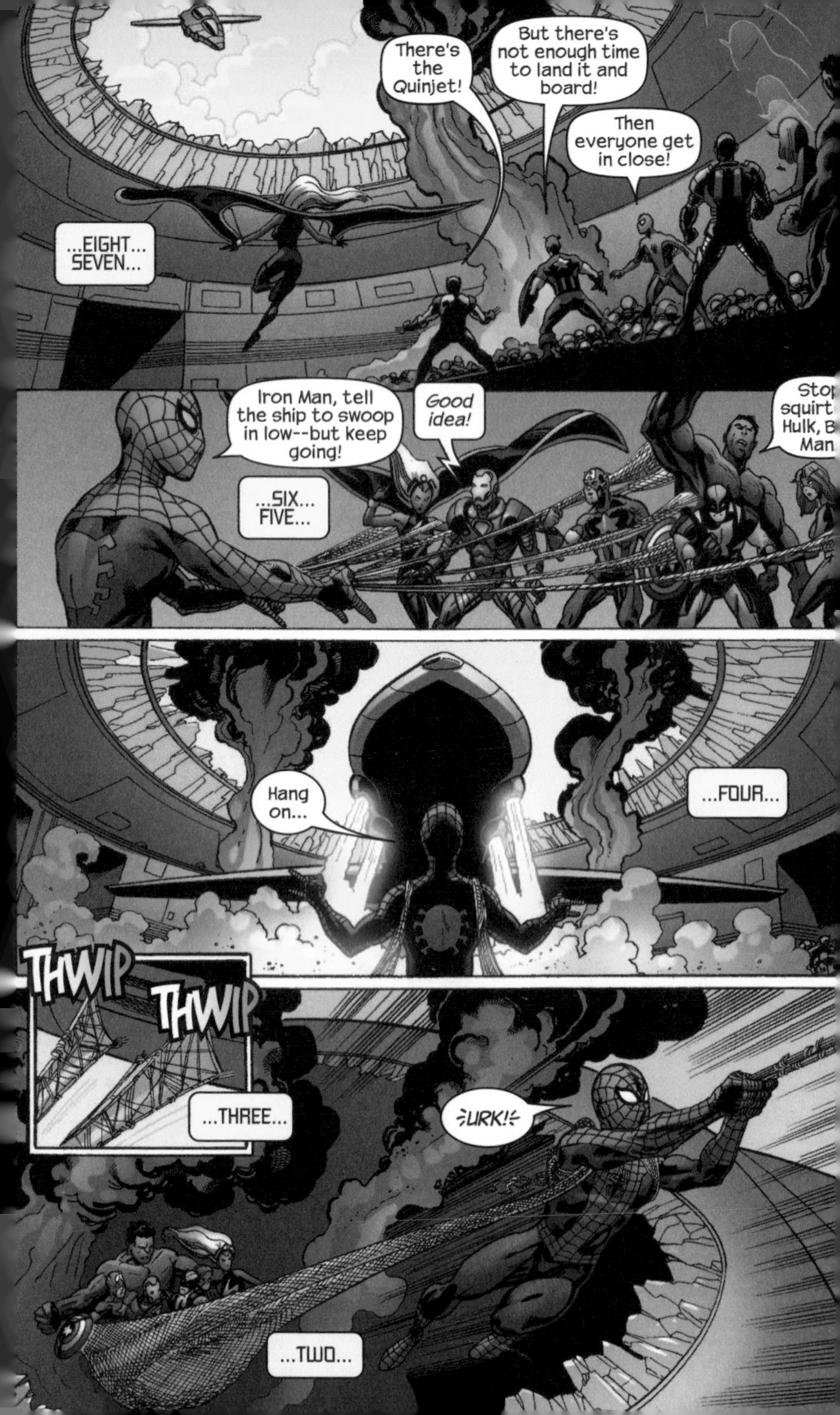
There's the Quinjet!
But there's not enough time to land it and board!
Then everyone get in close!
...EIGHT... SEVEN...
Iron Man, tell the ship to swoop in low--but keep going!
Good idea!
...SIX... FIVE...
Hang on...
...FOUR...
THWIP
THWIP
...THREE...
URK!
...TWO...

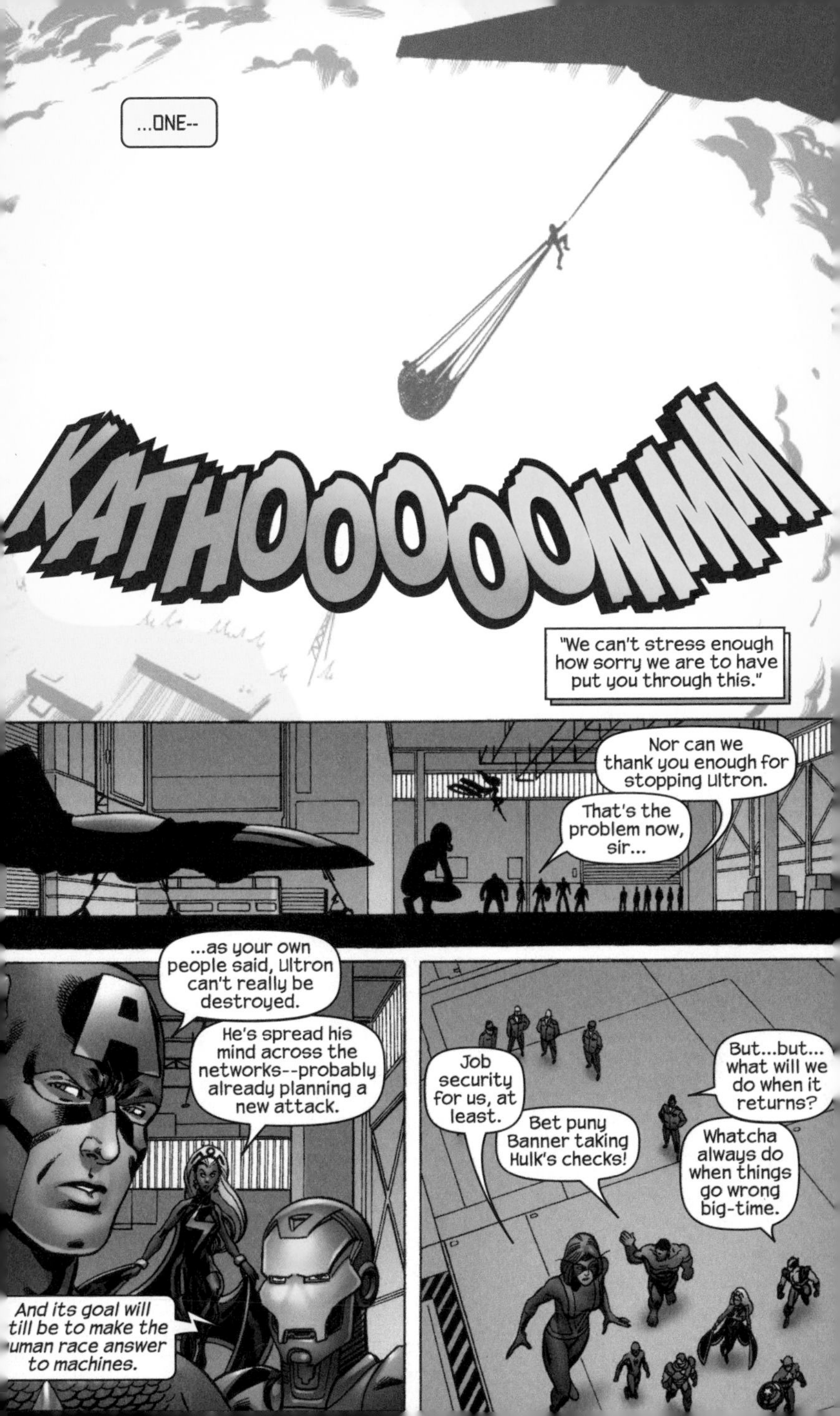
...ONE--
KATHOOOOOMMM
"We can't stress enough how sorry we are to have put you through this."
Nor can we thank you enough for stopping Ultron.
That's the problem now, sir...
...as your own people said, Ultron can't really be destroyed.
He's spread his mind across the networks--probably already planning a new attack.
And its goal will till be to make the uman race answer to machines.
But...but... what will we do when it returns?
Whatcha always do when things go wrong big-time.
Job security for us, at least.
Bet puny Banner taking Hulk's checks!

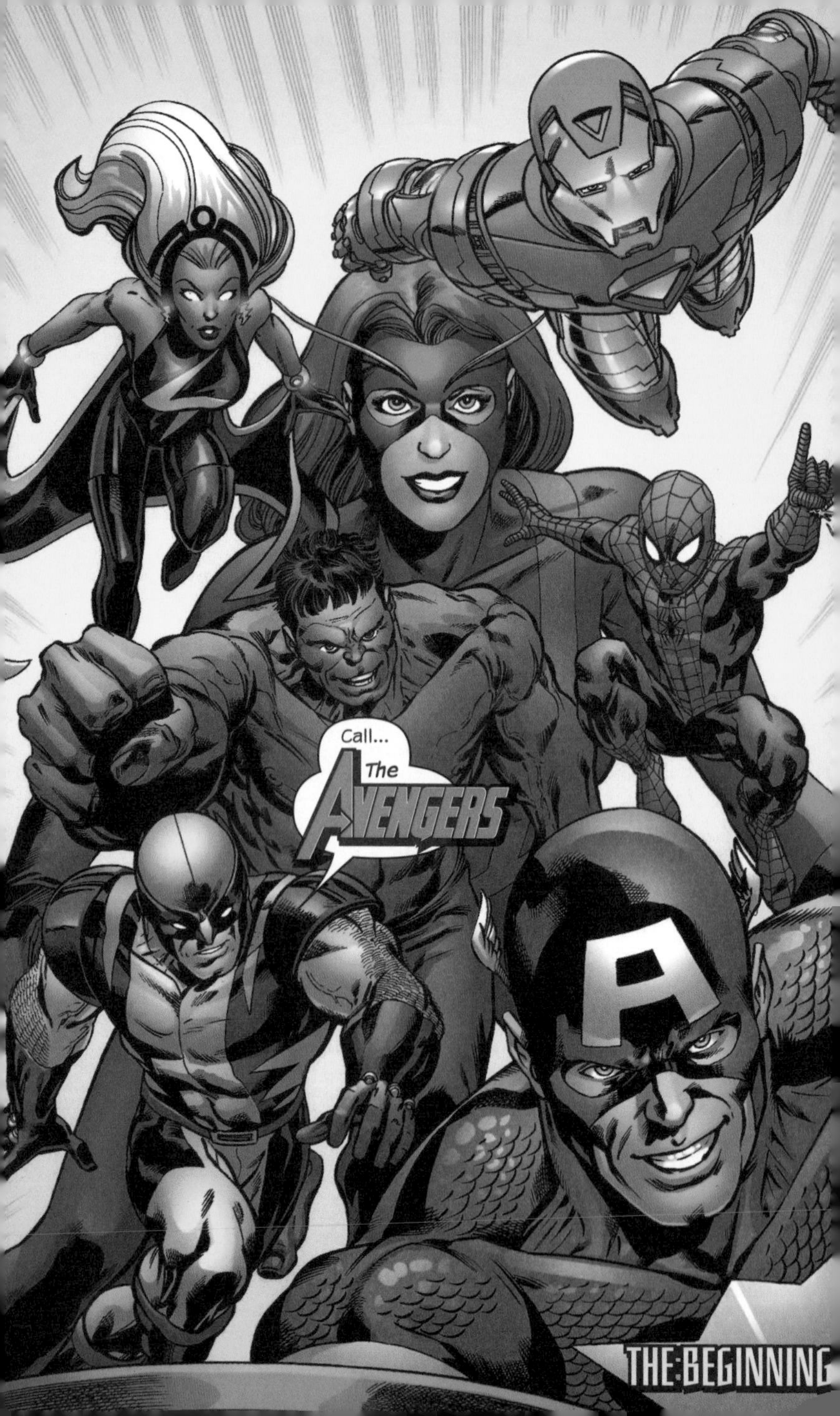
Call... The AVENGERS
THE BEGINNING

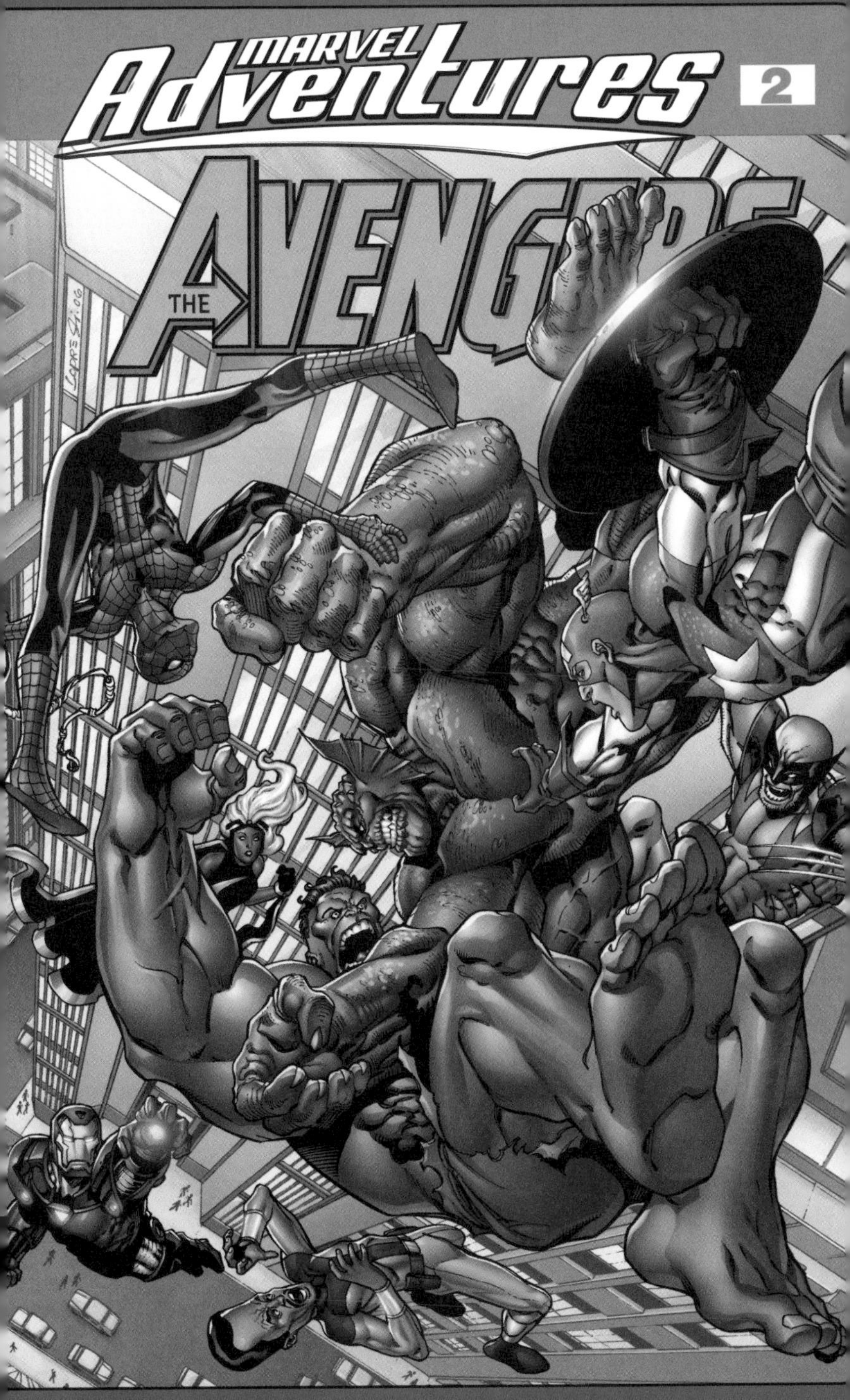
MARVEL
Adventures
2
THE
AVENGERS

SUPER-SOLDIER FROM WORLD WAR II. WEATHER GODDESS. SUPER-STRONG ALTER EGO OF SCIENTIST BRUCE BANNER. SPIDER-POWERED WEB-SLINGER. GIANT-SIZED CRIMEFIGHTER. BRILLIANT ARMORED INVENTOR. FERAL MUTANT BRAWLER. TOGETHER THEY ARE THE WORLD'S MIGHTIEST HEROES, BATTLING THE FOES THAT NO SINGLE SUPER HERO COULD WITHSTAND!

CAPTAIN AMERICA

STORM

HULK

SPIDER-MAN

GIANT-GIRL

IRON MAN

WOLVERINE

THE LEADER HAS A BIG HEAD

JEFF PARKER
CRANIUM

MANUEL GARCIA
HYPOTHALAMUS

SCOTT KOBLISH
CORPUS CALLOSUM

VAL STAPLES
COLORHEAD

DAVE SHARPE
BRAINTRUST

AARON LOPRESTI
and GURU eFX
COVER

KATE LEVIN
PRODUCTION

NATHAN COSBY
GRAY MATTER

MARK PANICCIA
TEMPORAL LOBE

JOE QUESADA
OVERMIND

DAN BUCKLEY
COSMIC CONSCIOUSNESS

Captain America created by Joe Simon and Jack Kirby

All ships and coastal traffic are advised to keep a 30-mile clearance of the Benchley Oceanic Research Station until further notice. The Avengers have been called in to handle the situation...warning: all ships and--

This menace shows every sign of being an accident of science, but I don't know. Something seems...*strange* about it all. Let the record show that I specifically did *not* say "fishy."

--that's right, sir, the sea life in one of the outside aquariums has mutated to become *gigantic.* The Avengers just arrived, that's how bad it is!

Well, they brought Dr. Bruce Banner too, but I don't think he'll be of much help--he's looking kind of green at the moment!

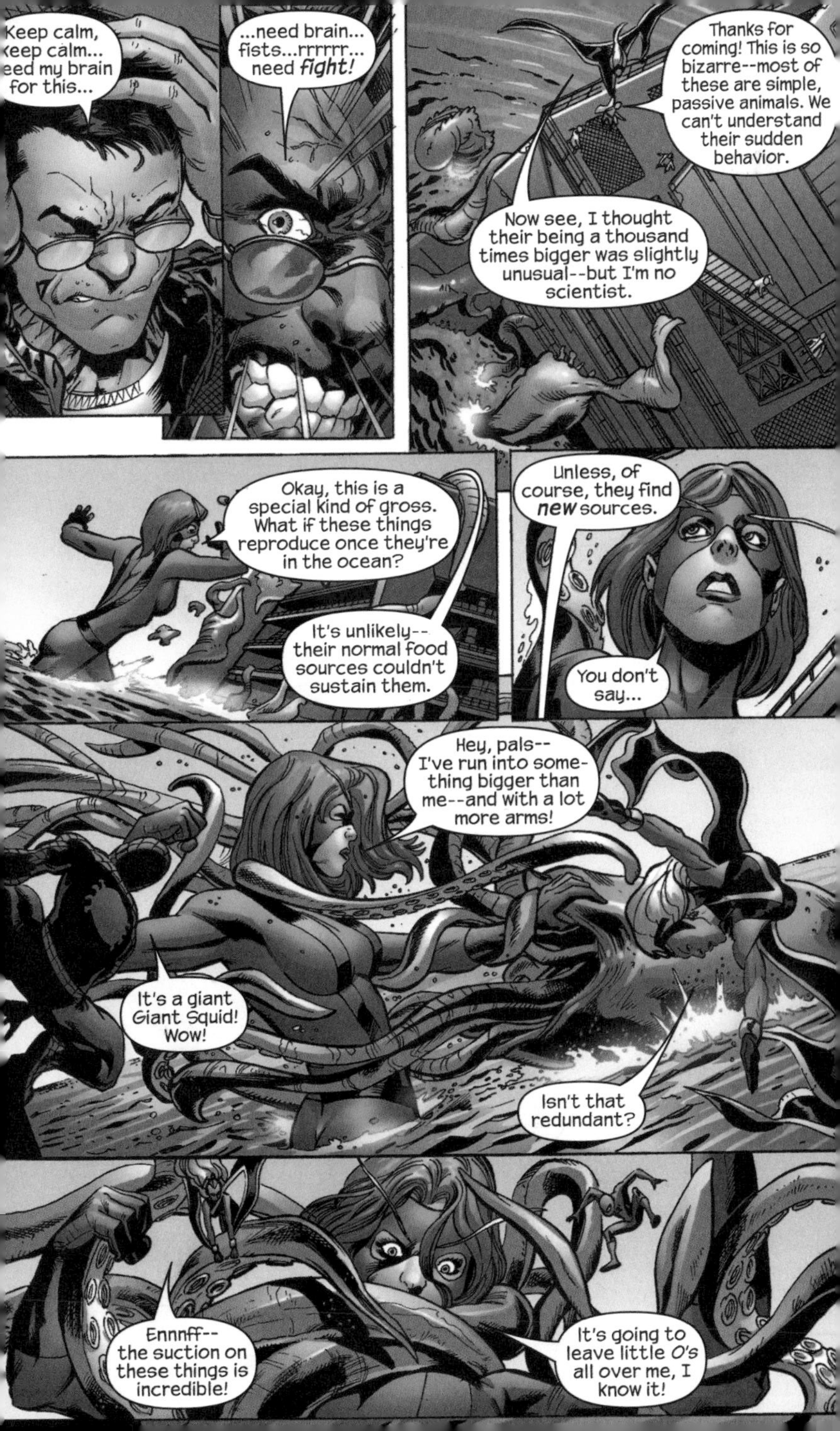
Keep calm,
keep calm...
need my brain
for this...
...need brain...
fists...rrrrrr...
need *fight!*
Thanks for
coming! This is so
bizarre--most of
these are simple,
passive animals. We
can't understand
their sudden
behavior.
Now see, I thought
their being a thousand
times bigger was slightly
unusual--but I'm no
scientist.
Okay, this is a
special kind of gross.
What if these things
reproduce once they're
in the ocean?
It's unlikely--
their normal food
sources couldn't
sustain them.
Unless, of
course, they find
new sources.
You don't
say...
Hey, pals--
I've run into some-
thing bigger than
me--and with a lot
more arms!
It's a giant
Giant Squid!
Wow!
Isn't that
redundant?
Ennnff--
the suction on
these things is
incredible!
It's going to
leave little *O's*
all over me, I
know it!

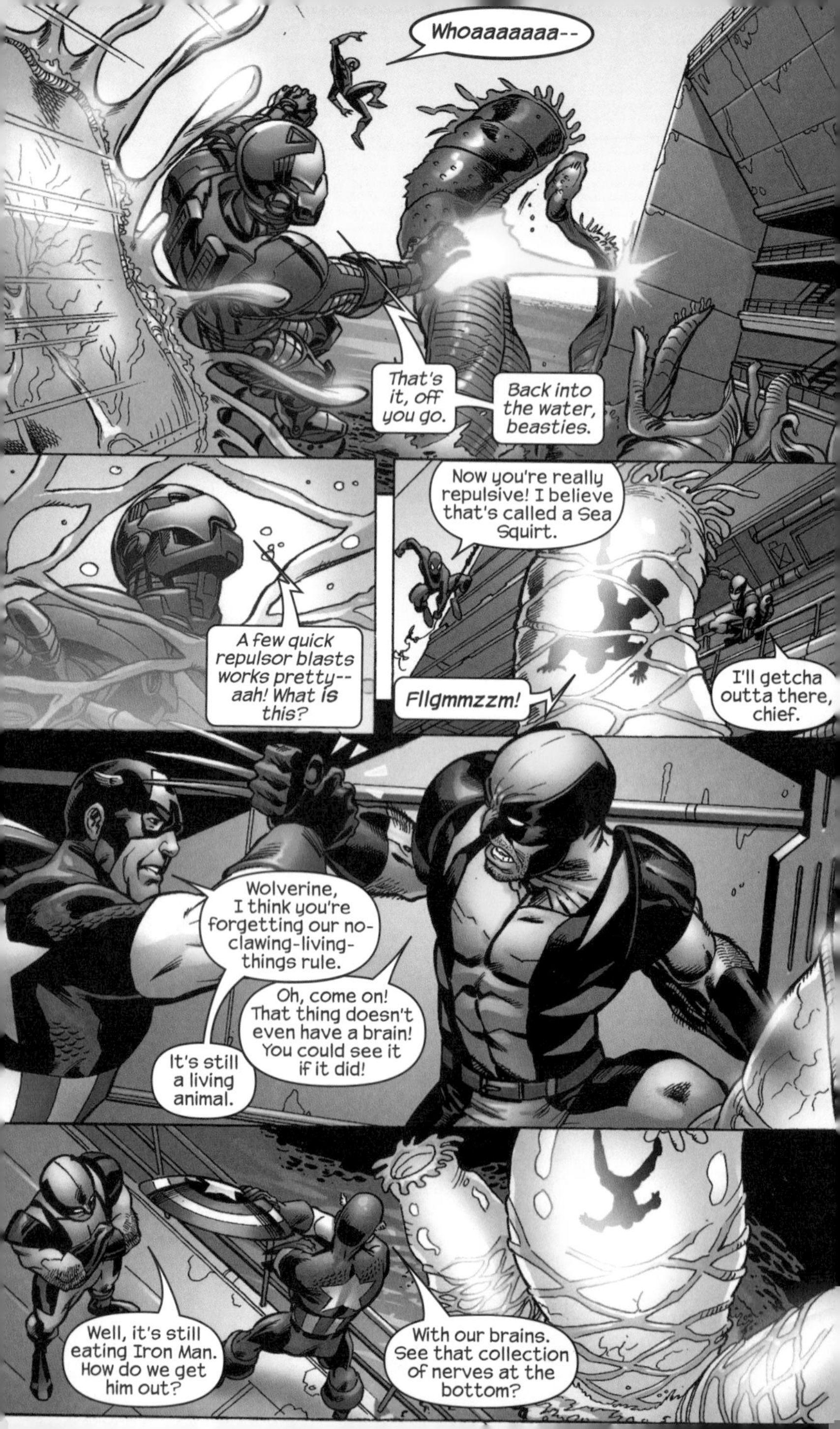

Whoaaaaaaa--
That's it, off you go.
Back into the water, beasties.
A few quick repulsor blasts works pretty-- aah! What is this?
Now you're really repulsive! I believe that's called a Sea Squirt.
Fllgmmzzm!
I'll getcha outta there, chief.
Wolverine, I think you're forgetting our no-clawing-living-things rule.
Oh, come on! That thing doesn't even have a brain! You could see it if it did!
It's still a living animal.
Well, it's still eating Iron Man. How do we get him out?
With our brains. See that collection of nerves at the bottom?

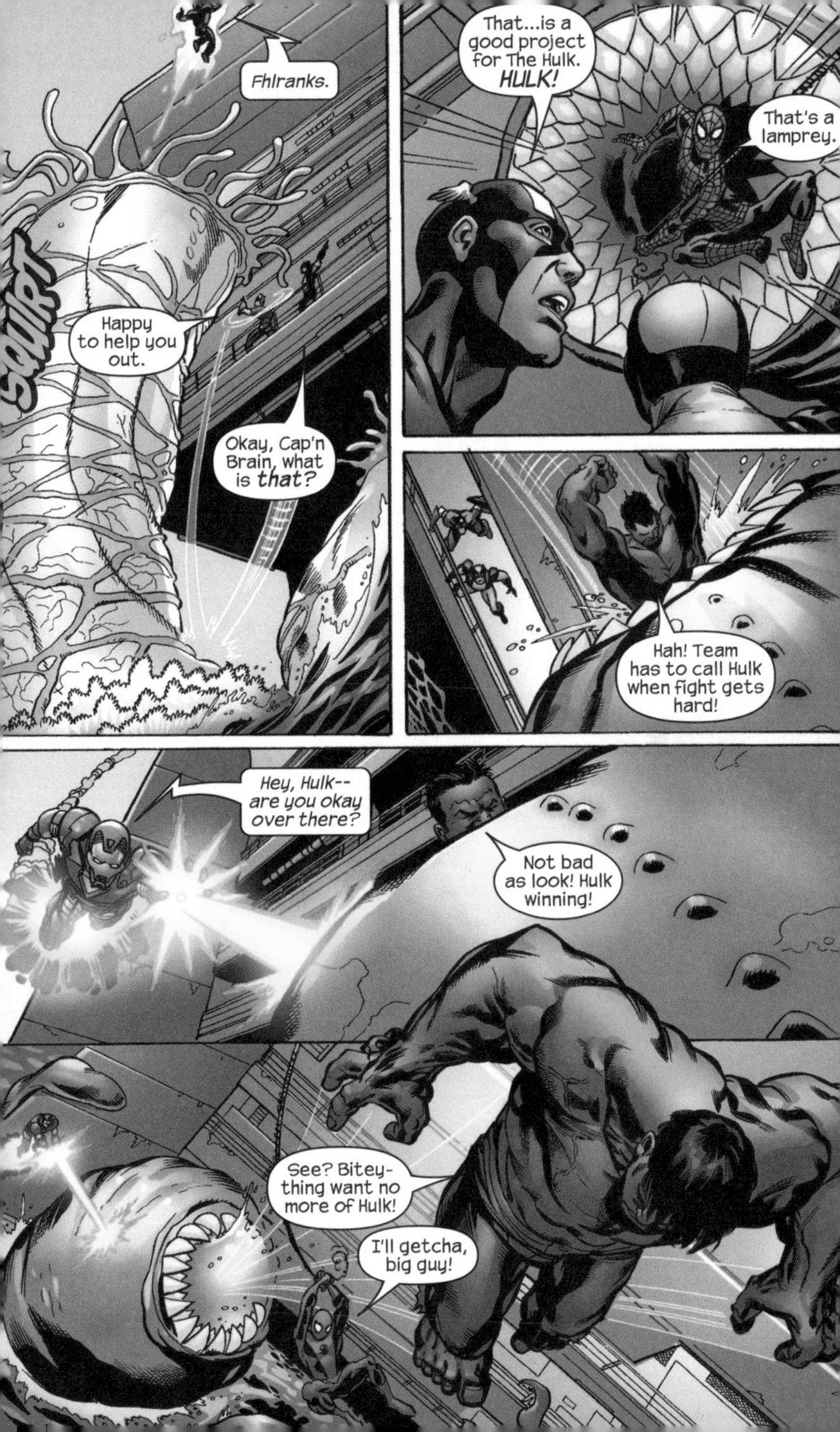
Fhlranks.
SQUIRT
Happy to help you out.
Okay, Cap'n Brain, what is *that*?
That...is a good project for The Hulk. HULK!
That's a lamprey.
Hah! Team has to call Hulk when fight gets hard!
Hey, Hulk-- are you okay over there?
Not bad as look! Hulk winning!
See? Bitey-thing want no more of Hulk!
I'll getcha, big guy!

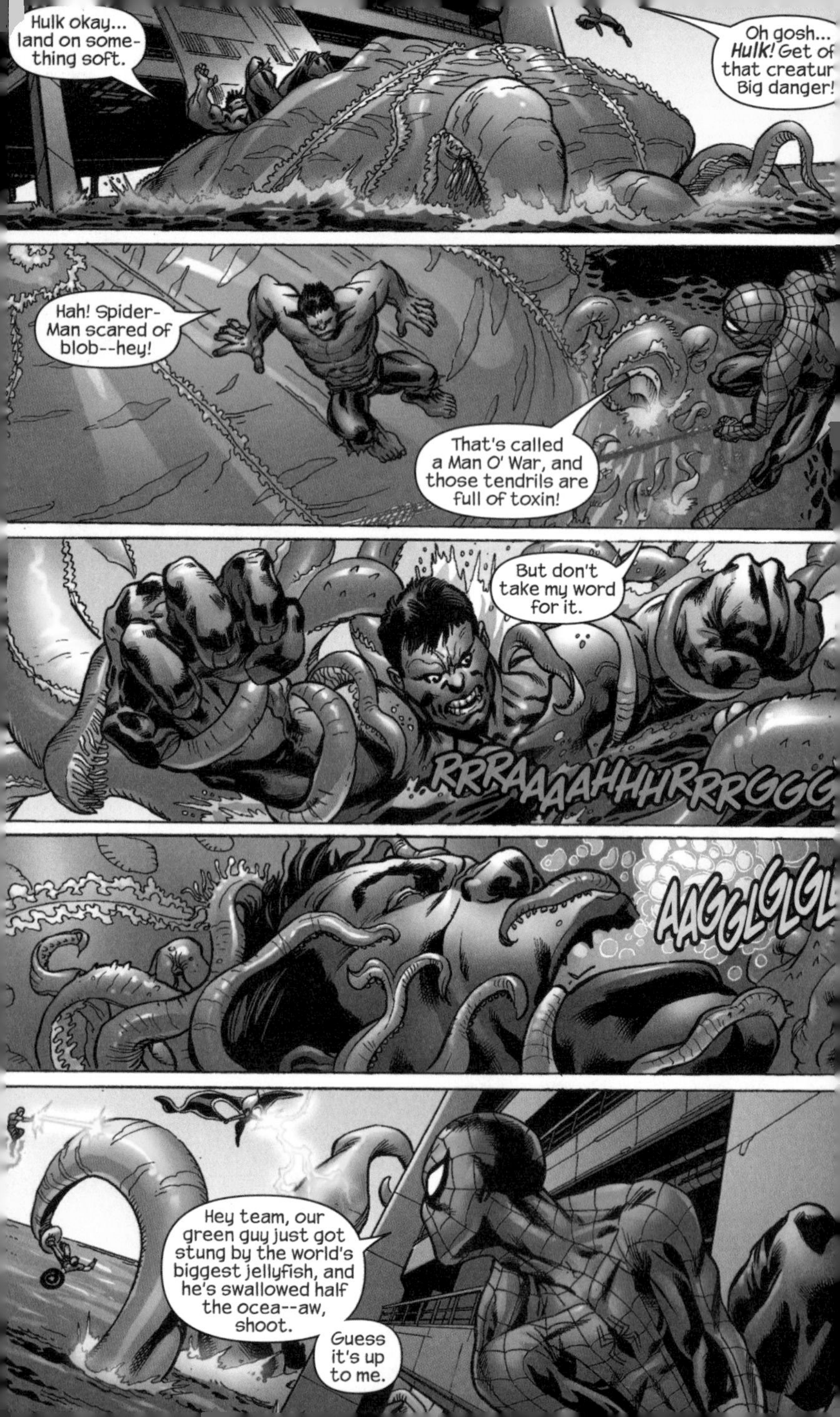
Hulk okay... land on some-thing soft.
Oh gosh... Hulk! Get of that creatur Big danger!
Hah! Spider-Man scared of blob--hey!
That's called a Man O' War, and those tendrils are full of toxin!
But don't take my word for it.
RRRAAAAHHHRRRGGG
AAGGLGLGL
Hey team, our green guy just got stung by the world's biggest jellyfish, and he's swallowed half the ocea--aw, shoot.
Guess it's up to me.

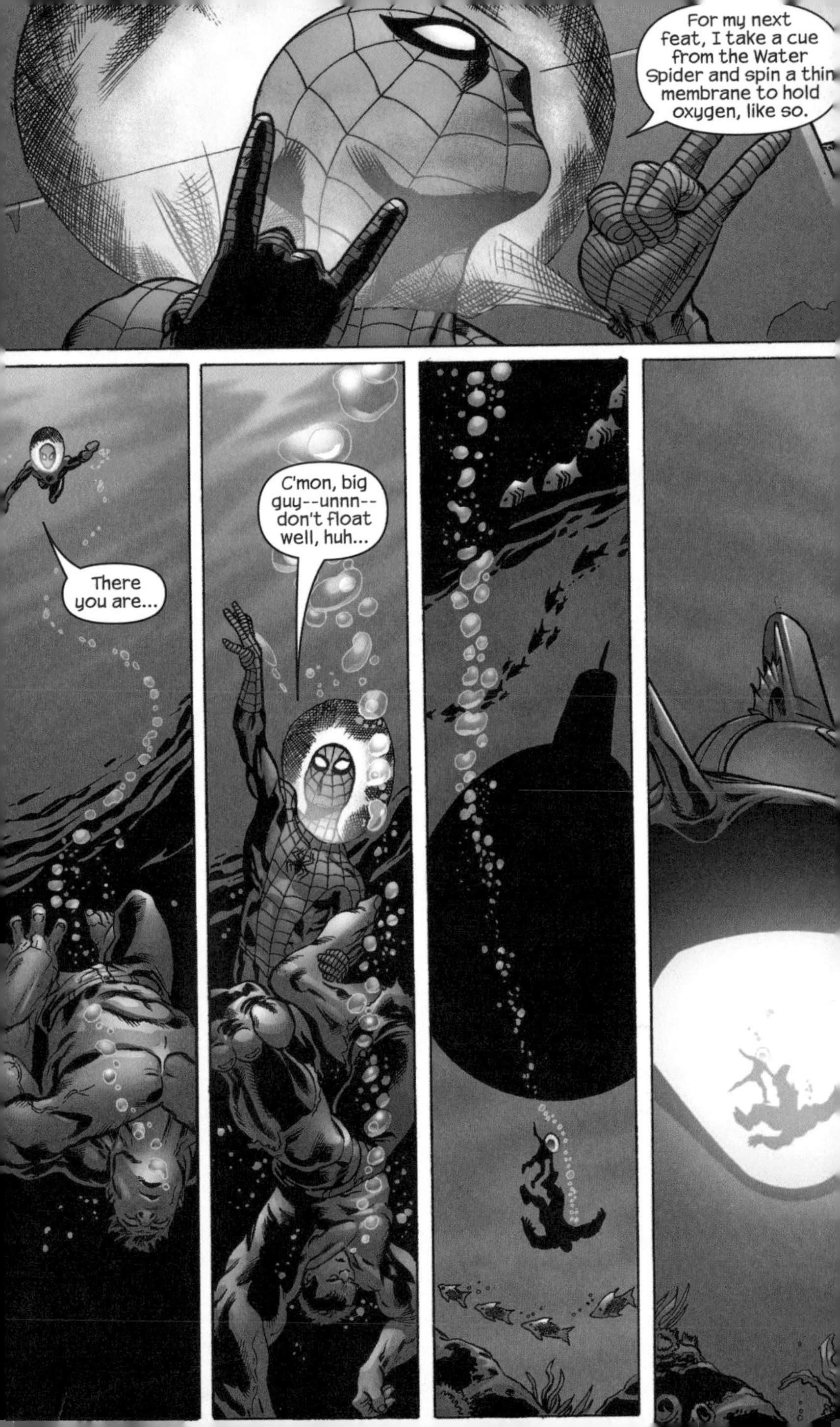
For my next feat, I take a cue from the Water Spider and spin a thin membrane to hold oxygen, like so.
There you are...
C'mon, big guy--unnn--don't float well, huh...

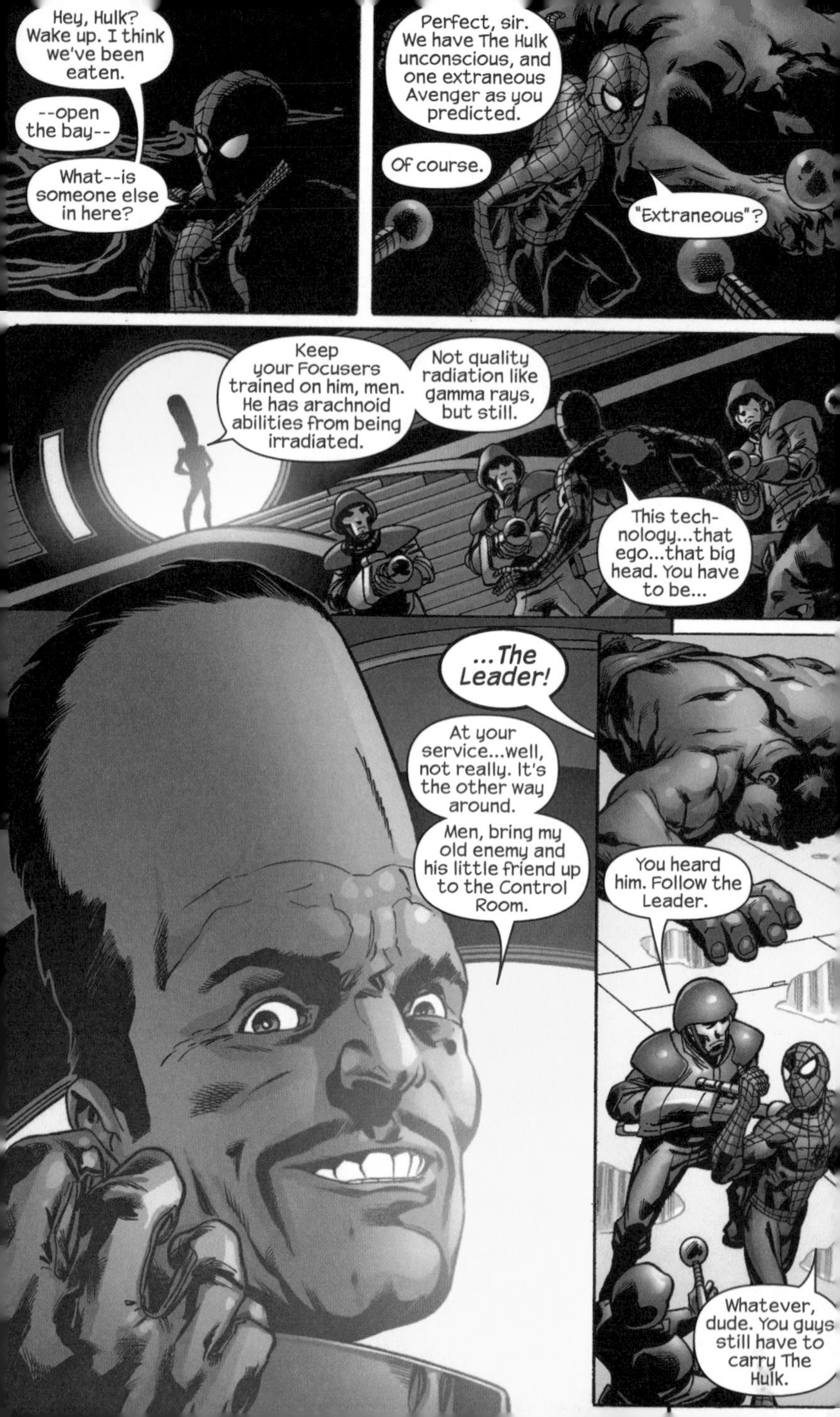
Hey, Hulk? Wake up. I think we've been eaten.
--open the bay--
What--is someone else in here?
Perfect, sir. We have The Hulk unconscious, and one extraneous Avenger as you predicted.
Of course.
"Extraneous"?
Keep your Focusers trained on him, men. He has arachnoid abilities from being irradiated.
Not quality radiation like gamma rays, but still.
This tech-nology...that ego...that big head. You have to be...
...The Leader!
At your service...well, not really. It's the other way around.
Men, bring my old enemy and his little friend up to the Control Room.
You heard him. Follow the Leader.
Whatever, dude. You guys still have to carry The Hulk.

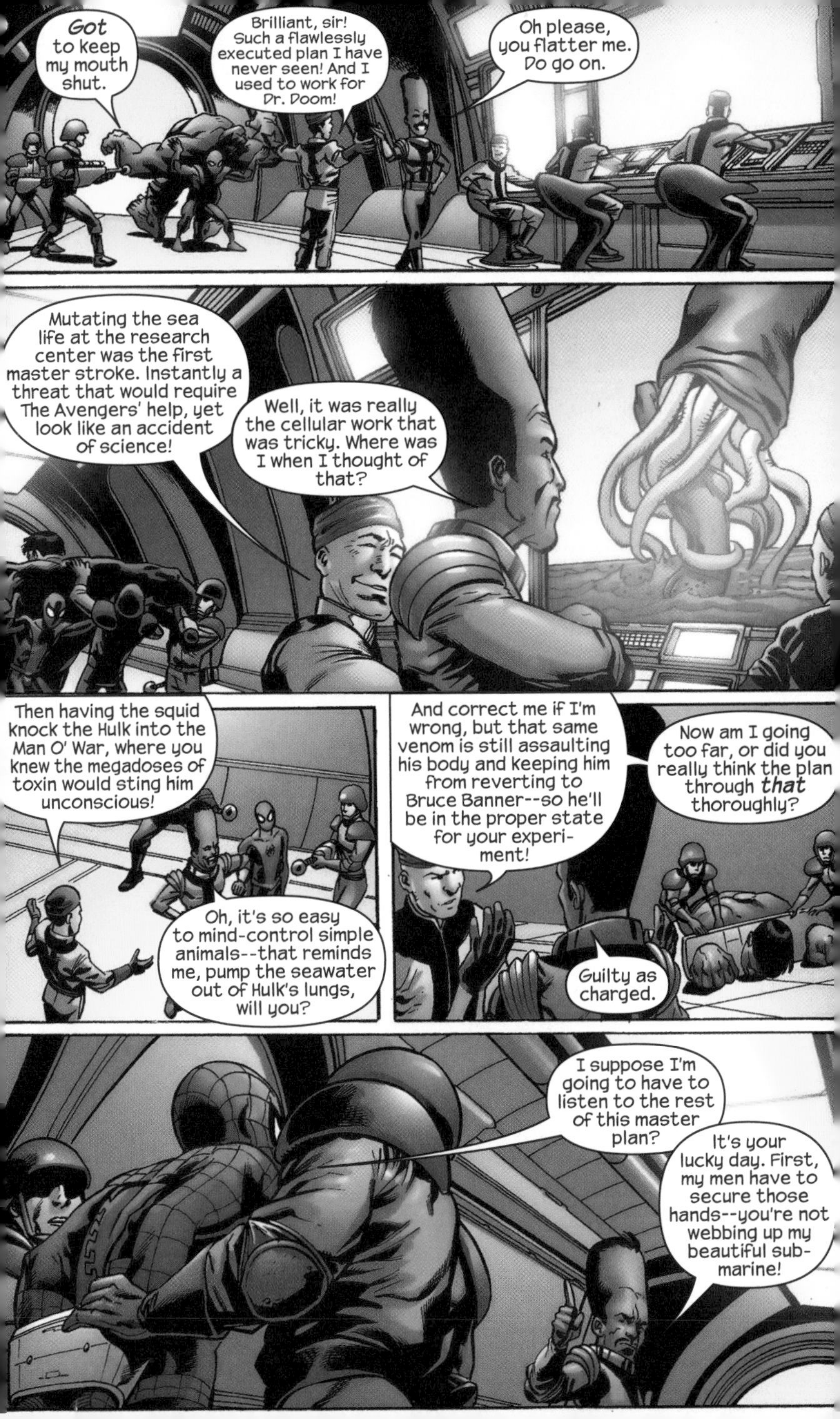

Got to keep my mouth shut.
Brilliant, sir! Such a flawlessly executed plan I have never seen! And I used to work for Dr. Doom!
Oh please, you flatter me. Do go on.
Mutating the sea life at the research center was the first master stroke. Instantly a threat that would require The Avengers' help, yet look like an accident of science!
Well, it was really the cellular work that was tricky. Where was I when I thought of that?
Then having the squid knock the Hulk into the Man O' War, where you knew the megadoses of toxin would sting him unconscious!
Oh, it's so easy to mind-control simple animals--that reminds me, pump the seawater out of Hulk's lungs, will you?
And correct me if I'm wrong, but that same venom is still assaulting his body and keeping him from reverting to Bruce Banner--so he'll be in the proper state for your experi-ment!
Now am I going too far, or did you really think the plan through *that* thoroughly?
Guilty as charged.
I suppose I'm going to have to listen to the rest of this master plan?
It's your lucky day. First, my men have to secure those hands--you're not webbing up my beautiful sub-marine!

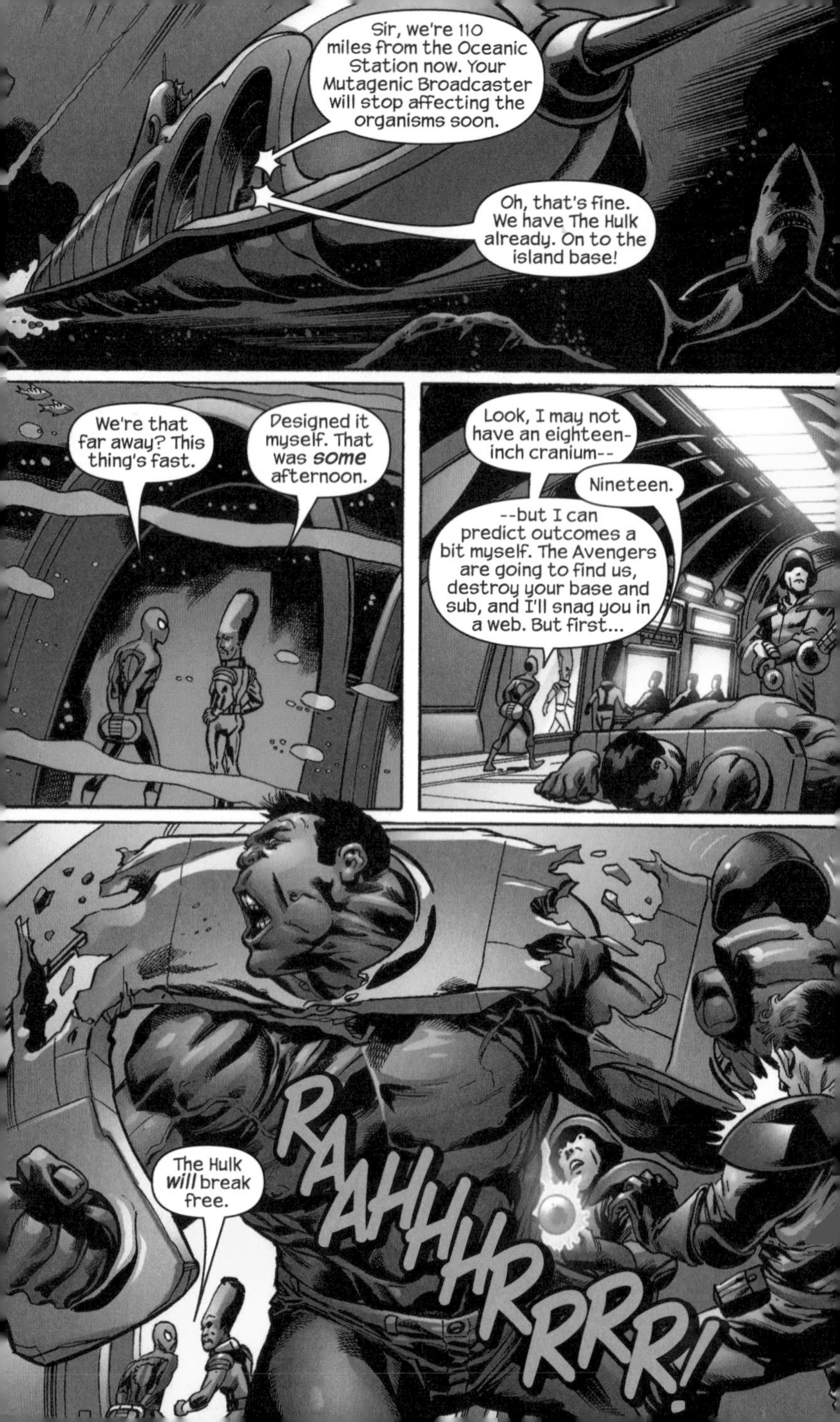
Sir, we're 110 miles from the Oceanic Station now. Your Mutagenic Broadcaster will stop affecting the organisms soon.
Oh, that's fine. We have The Hulk already. On to the island base!
We're that far away? This thing's fast.
Designed it myself. That was *some* afternoon.
Look, I may not have an eighteen-inch cranium--
Nineteen.
--but I can predict outcomes a bit myself. The Avengers are going to find us, destroy your base and sub, and I'll snag you in a web. But first...
The Hulk *will* break free.
RAAHHHRRRR!

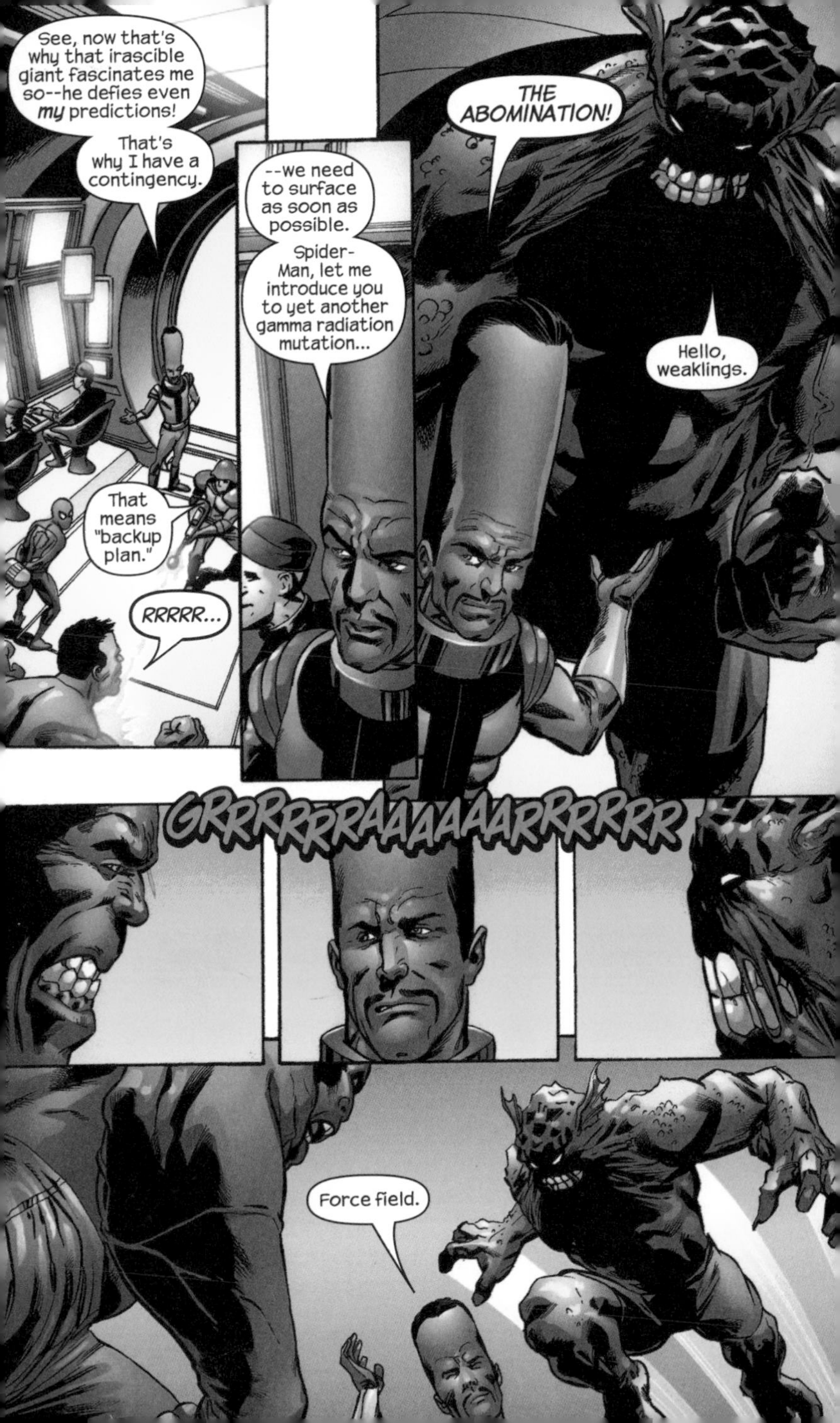
See, now that's why that irascible giant fascinates me so--he defies even *my* predictions!
That's why I have a contingency.
That means "backup plan."
RRRRR...
--we need to surface as soon as possible.
Spider-Man, let me introduce you to yet another gamma radiation mutation...
THE ABOMINATION!
Hello, weaklings.
GRRRRRRAAAAAAARRRRRR
Force field.

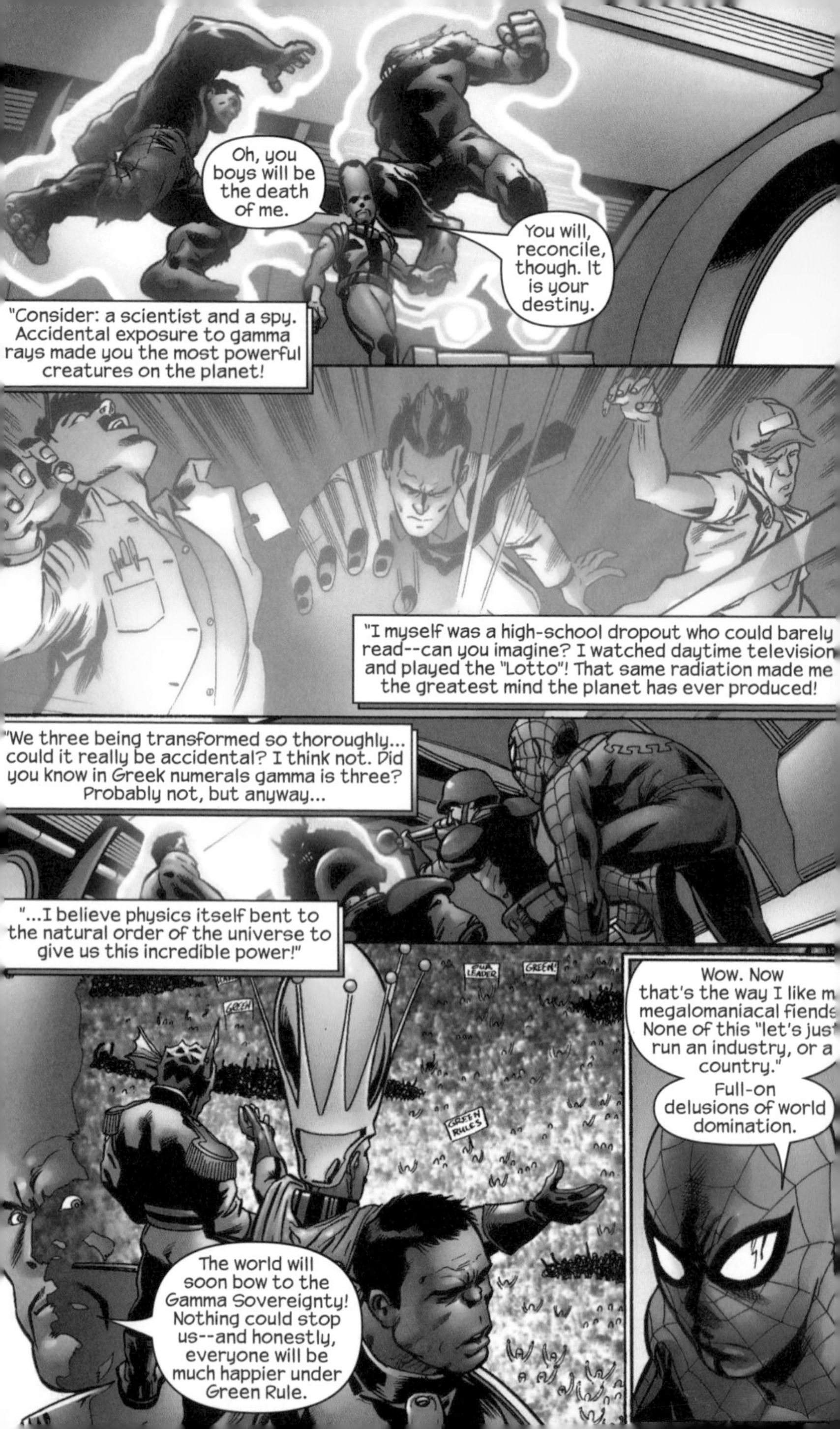
Oh, you boys will be the death of me.
You will, reconcile, though. It is your destiny.
"Consider: a scientist and a spy. Accidental exposure to gamma rays made you the most powerful creatures on the planet!
"I myself was a high-school dropout who could barely read--can you imagine? I watched daytime television and played the "Lotto"! That same radiation made me the greatest mind the planet has ever produced!
"We three being transformed so thoroughly... could it really be accidental? I think not. Did you know in Greek numerals gamma is three? Probably not, but anyway...
"...I believe physics itself bent to the natural order of the universe to give us this incredible power!"
GREEN!
GREEN RULES
The world will soon bow to the Gamma Sovereignty! Nothing could stop us--and honestly, everyone will be much happier under Green Rule.
Wow. Now that's the way I like m megalomaniacal fiends None of this "let's just run an industry, or a country."
Full-on delusions of world domination.

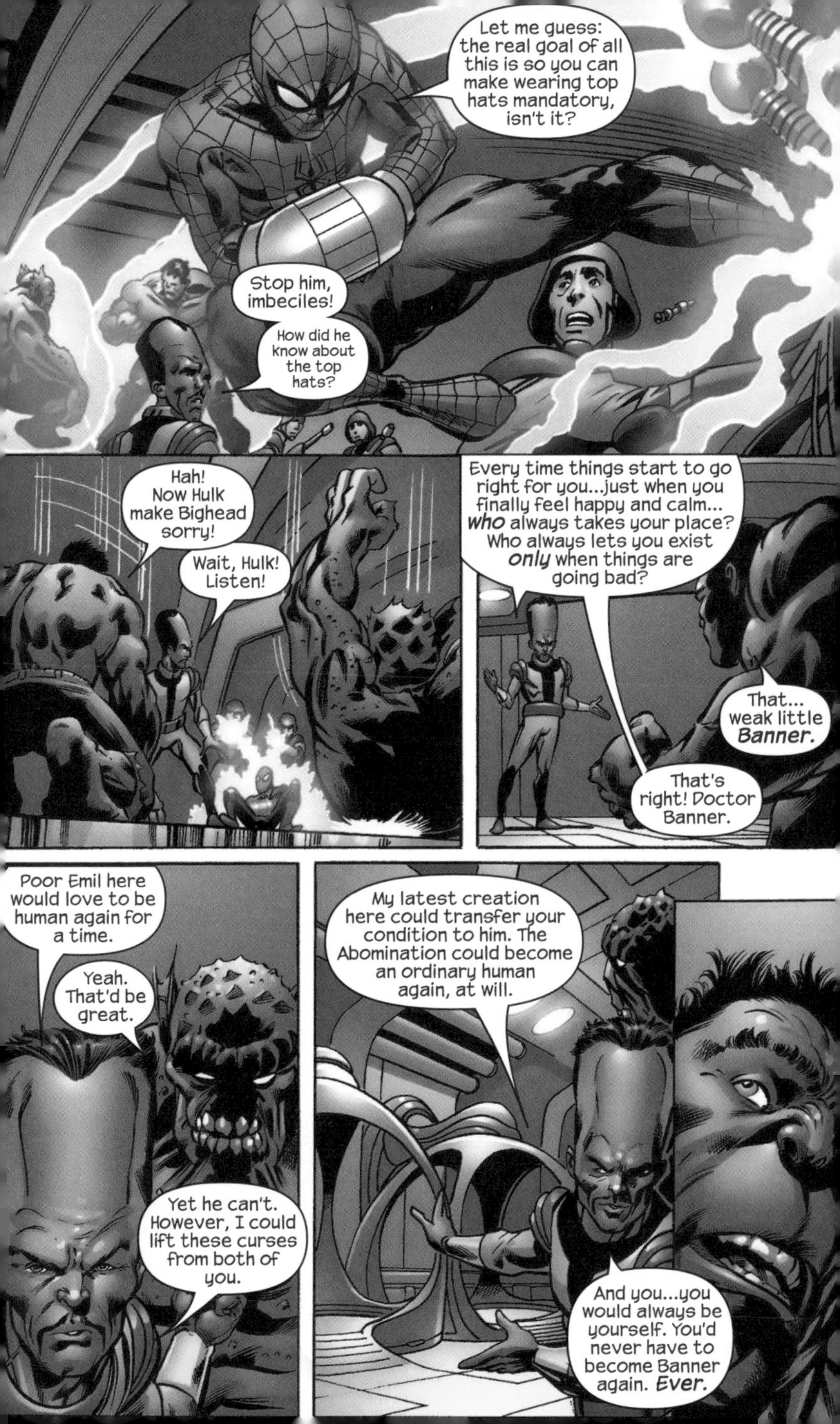
Let me guess: the real goal of all this is so you can make wearing top hats mandatory, isn't it?
Stop him, imbeciles!
How did he know about the top hats?
Hah! Now Hulk make Bighead sorry!
Wait, Hulk! Listen!
Every time things start to go right for you...just when you finally feel happy and calm... *who* always takes your place? Who always lets you exist *only* when things are going bad?
That... weak little *Banner.*
That's right! Doctor Banner.
Poor Emil here would love to be human again for a time.
Yeah. That'd be great.
Yet he can't. However, I could lift these curses from both of you.
My latest creation here could transfer your condition to him. The Abomination could become an ordinary human again, at will.
And you...you would always be yourself. You'd never have to become Banner again. *Ever.*

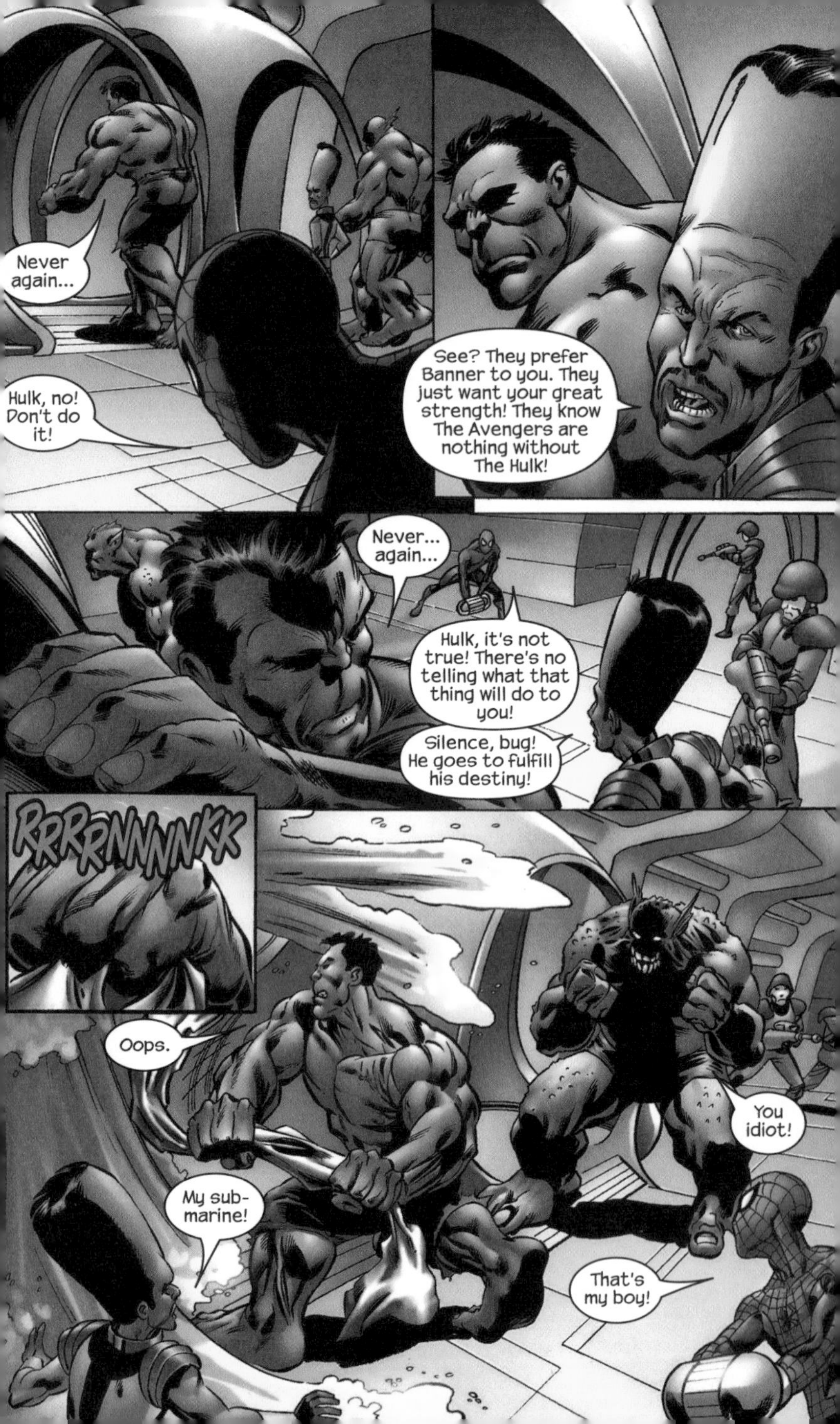
Never again...
Hulk, no! Don't do it!
See? They prefer Banner to you. They just want your great strength! They know The Avengers are nothing without The Hulk!
Never... again...
Hulk, it's not true! There's no telling what that thing will do to you!
Silence, bug! He goes to fulfill his destiny!
RRRRNNNNKK
Oops.
You idiot!
My sub-marine!
That's my boy!

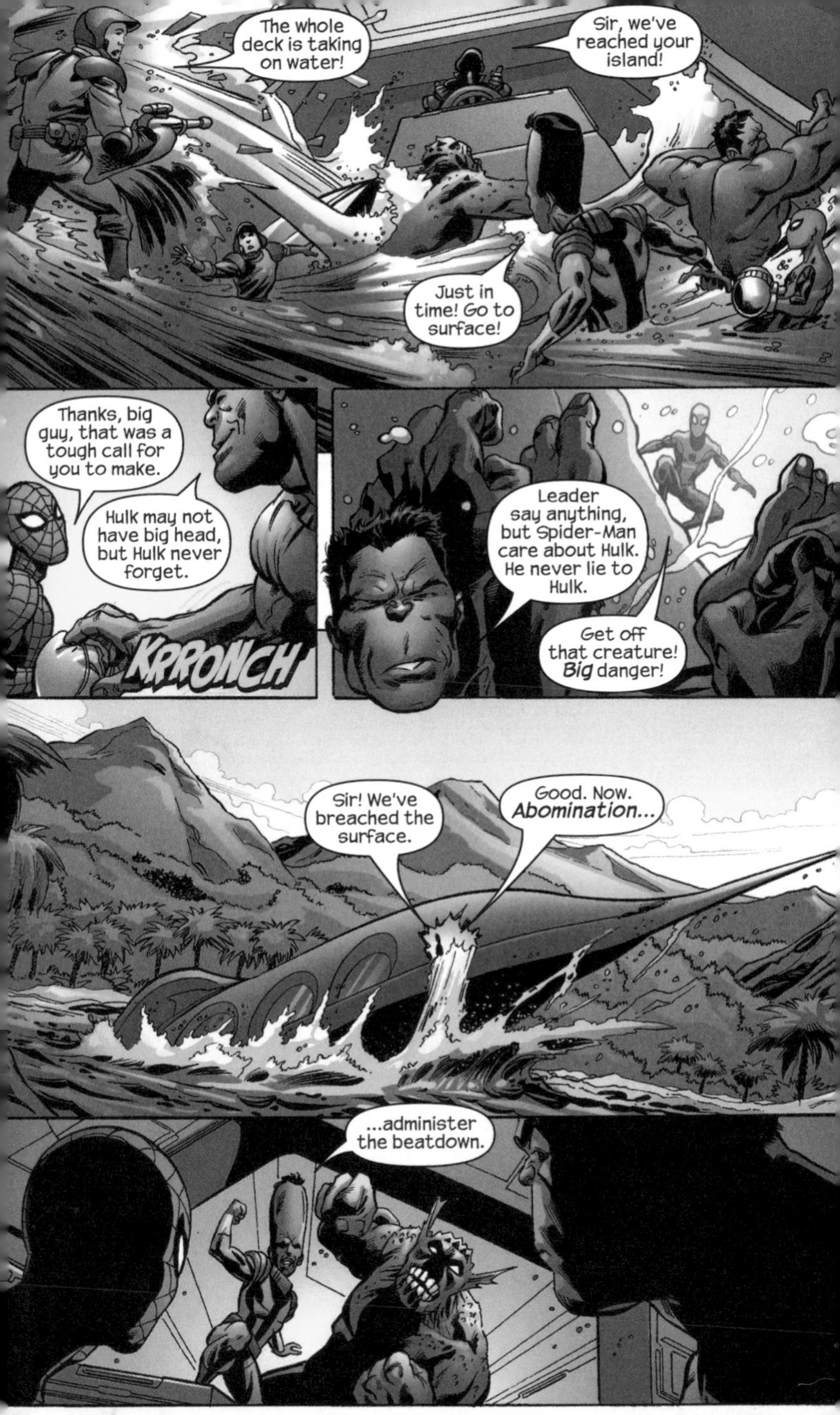
The whole deck is taking on water!
Sir, we've reached your island!
Just in time! Go to surface!
Thanks, big guy, that was a tough call for you to make.
Hulk may not have big head, but Hulk never forget.
KRRONCH
Leader say anything, but Spider-Man care about Hulk. He never lie to Hulk.
Get off that creature! *Big* danger!
Sir! We've breached the surface.
Good. Now. *Abomination...*
...administer the beatdown.

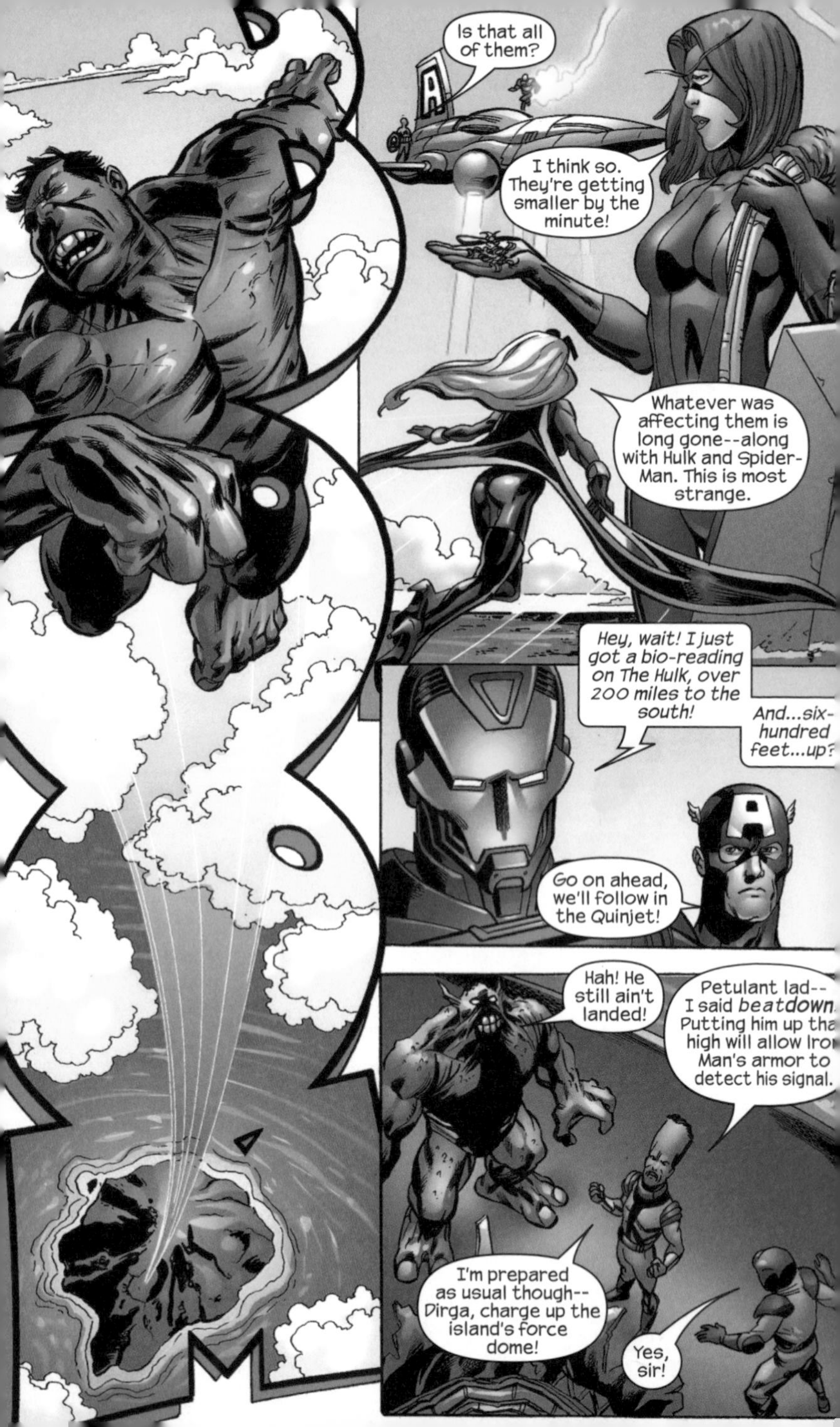
Is that all of them?
I think so. They're getting smaller by the minute!
Whatever was affecting them is long gone--along with Hulk and Spider-Man. This is most strange.
Hey, wait! I just got a bio-reading on The Hulk, over 200 miles to the south!
And...six-hundred feet...up?
Go on ahead, we'll follow in the Quinjet!
Hah! He still ain't landed!
Petulant lad-- I said *beatdown*. Putting him up that high will allow Iron Man's armor to detect his signal.
I'm prepared as usual though-- Dirga, charge up the island's force dome!
Yes, sir!

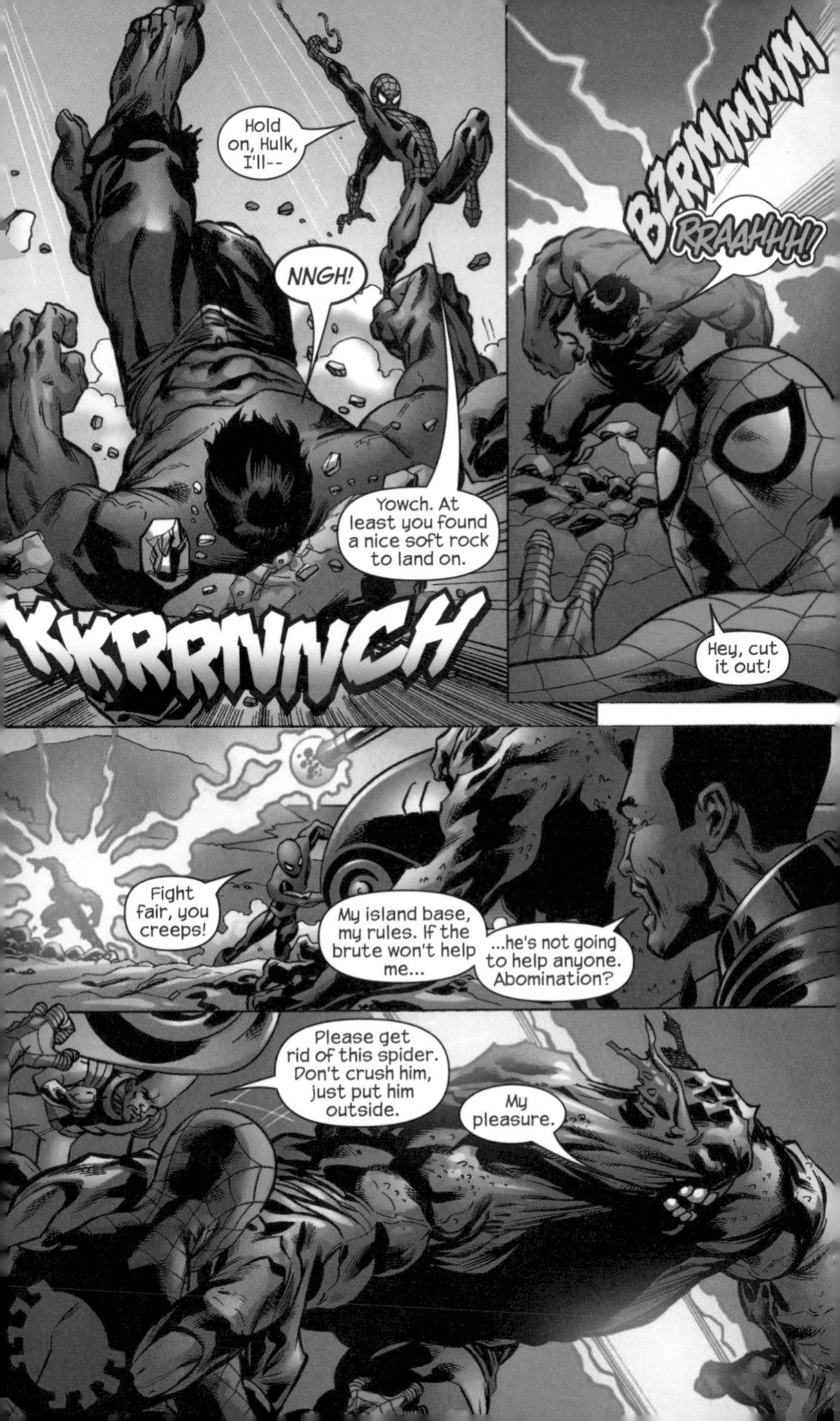
Hold on, Hulk, I'll--
NNGH!
Yowch. At least you found a nice soft rock to land on.
KKRRNNCH
BZRMMMM
RRAAHHH!
Hey, cut it out!
Fight fair, you creeps!
My island base, my rules. If the brute won't help me...
...he's not going to help anyone. Abomination?
Please get rid of this spider. Don't crush him, just put him outside.
My pleasure.

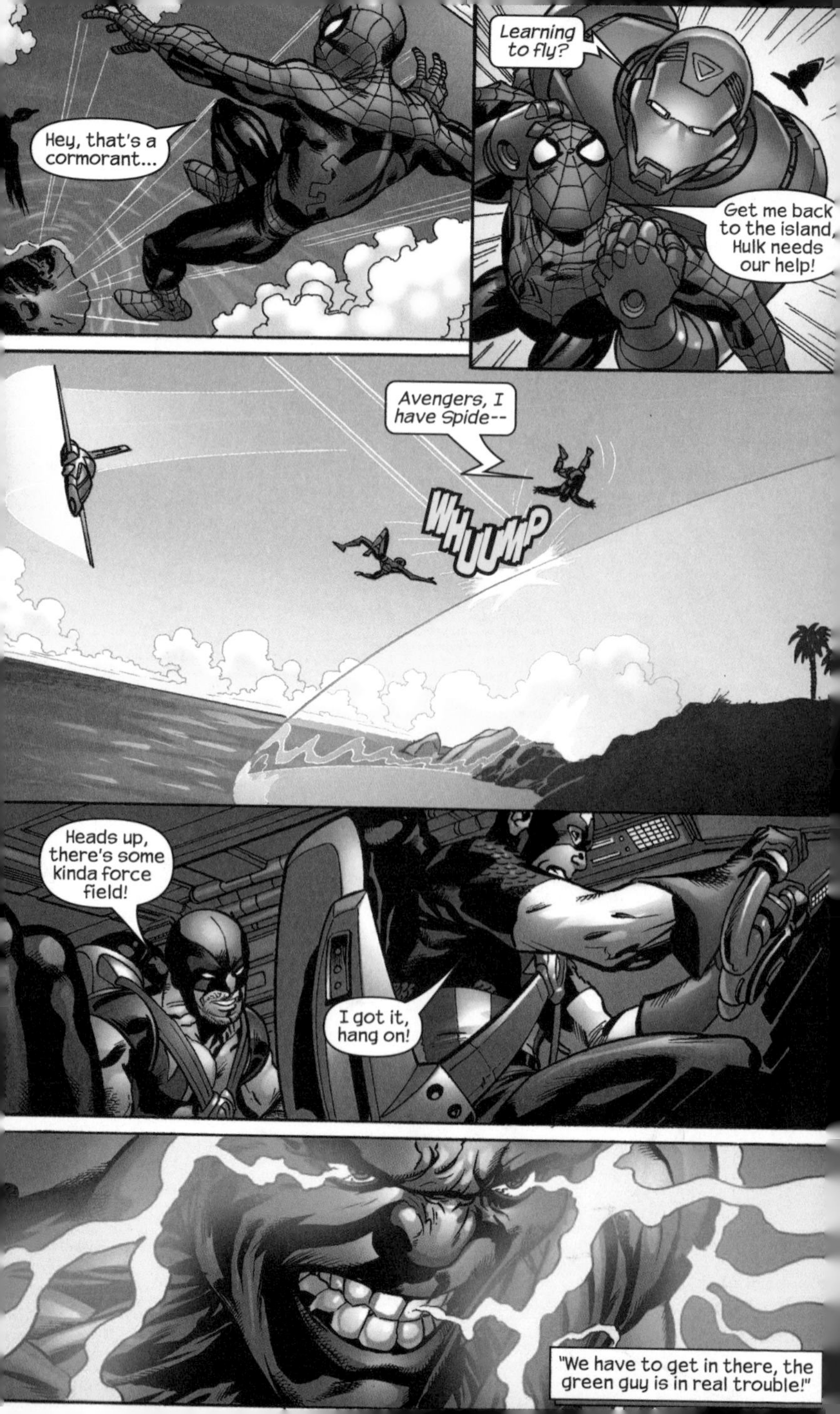
Hey, that's a cormorant...
Learning to fly?
Get me back to the island, Hulk needs our help!
Avengers, I have Spide--
WHUUMP
Heads up, there's some kinda force field!
I got it, hang on!
"We have to get in there, the green guy is in real trouble!"

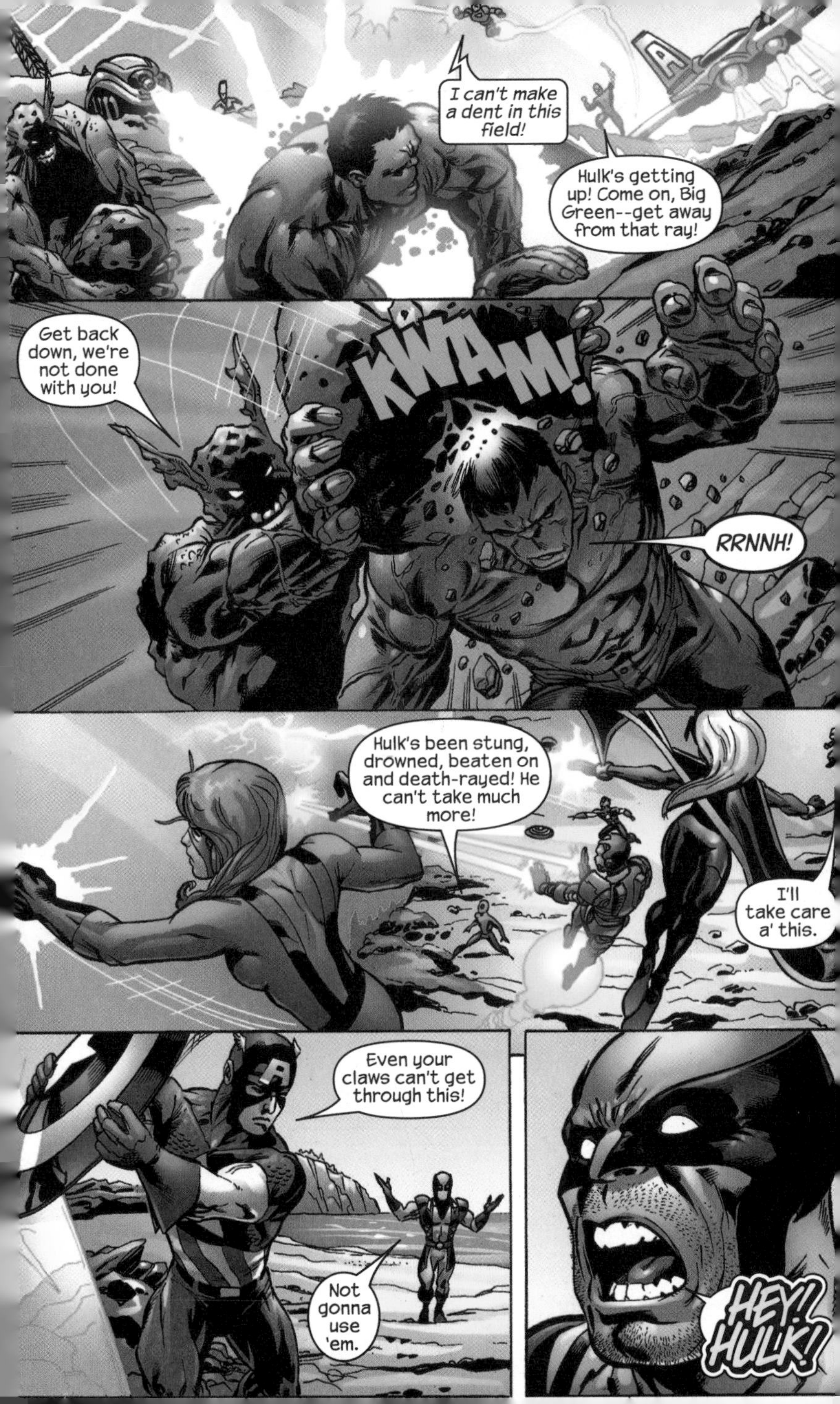
I can't make a dent in this field!
Hulk's getting up! Come on, Big Green--get away from that ray!
Get back down, we're not done with you!
KWAM!
RRNNH!
Hulk's been stung, drowned, beaten on and death-rayed! He can't take much more!
I'll take care a' this.
Even your claws can't get through this!
Not gonna use 'em.
HEY! HULK!

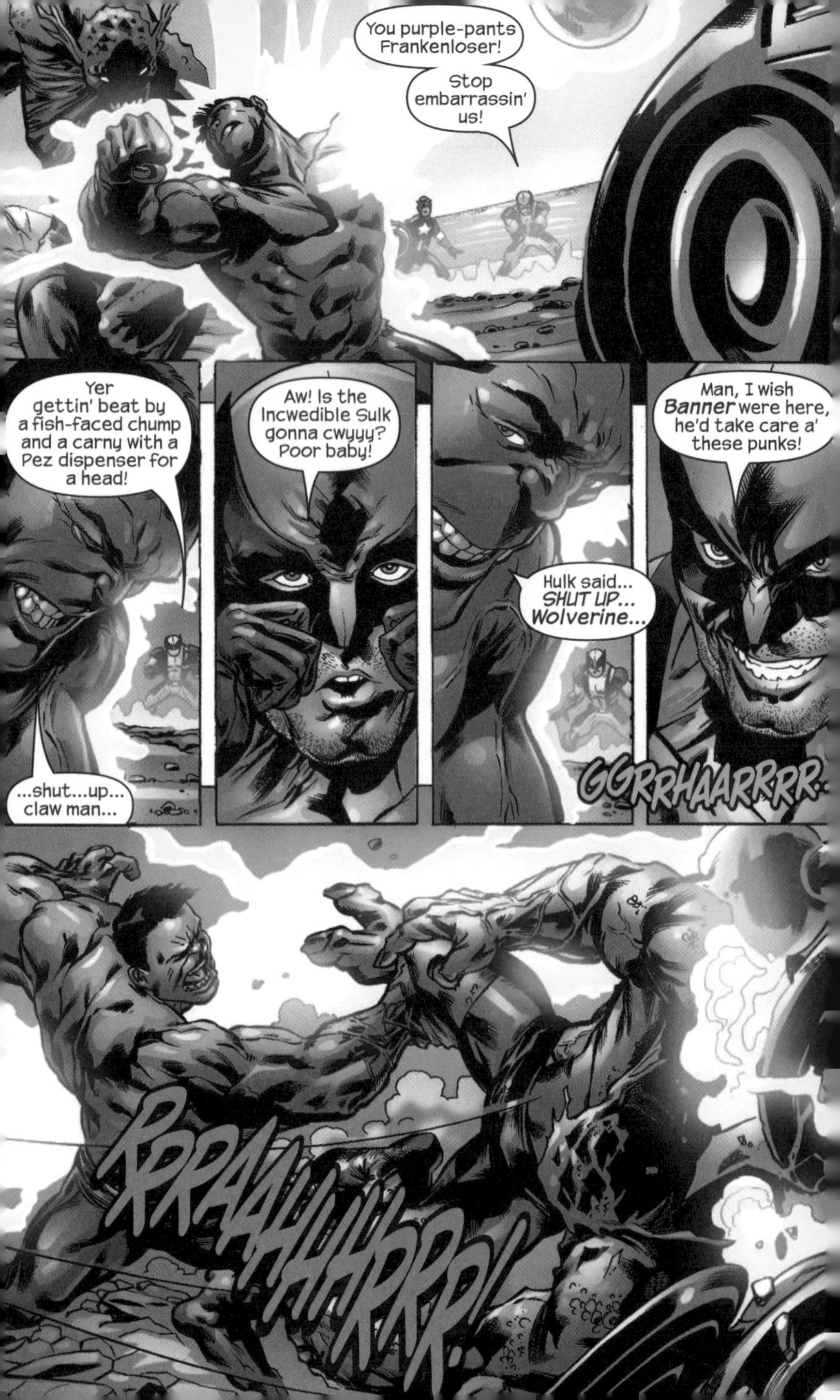
You purple-pants Frankenloser!
Stop embarrassin' us!
Yer gettin' beat by a fish-faced chump and a carny with a Pez dispenser for a head!
...shut...up... claw man...
Aw! Is the Incwedible Sulk gonna cwyyy? Poor baby!
Hulk said... SHUT UP... Wolverine...
Man, I wish Banner were here, he'd take care a' these punks!
GGRRHAARRRR
RRRAAHHHRRR!

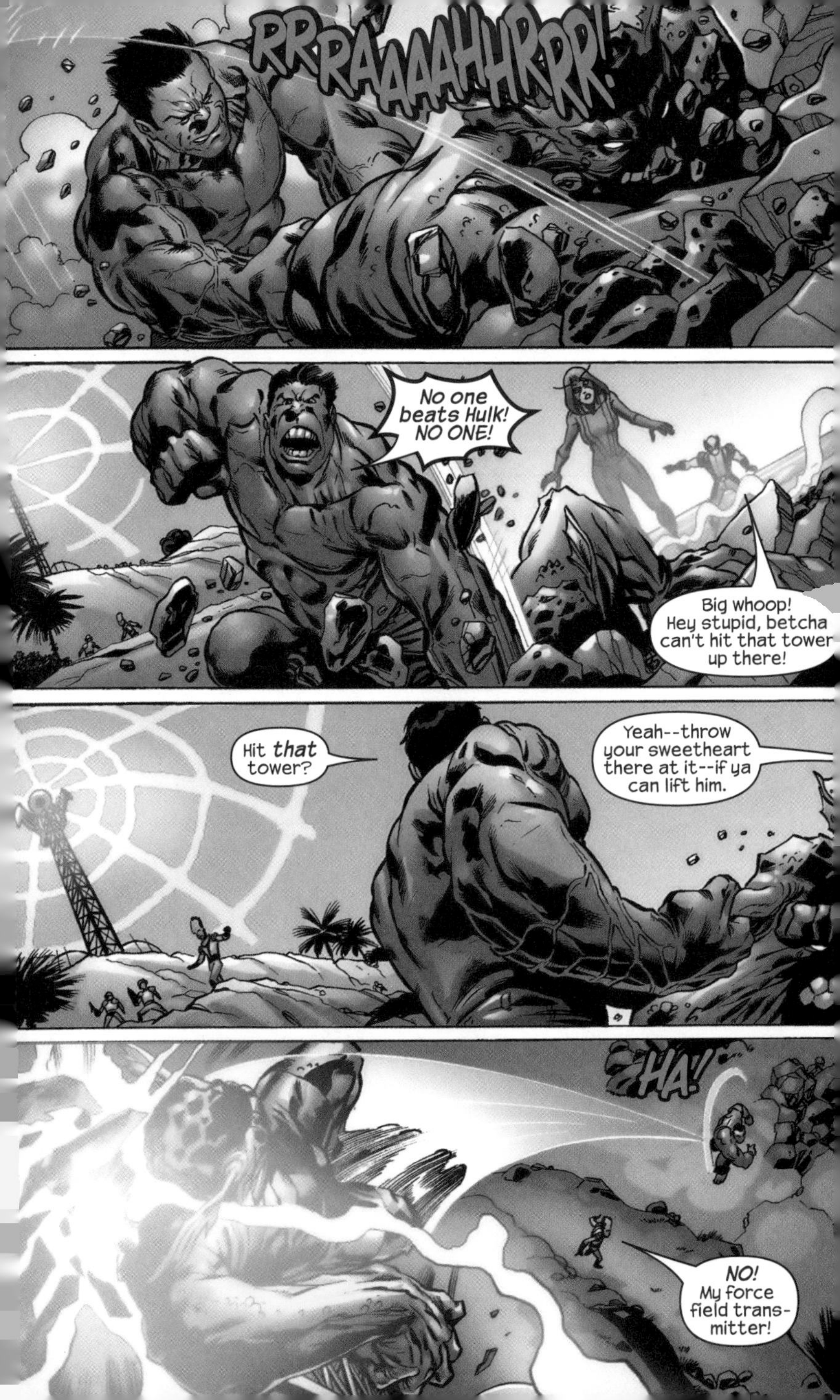

RRRAAAAHHRRR!
No one beats Hulk! NO ONE!
Big whoop! Hey stupid, betcha can't hit that tower up there!
Hit *that* tower?
Yeah--throw your sweetheart there at it--if ya can lift him.
HA!
NO! My force field trans-mitter!

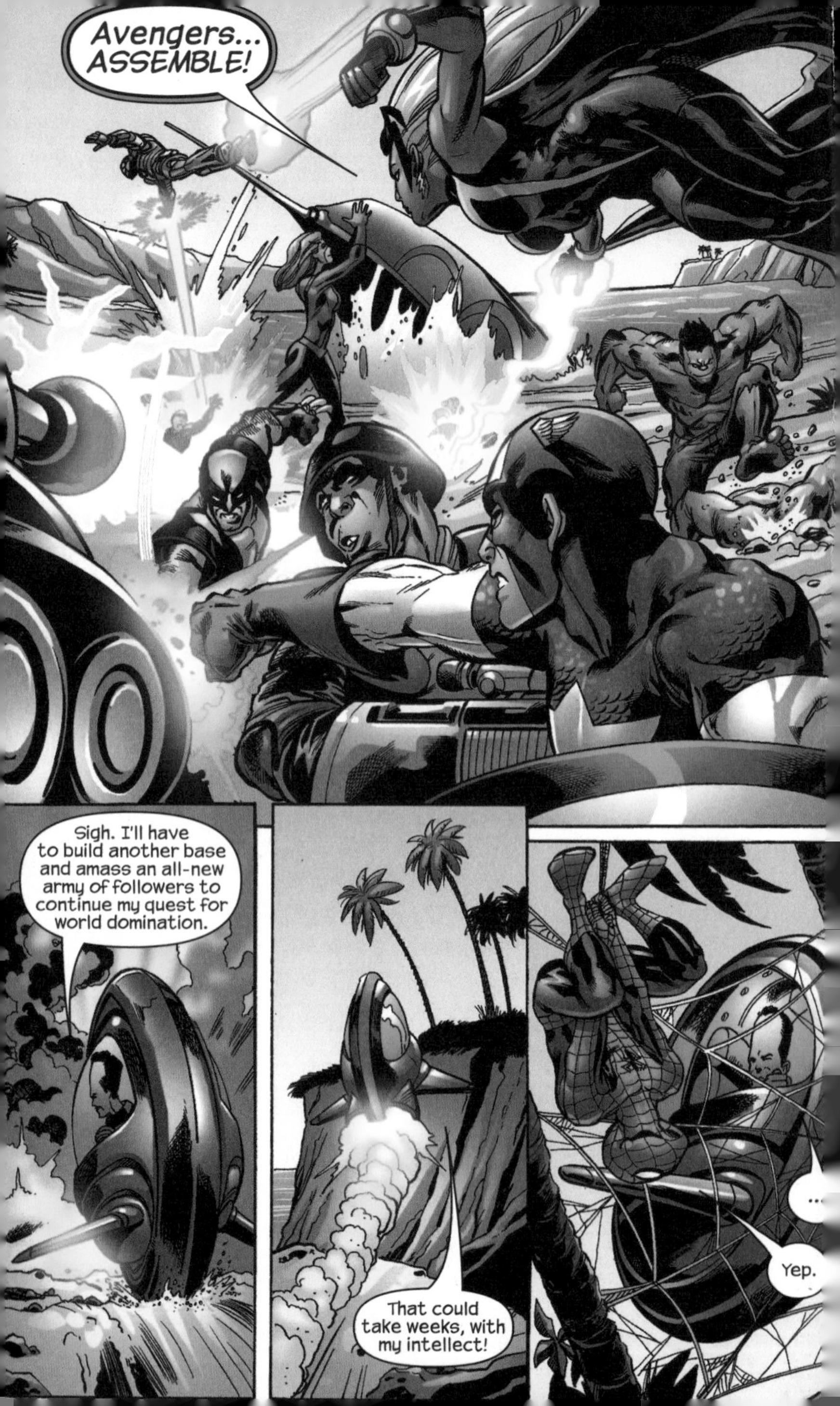
Avengers... ASSEMBLE!
Sigh. I'll have to build another base and amass an all-new army of followers to continue my quest for world domination.
That could take weeks, with my intellect!
...
Yep.

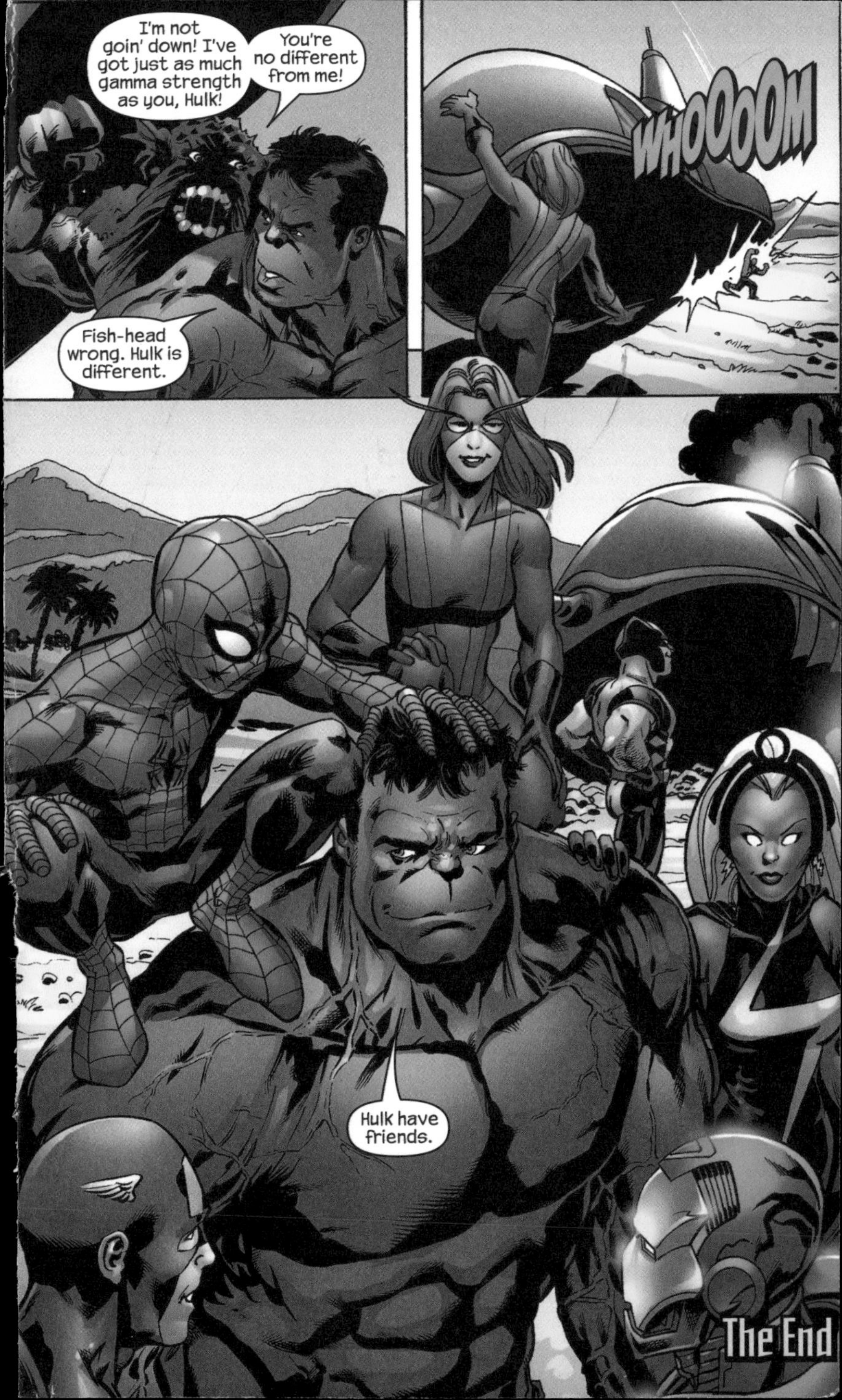
I'm not goin' down! I've got just as much gamma strength as you, Hulk!
You're no different from me!
Fish-head wrong. Hulk is different.
WHOOOOM
Hulk have friends.
The End